Charlottesville Lodge

No 55

Charlottesville

Va

1874

Yours fraternally

Jno Dove

Lith. by A. Hoen & Co. Balto.

THE

VIRGINIA TEXT-BOOK:

CONTAINING A

HISTORY OF MASONIC GRAND LODGES,

AND THE

CONSTITUTION OF MASONRY,

OR

AHIMAN REZON:

TOGETHER WITH A

DIGEST OF THE LAWS, RULES AND REGULATIONS

OF THE

GRAND LODGE OF VIRGINIA;

ALSO,

A COMPLETE COMPILATION OF THE ILLUSTRATIONS OF MASONIC WORK, AS DRAWN FROM

PRESTON, WEBB, READ AND OTHERS,

BY JOHN DOVE,

GRAND SECRETARY OF THE GRAND LODGE OF VIRGINIA.

THIRD EDITION.

RICHMOND:

PRINTED BY JAMES E. GOODE.

1866.

PREFACE.

In obedience to the orders of the Most Worshipful Grand Lodge of Virginia, I present to my Brethren the Third Edition of the Virginia Masonic Text-Book at a rather earlier period than anticipated. By the melancholy conflagration, which laid a very large part of the business portion of the City of Richmond in ruins on the ever-memorable 3rd day of April, 1865, when the Confederate army surrendered the city to the Federal troops, the entire remnant of the Second Edition was consumed, and the present rendered necessary.

I need not, and therefore will not detain the reader by an elaborate Preface, setting forth all the excellencies of this work, but will proceed at once to point out a few which have stood the test of time and practice.

The Ritual of this Text-Book has stood the scrutiny of forty-six years' experience of the various Working Committees of the Grand Lodge of this State; the severe criticism of the Baltimore Convention in 1843, of which I was the President; and been sanctioned by the approval either expressed or implied of most of the Grand Lodges in correspondence with this.

The Code of Laws, as laid down in the Methodical Digest, and predicated on the Ahiman Rezon, or Book of Constitutions, is so nearly perfect, as in most instances to have acted as the Book of Reference by which many of the questions of Jurisprudence which have agitated the Grand Lodges of this Continent have seemingly been settled. The beautiful efficiency of this Code is fully exemplified in the Brotherly harmony and quiet which has prevailed throughout our Jurisdiction for nearly a century.

The Historical part, which abounds in useful and instructive matter, as drawn from the writings of Preston, Webb, Read, Mackey and others, will amply compensate the reader for the time devoted to its careful perusal.

J. D.

RICHMOND, NOVEMBER, A. L. 5866, A. D. 1866.

PREFACE TO FIRST EDITION.

In presenting to the Masonic Fraternity the following Manual or Text-Book, as the Organ of the Grand Lodge of Virginia, I am compelled to throw myself on their indulgence for any errors which they may detect either in style or arrangement, and to plead that the work has been begun, continued and finished while under the constant interruptions incident to a professional life, and must beg to assure them that no inducement short of a sense of imperious duty could have brought me to accept the arduous task of compiling and editing a work on Masonry bearing the authoritative and imposing title of a Text-Book. The responsibility, however, which attaches to the undertaking has been greatly lightened by the severe criticism and subsequent approval which it has received at the hands of two of the most enlightened committees appointed by the Grand Lodge for that purpose, and to whose reports embodied in the work, I beg to refer the reader.

For the History of Masonry, its origin, antiquity and present development, I stand pledged to prove by authentic and indubitable records now in my possession, that the statements made are verified, and have received the sanction of virtuous and enlightened men in every age down to the present; I have contented myself with merely giving the heads or outlines of those facts which will induce and enable the studious Mason to inform himself and become learned and useful in his profession, by consulting those authorities, both sacred and profane, on which those statements rest.

The Book of Constitutions or Ahiman Rezon, is a literal transcript of that which was collated from old and authentic sources by the M. W. Grand Lodge of England in the beginning of the last century, and by her promulgated to the whole world, so that it is now in every language and in every civilized portion of the globe, the *basis* on which the superstructure of Free Masonry *must be erected;* and any departure from them constitutes a removal of those Ancient Land-Marks which all authority, holy and profane, severely censure. This being the fact, how important is it that every Mason should make himself intimately acquainted with all its requirements, not only as a safeguard against any, the smallest violation thereof on his own part, but to enable him to prevent the mischievous consequences of errors of omission in others to whom may be entrusted the exercise of its high behests. No reflecting Mason can rise from a perusal of the requirements of this Constitution without being forcibly reminded how far short the most zealous votary of our time-honored Institution falls from the performance of those duties and obligations therein enjoined, a just and due appreciation of which induced our Illustrious Brother George Washington to say in a letter addressed to the Grand Lodge of Massachusetts, dated in 1792, on the occasion of receiving a copy of the Constitutions from that Grand Lodge:—" Flattering as it may be to the human mind, and truly honorable as it is, to receive from our fellow-citizens testimonies of approbation for exertions to promote the public welfare, *it is not less pleasing to know that the milder virtues of the heart are highly respected by a Society,* WHOSE LIBERAL PRINCIPLES ARE FOUNDED ON THE IMMUTABLE LAWS OF TRUTH AND JUSTICE.

"To enlarge the sphere of social happiness is worthy the benevolent design of a Masonic Institution; and it is most fervently to be wished that the conduct of every member of the Fraternity, as well as those publications that discover the principles that actuate them, may tend to convince mankind, THAT THE GRAND OBJECT OF MASONRY IS TO PROMOTE THE HAPPINESS OF THE HUMAN RACE."

For the work and illustrations of Masonry, I have pursued as closely as possible those Illustrious Beacon Lights, William Preston of the Lodge of Antiquity, London, and Thomas S. Webb, P. G. Master of Rhode Island, which having been in use in this country now nearly a century, stamp at once their antiquity and consequent value.

In compiling the Laws of the Grand Lodge, I have drawn upon the labors of the R. W. John K. Read, P. D. Grand Master, and R. W. James Henderson, P. J. Grand Warden of the Grand Lodge of Virginia, but more especially on the latter, whose highly gifted and methodic mind prepared the Methodical Digest of those Laws, which being based upon the Constitution of Masonry, and in strict accordance with the usages of the Fraternity, have stood the test of sixty years' experience in their practical operations on the Government of the Craft, and will be found equally applicable to other Grand Jurisdictions.

For the benefit of my Brethren who may be concerned in forming new Lodges, or revising Laws of the old ones, I have subjoined a copy of the By-Laws of Richmond Randolph Lodge No. 19, which having been framed in 1794, by our venerable Brother, William H. Fitzwhylsonn, afterwards, and for twenty-five years Grand Secretary, aided by others equally skilled in Masonry, and having been in constant use since that time in the government of that Lodge, entitle them to the appellation of a CODE, as nearly *perfect* as can be necessary for practical purposes.

I have thus endeavored, in due obedience to the orders of the Grand Lodge of Virginia, to present my Masonic Brethren a Book of purely practical character, which every Mason ought to make himself intimately acquainted with, in order that he may be qualified to act well his part in any situation to which the partiality of his Brethren may call him. Whether I have succeeded or not, time alone must determine.

THE AUTHOR.

RICHMOND, VA., Sept. A. L. 5846, A. D. 1846.

CONTENTS.

THE VIRGINIA MASONIC TEXT-BOOK.

CHAPTER I.

ORIGIN OF MASONRY.

With a view to the discussion and settlement of this question, it becomes primarily necessary to assert what Masonry is. At the present day, among all enlightened members of the Fraternity, it has two meanings, under the style of *Operative* and *Speculative* Masonry. By the former it is, under its synonyme, Geometry, made to conduce to man's temporal wants by furnishing shelters from the weather, and by the appliances of architectural symmetry, varied by the taste and talents of succeeding generations, has imprinted its existence in every country and clime where civilization prevails, by those magnificent structures which are the pride and admiration of every nation.

By *Speculative* Masonry, we mean *Virtue* in its most extended sense, as taught by the daily exercise of Brotherly Love, Relief and Truth, and which compels or requires the initiated to subdue the passions, act upon the square, keep a tongue of good report, maintain secrecy and practise charity. It is so intimately interwoven with religion as to lay its professors under the strongest obligation to pay to the Deity that rational and heart-emanating homage which at once constitutes their duty and happiness. Reasoning, then, on these acknowledged data, it will not be necessary to detain the reader with a long account of the *Origin* of Masonry. Certain it is, and must be, that when the first man was formed in the image of God, the

Principles of Masonry, as a Divine gift from Heaven were stamped upon his heart by the Great Architect of the Universe.

With this explanation of what Masonry is, we may be permitted to add the beautiful description of its origin by that greatly learned and truly zealous Brother, William Preston, of the Lodge of Antiquity in London, who says:

"From the commencement of the world, we may trace the foundation of Masonry. Ever since symmetry began, and harmony displayed her charms, our Order has had a being. During many ages, and in many different countries, it has flourished. No art, no science preceded it. In the dark periods of antiquity, when literature was in a low state, and the rude manners of our forefathers withheld from them that knowledge we now so amply share, Masonry diffused its influence. Thus science unveiled, arts arose, civilization took place, and the progress of knowledge and philosophy gradually dispelled the gloom of ignorance and barbarism. Government being settled, authority was given to laws, and the assemblies of the Fraternity acquired the patronage of the great and the good, while the tenets of the profession diffused unbounded utility.

"Abstracting from the pure pleasures which arise from friendship, so wisely constituted as that which subsists among Masons, and which it is scarcely possible that any circumstance or occurrence can erase, Masonry is a science confined to no particular country, but extends over the whole terrestrial globe. Wherever arts flourish, there it flourishes too. Add to this, that by secret and inviolable signs, carefully preserved among the Fraternity, it becomes an universal language. Hence many advantages are gained: The distant Chinese, the wild Arab and the American Savage will embrace a brother Briton, and will know, that beside the common ties of humanity, there is still a stronger obligation to induce him to kind and friendly offices. The spirit of the fulminating priest will be tamed; and a moral brother, though of a different persuasion, engage his esteem; for mutual toleration in religious opinions is one of the most distinguishing and valuable characteristics of the Craft. As all religions teach morality, if a brother be found to act the part of a truly honest man, his private speculative opinions are left to God and himself. Thus, through the influence of Masonry, which is reconcilable to the best policy, all those disputes which embitter life, and sour the tempers of men, are avoided, while the common good, the general object, is zealously pursued.

"From this view of our system, its utility must be sufficiently obvious. The universal principles of the art unite, in one indissoluble bond of affection, men of the most opposite tenets, of the most distant countries, and of the most contradictory opinions, so that in every nation a Mason will find a *friend*, and in every clime a *home*.

"Such is the nature of our institution, that in the Lodge, union is cemented by sincere attachment, and pleasure is reci: rocally communicated in the cheerful observance of every obliging office. Virtue, the grand object in view, luminous as the meridian sun, shines refulgent on the mind, enlivens the heart, and heightens cool approbation into warm sympathy and cordial attention."

CHAPTER II.

ANTIQUITY OF MASONRY, AS DERIVED FROM HOLY WRIT.

That Adam, our great progenitor, was ignorant of the principles of geometry can hardly be supposed, for after his expulsion from the garden of Eden, he built an habitation for himself and family, and no doubt instructed his descendants in that noble science, and its application to whatsoever crafts were convenient for those early times.

Cain, with his family and adherents, being prëinstructed in the principles of geometry and architecture, built a strong city and called it Dedicate or Consecrate, after the name of his eldest son Enoch, whose race, following his example, improved themselves not only in geometry and masonry, but made discoveries of several other useful arts.

The descendants of Seth came nothing behind those of Cain, in the cultivation of geometry and masonry. This patriarch greatly profited in those noble sciences, under the tuition of Adam, with whom he lived till the year of the world 930, and succeeded him in the direction of the Craft; who, as a monument of his superior abilities, and love to posterity, foreseeing the universal desolation which would happen by fire or water, and deprive mankind of those arts and sciences at that time existing, raised two pillars of stone, and inscribed thereon an abridgement of the arts and sciences, particularly geometry or masonry, in order to withstand the overthrow of the flood, which Josephus, the historian, informs us were to be seen in his time, in the land of Siriad, by the name of Seth's or Enoch's pillars.

Methuselah, with his son Lamech and grandson Noah, retired from the corrupt world, and in their own peculiar family preserved the religion of the promised Messiah pure, and also the art of Masonry till the flood.

The ark was built on principles of geometry. Noah and his family, besides a number of all created beings, were saved from the general deluge; he and his three sons are, therefore, the progenitors of the present race of mankind.

From the Sacred Writings we learn, that Noah and his sons, being all of one language and speech, it came to pass as they journeyed from the *East* to the *West*, they found a plain in the land of Shinar, and dwelt there together as *Noachidae* or sons of Noah, the first name of Masons, and under which name many brethren are known in France up to the present day.

In following that great luminary of the Craft, the Holy Bible, we find the tower of Babel is built, and before its entire completion, by the will of the Divine Architect, the language of the builders is confounded and the people dispersed, all of which shows that, after the dispersion, they still carried with them the knowledge of Masonry, and improved it to a great degree of perfection.

Nimrod or Belus, the son of Cush, the eldest son of Ham, and founder of the Babylonian monarchy, kept possession of the plain, and founded the first great empire at Babylon.

From Shinar the science and the art were carried to distant parts of the world, notwithstanding the confusion of the dialects, and which is presumed to have given rise to the universal practice of conversing without speaking, and communications between Masons by tokens or signs.

Mizraim, the second son of Ham, carried to, and preserved in Egypt, the original skill, and cultivated the arts—monuments of which are still extant in that country under the name of Pyramids, which are, and have been, the universal admiration of succeeding ages. The successors of Mizraim, who were styled the sons of ancient kings, encouraged the art, down to the last of their race, the learned king *Amasis.*

It is presumed that the offspring of Shem propagated the science as far as China and Japan.

Abraham, born two years after the death of Noah, had learned the science, before the Grand Architect of the universe called him to travel from Ur of the Chaldees. He communicated it to the Canaanites, for which they honored him as a prince.

Isaac, Ishmael and Jacob, no doubt were taught the science by their progenitor. Joseph was also well instructed by his father, for the Scripture informs us he excelled the Egyptians in knowledge, and was installed by Pharaoh himself as a ruler over the people.

It is well known, and needs no comment here, that Melchizedeck is recognized amongst us as one of the most venerable patrons of the Order.

That the Israelites practised Masonry in Egypt is a well authenticated fact from the Bible. We read "they were trained up" to the building of two cities with stone and brick for the Egyptians, and it undoubtedly was the design of the Most High to make them expert Masons before they should possess the promised land.

In their peregrinations through the wilderness, after their singular deliverance from Egyptian bondage, on their voyage to the land which was promised they should possess for an inheritance forever, God was pleased to inspire Moses, and gave him the decalogue, which can be summed up in those two doctrines, honor God and love thy neighbor, (and in what society are those two precepts better exemplified than among Masons?) When Moses, after a sojourn of forty days on Mount Sinai, came down with the laws, he entered into his tent. Aaron, his brother, who afterwards became high priest, came to visit him, and Moses acquainted him with the laws he had received from God with the explanation of them. After this Aaron placed himself at the right hand of Moses, and Eleazer and Ithamar (sons of Aaron) were admitted, to whom Moses repeated what he had said to Aaron. Moses afterwards declared the same over to the elders of the Sanhedrim, composed of seventy members, after which instruction he reduced the law to writing, except the explanations; these he thought sufficient to commit and entrust to their memories, with instructions to teach them to their children and their offspring. He also ordered the more skilful to meet him as in a lodge or tabernacle, and gave them wise charges and regulations, from which they should not deviate.

Joshua, the faithful follower of Moses, succeeded him, with Caleb and Eleazer, the high priest, and Phineas, his deputy.

After the conquest and settlement of the promised land, the Israelites made further progress in the study of geometry and architecture, having many expert artists.

The city of Tyre or Tsor was built by a great body of Sidonian Masons from *Gabala*, under a Grand Master and a number of princes.

In after times, Ahibal, King of Tyre, repaired and beautified that city, and so did his son Hiram, being also a Mason. He became one of the principal architects of that stupendous edifice which has been and always will remain the admiration of the world, viz: Solomon's temple.

CHAPTER III.

ANTIQUITY OF MASONRY, AS DERIVED FROM A NUMBER OF EXTRACTS OF OLD MANUSCRIPTS AND RECORDS IN GREAT BRITAIN.

I.

An old manuscript, which was destroyed with many others in 1720, said to have been in the possession of Nicholas Stone, a curious sculptor under Inigo Jones, contains the following particulars:

"St. Albans loved Masons well, and cherished them much, and made their pay right good; for he gave them 2 shillings per weeke, and 3d. to their cheer; whereas, before that time, in all the land, a Mason had but a penny a day and his meat, until St. Albans mended itt, and he gott them a charter from the king and his counsell for to hold a general counsell, and gave itt to name assemblie. Thereat he was himselfe, and did helpe to make Masons, and gave them good charges."

II.

A record of the society, written in the reign of Edward IV., formerly in possession of the famous Elias

Ashmole, the founder of the Museum of Oxford, England:

"Though the ancient records of the Brotherhood in England were many of them destroyed or lost in the wars of the Saxons and Danes, yet King Athelstane, (the grandson of King Alfred the Great, a mighty architect,) the first annointed King of England, and who translated the Sacred Scriptures into the Saxon tongue, (A. D. 930,) when he had brought the land into rest and peace, built many great works, and encouraged many Masons from France, who were appointed overseers thereof, and brought with them the charges and regulations of the Lodges, preserved since the Roman times; who also prevailed with the king to improve the Constitution of the English Lodges according to the foreign model, and to increase the wages of the working Masons.

"The said king's brother, Prince Edwin, being taught Masonry, and taking upon him the charges of a Master Mason, for the love he had to the said Craft, and the honorable principles whereon it is grounded, purchased a free charter of King Athelstane, for the Masons having a correction among themselves, (as it was anciently expressed,) or a freedom and power to regulate themselves, to amend what might happen amiss, and to hold a yearly communication and General Assembly.

"Accordingly, Prince Edwin summoned all the Masons in the realm to meet him in a congregation at York,* who came and composed a general Lodge, of which he was Grand Master; and having brought with him all the writings and records extant, some in Greek, some in Latin, some in French, and other languages, from the contents thereof the assembly did frame the Constitution and charges of the Ancient English Lodge; they made a law to preserve and observe the same in all time coming, and ordained good pay for working Masons, &c. And he made a book thereof, how the Craft was founded; and he himself ordered and commanded that it should be read, and told when any Mason should be made, and for to give him his charges. And from that day until this time, manners of Masons have been kept in that form, as well as men might govern.

"Furthermore, however, at diverse assemblies certain charges have been made and ordained by the best advice of Masters and fellowes, as the exigencies of the Craft made necessarie."

* Hence the origin of Ancient York Masonry.

III.

In the reign of King Edward the Third, when Lodges were more frequent, the Right Worshipful the Master and fellows, with the consent of the lords of the realm, (for most great men were then Masons,) ordained as follows:

"That for the future, at the making or admission of a Brother, the Constitution and the ancient charges should be read by the Master or Wardens.*

"That such as were to be admitted Master Masons, or Masters of the Work, should be examined whether they be able* to serve their respective lords, as well the lowest as the highest, to the honor and worship of the aforesaid art, and to the profit of their Lord or Master, for they be their Lords or Masters that employ and pay them for their service and travel."

IV.

The following particulars are also contained in a very old manuscript, of which a copy was in the possession of the Right Worshipful George Payne, Grand Master, in 1718:

"That when the Master and Wardens meet in a Lodge, if need be, the sheriff of the county, or the mayor of the city, or aldermen of the town, in which the congregation is held, should be made fel low and sociate to the Master, in help of him against rebels, and for upbearing the rights of the realm.

"That entered prentices, at their making, were charged not to be thieves, or thieves' maintainers; that they should travel honestly for their pay, and love their fellowes as themselves, be true to the King of England, to the realm and to the Lodge.

"That at such congregations it shall be required, whether any Master or fellow has broken any of the articles agreed to; and if the offender, being duly cited to appear, prove rebel, and will not attend, then the Lodge shall determine against him, that he shall forswear (or renounce) his Masonry, and shall no more use this

* This good rule ought to be always enforced.

Craft, the which if he presume for to do, the sheriff of the county shall prison him, and shall take all his goods into the king's hands, until his grace be granted him and issued. For this cause principally have these congregations been ordained, that as well the lowest as the highest should be well and truly served in the aforesaid art, throughout all the Kingdom of England. Amen—so mote it be."

V.

The Latin register of William Molart, Prior of Canterbury, in manuscript paper 88, dated 1429, informs us, that in the year 1429, during the minority of Henry the Sixth, a respectable Lodge was held at Canterbury, under the patronage of Henry Chicheley, the Archbishop, at which were present Thomas Stapylton, the Master, John Morris, Custos de la Loge Lathomorum, or Warden of the Lodge of Masons, with fifteen fellow-crafts, and three entered apprentices, all of whom are particularly named.

A record of the same period says:

"The Company of Masons, being otherwise termed Free Masons, of auntient staunding, and gude reckoninge, by means of affable and kind meetings dyverse tymes, and as a loving brotherhood used to do, did frequent this mutual assembly in the time of Henry the 4th, in the 12th year of his reign, A. D. 1434.*

The same record in another part says:

"That the charges and laws of the Free Masons have been seen and perused by our late sovereign, King Henry the 6th, and by the lords of his most honourable council, who have allowed them and declared, that they be right good and reasonable to be holden, as they have been drawn out and collected from the records of auntient tymes, &c. &c."

VI.

Ancient Charges.—"Ye shall be true to the King, and the master you serve, and to the fellowship whereof you are admitted. Ye

* Extract of Stowe's Survey, chap. v. p. 215.

shall be true to and love eidher odher. Ye shall call eidher odher Brother or Fellow, not slave, nor any unkind name.

"Ye shall ordain the wisest to be master of the work; and neither for love nor lineage, riches nor favour, set one over the work who hath but little knowledge; whereby the master would be evil served, and ye ashamed, and also ye shall call the governour of the work master in the time of working with him; and ye shall truly deserve your reward of the master ye serve.

"All the Freres* shall treat the peculiarities of eidher odher with the gentleness, decencie, and forbearance he thinks due to his own.

"Ye shall have a reasonable pay, and live honestly.

"Once a year ye are to come and assemble together, to consult how ye may best work to serve the craft, and to your own profit and credit."

VII.

A manuscript copy of an examination of some of the Brotherhood, taken before King Henry the 6th, was found by the learned John Locke, Esq., in the Bodleian library. This dialogue possesses a double claim to our regard: first for its antiquity, and next for the ingenious notes and conjectures of Mr. Locke upon it; some of which we have retained. The approbation of a philosopher of as great merit and penetration as the English nation ever produced, added to the real value of the piece itself, must give it a sanction, and render it deserving a serious and candid examination. This ancient manuscript is as follows:

"A certayne questyons, with answeres to the same, concernynge the mysterye of Maconrye: wryttene by the hande of King Henrye, the Sixthe of the name, and faythfullye copyed by me Johann Leylande,† Antiquarius, by the command of his Highnesse.‡

* *Freres.* French, signifying Brethren.

† "*John Leylande* was appointed by King Henry the eighth, at the dissolution of the monasteries, to search for, and save such books and records as were valuable among them. He was a man of great labour and industry."

‡ "*His Highness*, meaning the said King Henry the eighth. Our Kings had not then the title of Majesty."

"They be as followethe:

"*Quest.* What mote ytt be?

"*Answ.* Ytt beeth the Skylle of nature, the understondynge of the myghte that is hereynne, and its sondrye werckynges; sonderlyche, the Skylle of rectenyngs, of waightes, and metynges, and the treu manere of faconnynge al thynges for mannes use, headlye, dwellynges, and buyldynges of alle kindes, and al odher thynges that make gudde to manne.

"*Quest.* Where did ytt begyne?

"*Answ.* Ytt dyd begynne with the fyrste menne yn the este, whych were before the ffyrste manne of the weste, and comynge westlye, ytt hath broughte herwyth alle comforts to the wylde and comfortlesse.

"*Quest.* Who dyd brynge ytt westlye?

"*Answ.* The Venetians,* whoo begynge grate merchaundes, comed ffyrste ffromme the este ynn Venetia, ffor the commodytye of marchaundysynge beithe este and weste, bey the Redde and Myddlelonde Sees.

"*Quest.* Howe comede ytt yn Engelonde?

"*Answ.* Peter Gower,† a Grecian, journeyedde ffor kunnynge yn Egypte, and yn Syria, and in everyche londe whereat the Venetians hadde plauntedde Maconrye, and wynnynge entrance yn al Lodges of Macconnes, he lerned muche, and retournedde, and worked yn

* *The Venetians*, &c. "In times of ignorance, it is no wonder that the *Phenicians* should be mistaken for the *Venetians*. Or, perhaps, if the people were not taken one for the other, similitude of sound might deceive the clerk who first took down the examination. The Phenecians were the greatest voyagers among the ancients, and were in Europe thought to be the inventors of letters, which perhaps they brought from the east with other arts."

† *Peter Gower*. "This must be another mistake of the writer. I was puzzled at first to guess who Peter Gower should be, the name being perfectly English; or how a Greek should come by such a name; but as soon as I thought of Pythagoras, I could scarce forbear smiling to find that philosopher had undergone a metempsychosis he never dreamt of. We need only consider the French pronunciation of this name Pythagore, that is, Petegore, to conceive how easily such a mistake might be made by an unlearned clerk. That Pythagoras travelled for knowledge into Egypt, &c., is known to all the learned, and that he was initiated into several different orders of Priests, who in those days kept all their learning secret from the vulgar, is as well known. Pythagoras, also, made every geometrical theorem a secret, and admitted only such to the knowledge of them, as had first undergone a five years' silence. He is supposed to be the inventor of the xlvii*th* of the first book of Euclid, for which, in the joy of his heart, it is said he sacrificed a hecatomb. He also knew the true system of the world lately revived by Copernicus, and was certainly a most wonderful man. See his life by Dion Hal."

Grecia Magna,* wachsynge, and becommynge a myghtye wyseacre,† and gratelyche renowned, and here he framed a great Lodge at Groton,‡ and maked manye Maconnes, some whereofte dyd journnye yn Fraunce, and maked manye Maconnes, wherefromme, in processe of tyme, the arte passed yn Engelonde.

"*Quest.* Dothe Maconnes descouer here arts unto odhers?

"*Answ.* Peter Gower, when he journeyedde to lernne, was ffyrste made, and anonne techedde, even soe shulde all odhers be and teche. Maconnes§ hauthe always yn everyche tyme from tyme to tyme communycatedde to mankynde soche of her secrettes as generallyche myghte be usefulle; they haueth keped backe soche allein as shulde be harmfulle yff they commend yn euylle haundes, oder soche as ne myghte be holpynge wythouten the techynges to be joynedde herwythe in the Lodge, oder soche as do bynde the Freres more strongelyche togeder, bey the profytte, and commodyte comynge to the Confrerie herfromme.

"*Quest.* Whatte artes haueth the Maconnes techedde mankynde?

"*Answ.* The Artes Agricultura, Architectura, Astronomia, Geometria, Numeries, Musica, Poesie, Kymistrye, Governmente and Relygyonne.

"*Quest.* How commethe Maconnes more teachers than odher men?

"*Answ.* They hemselfe haueth allein the arte of fyndyng neue artes, whyche arte the ffyrste Maconnes receaued from Godde; by the whyche they fyndethe whatte artes hem plesethe, and the true way of techynge the same. Whatt odher menne doethe ffynde out, ys onelyche bey chaunce, and herfore but lytel I tro.

"*Quest.* What dothe the Maconnes concele and hyde?

"*Answ.* Thay concelethe the art of ffynding neue artes, and thattys for here owne proffytte, and preise. Thay conceleth the art of kepynge secrettes, that soe the worlde mayeth nothinge concele

* *Grecia Magna.* "A part of Italy, formerly so called, in which the Greeks had settled a large colony."

† "*Weisager*, in the old Saxon, is philosopher, wiseman or wizard."

‡ *Groton.* "Groton is the name of a place in England. The place here meant is Crotona, a city of Grecia Magna, which in the time of Pythagoras was very populous."

§ *Maconnes havethe communicatedde*, &c. "This paragraph hath something remarkable in it. It contains a justification of the secresy so much boasted of by Masons, and so much blamed by others, asserting that they have in all ages discovered such things as might be useful, and that they conceal such only as would be hurtful either to the world or themselves. What these secrets are, we see afterwards."

from them. They concelethe the art of wunderwerckynge, and of fore sayinge thynges to come, thatt so thay same artes may not be usedde of the wyckedde to an euylle ende; thay also conceuthe the arte of chaunges,* the wey of wynnyng the faculty of Abrac,† the skylle of becommynge gude and parfyghte withouten the holpynges of fere and hope, and the universelle‡ longage of Maconnes.

"*Quest.* Wylle he teche me thay same artes?

"*Answ.* Ye shalle be techedce yff ye be werthye and able to lerne.

"*Quest.* Dothe alle Maconnes kunne more then odher menne?

"*Answ.* Not so. Thay onlyche haueth recht, and occasyonne more then odher menne to kunne, butt manye doeth fale yn capacitye, and many more doth want industrye, that ys pernecessarye for the gaynynge all kunnynge.

"*Quest.* Are Maconnes gudder menne then odhers?

"*Answ.* Some Maconnes are not so vertuous as some odher menne; but yn the moste parte, they be more gude than they woulde be yf thay war not Maconnes.

"*Quest.* Doth Maconnes love eidther odher myghtylye as beeth sayde?

"*Answ.* Yea verylyche, and yt may not otherwyse be; for gude menne and true kennynge eidher odher to be soche, doeth always love the more as they be more gude.

"Here endethe the Questyonnes and Answeres." §

* The transmutation of metals.

† *Facultye of Abrac.* An abbreviation of the word Abracadabra. In the days of Ignorance and Superstition, that word had a magical signification, but the explanation of it is now lost.

‡ The being able by secret and inviolable signs, carefully preserved among the Fraternity throughout the world, to express themselves intelligibly to men of all languages and nations. "A man who has all these arts and advantages is certainly in a condition to be envied; but we are told that this is not the case with all Masons, for though these arts are among them, and all have a right and an opportunity to know them, yet some want capacity and others industry to acquire them. However, of all their arts and secrets, that which I most desire to know is, *The skylle of becommynge gude and parfyghte;* and I wish it were communicated to all mankind, since there is nothing more true than the beautiful sentence contained in the last answer, 'that the better men are, the more they love one another.' Virtue having in itself something so amiable as to charm the hearts of all that behold it."

§ *Glossary, to explain the Old Words in the foregoing Manuscript.*—Allein, *only;* alweys, *always;* beithe, *both;* commodyte, *conveniency;* confrerie, *fraternity;* faconnynge, *forming;* fore saying, *prophesying;* freres, *brethren;* headlye, *chiefly;* hem pesethe, *they please;* hemselfe, *themselves;* her, *there, their;* hereynne, *therein;* herwyth, *with it;* holpynge, *beneficial;* kunne, *know;* kunnynge, *knowledge;* make gudde, *are beneficial;* metynges, *measures;* mote, *may;* myddlelonde, *Mediterra-*

A letter from Mr. Locke to the Right Honorable Thomas Earl of Pembroke, to whom he sent this ancient manuscript, concludes as follows:

"I know not what effect the sight of this old paper may have upon your Lordship, but for my own part I cannot deny that it has so much raised my curiosity, as to induce me to enter myself into the Fraternity, which I am determined to do (if I may be admitted) the next time I go to London, (and that will be shortly.)

I am, my Lord, your Lordship's

Most obedient and humble servant,

JOHN LOCKE."

VIII.

Ancient Charges at the Constitution of a Lodge, extracted from a manuscript in the possession of the Lodge of Antiquity in London, written in the time of James the Second:

"* * * * And furthermore, at diverse assemblies have been put and ordained diverse crafties by the best advice of magistrates and Fellows. *Tunc unus ex senioribus tenet, librum, et ille ponet manum suam, super librum.*

"Every man that is a Mason take good heed to these charges (we pray) that if any man find himselfe guilty of any of these charges, that he may amend himselfe, or principally for dread of God, you that be charged to take good heed that you keepe all these charges well, for it is a great evill for a man to forswear himselfe upon a book.

"The first charge is, that yee shall be true men to God and the holy church, and to use no error or heresie by your understanding and by wise men's teaching. Allso,

"Secondly, That yee shall be true liege men to the King of England, without treason or any falsehood, and that yee know no treason or treachery, but ye shall give knowledge thereof to the king or

nean; myghte, *power;* occasyonne, *opportunity;* oder, *or;* onelyche, *only;* pernecessarye, *absolutely necessary;* precise, *honor;* recht, *right;* reckenyngs, *numbers;* sonderlyche, *particularly;* skylle, *knowledge;* wachsynge, *growing;* werck, *operation;* wey, *way;* whereas, *where;* woned, *dwelt;* wunderwerckynge, *working miracles;* wylde, *savage;* wynnynge, *gaining;* ynn, *into.*

to his counsell; allso yee shall be true one to another, that is to say, every Mason of the Craft that is Mason allowed, yee shall doe to him as yee would be done unto yourselfe.

"Thirdly, And yee shall keepe truely all the counsell that ought to be kept in the way of Masonhood, and all the counsell of the Lodge or of the chamber. Allso, that ye shall be no thiefe or thieves to your knowledge free; that yee shall be true to the King, Lord or Master that yee serve, and truely to see and worke for his advantage.

"Fourthly, Yee shall call all Masons your Fellows, or your Brethren, and no other names.

"Fifthly, Yee shall not take your Fellow's wife in villainy, nor deflower his daughter or servant, nor put him to no disworship.

"Sixthly, Yee shall truely pay for your meat or drinke wheresoever ye go, to table or bord. Also, yee shall do no villainy there, whereby the Craft or Science may be slandered.

"These be the charges general to every true Mason, both Masters and Fellowes.

"Now will I rehearse other charges single for Masons allowed or accepted.

"First, That no Mason take on him no Lord's worke, nor any other man's, unlesse he know himselfe well able to perform the worke, so that the Craft have no slander.

"Secondly, Allso, that no Master take worke but that he take reasonable pay for itt; so that the Lord may be truly served, and the Master to live honestly, and to pay his Fellows truely. And that no Master or Fellow supplant others of their worke; that is to say, that if he hath taken a worke, or else stand Master of any worke, that he shall not put him out, unless he be unable of cunning to make an end of his worke. And no Master nor Fellow shall take no apprentice for less than seaven yeares. And that the apprentice be free born, and of limbs whole, as a man ought to be, and no bastard. And that no Master or Fellow take no allowance to be made Mason without the assent of his Fellows, at the least six or seaven.

"Thirdly, That he that be made be able in all degrees; that is, free born, of a good kindred, true and no bondsman, and that he have his right limbs, as a man ought to have.

"Fourthly, That a Master take no apprentice without he have occupation to occupy two or three Fellows at the least.

"Fifthly, That no Master or Fellow put away any Lord's worke to taske that ought to be journey worke.

"Sixthly, That every Master give pay to his Fellows and servants as they may deserve, so that he be not defamed with false workeing: And that none slander another behind his backe, to make him loose his good name.

"Seventhly, That no Fellow in the house or abroad answer another ungodly or reproveably without a cause.

"Eighthly, That every Master Mason doe reverence his elder, and that a Mason be no common plaier at the cards, dice or hazzard, nor at any other unlawful plaies, through the which the Science and Craft may be dishonoured or slandered.

"Ninthly, That no Fellow goe into the town by night, except he have a Fellow with him, who may beare him record that he was in an honest place.

"Tenthly, That every Master and Fellow shall come to the assemblie, if itt be within fifty miles of him, if he have any warning. And if he have trespassed against the Craft, to abide the award of Masters and Fellows.

"Eleventhly, That every Master Mason and Fellow that hath trespassed against the Craft shall stand to the correction of other Masters and Fellows to made him accord, and if they cannot accord, to go to the common law.

"Twelfthly, That a Master or Fellow make not a mould stone, square, nor rule, no to lowen, nor let no lowen worke within their Lodge, nor to mould stone.

"Thirteenthly, That every Mason receive and cherish strange Fellowes when they come over the countrie, and set them on worke, if they will worke, as the manner is; that is to say, if the Mason have any mould stone in his place, he shall give him a mould stone, and sett him on worke; and if he have none, the Mason shall refresh him with money unto the next Lodge.

"Fourteenthly, That every Mason shall truely serve his Master for his pay.

"Fifteenthly, That every Master shall truely make an end of his worke, taske or journey, whethersoe it be.

"These be all the charges and covenants that ought to be read at the installment of Master, or making of a Free Mason or Free Masons. The Almighty God of Jacob, who ever have you and me in his keeping, bless us now and ever. Amen."

IX.

Extract from the Diary of Elias Ashmole, a learned antiquary:

"I was made a Free Mason at Warrington, Lancashire, with Colonel Henry Mainwaring, or Kerthingham, in Cheshire, by Mr. Richard Penket, the Warden, and the Fellow Crafts (all of whom are specified) on the 16th October, 1646."

In another place of his Diary, he says:

"On March the 10th, 1682, about 5 hor. post. merid. I received a summons to appear at a Lodge to be held the next day at Masons' Hall in London. March 11, accordingly I went, and about noon were admitted into the fellowship of Free Masons, Sir William Wilson, Knt., Capt. Richard Borthwick, Mr. William Woodman, Mr. William Gray, Mr. Samuel Taylour, and Mr. William Wise. I was the senior Fellow among them, it being thirty-five years since I was admitted. There were present, beside myself, the Fellows after named: Mr. Thomas Wise, Master of the Masons' company this present year, Mr. Thomas Shorthose, and seven more old Free Masons. We all dined at the Half Moon Tavern, Cheapside, at a noble dinner prepared at the charge of the new accepted Masons."

An old record of the Society describes a coat of arms much the same with that of the London company of Freemen Masons; whence it is generally believed that this company is a branch of that ancient Fraternity; and in former times, no man, it also appears, was made free of that company, until he was initiated in some Lodge of Free and Accepted Masons, as a necessary qualification. This practice still prevails in Scotland among the operative Masons.

The writer of Mr. Ashmole's Life, who was not a Mason, before his History of Berkshire, p. 6, gives the following account of Masonry:

"He (Mr. Ashmole) was elected a Brother of the company of Free Masons, a favor esteemed so singular by the members, that

Kings themselves have not disdained to enter themselves of this Society. From these are derived the Adopted Masons, Accepted Masons, or Free Masons, who are known to one another all over the world by certain signals and watchwords known to them alone. They have several Lodges in different countries for their reception, and when any of them fall into decay, the Brotherhood is to relieve them. The manner of their adoption or admission is very formal and solemn, and with the administration of an oath of secrecy, which has had better fate than all other oaths, and has ever been most religiously observed, nor has the world yet been able, by the inadvertency, surprise or folly of any of its members, to dive into this mystery, or make the least discovery."

In some of Mr. Ashmole's manuscripts, there are many valuable Collections relating to the History of the Free Masons, as may be gathered from the letters of Dr. Knipe, of Christ Church, Oxford, to the publisher of Ashmole's Life; the following extracts from which will authenticate and illustrate many facts in the following history:

"As to the ancient Society of Free Masons, concerning whom you are desirous of knowing what may be known with certainty, I shall only tell you, that if our worthy Brother E. Ashmole, Esq., had executed his intended design, our Fraternity had been as much obliged to him as the Brethren of the most noble Order of the Garter. I would not have you surprised at this expression, or think it at all too assuming. The Sovereigns of that Order have not disdained our fellowship, and there have been times when Emperors were also Free Masons. What from Mr. Ashmole's collection I could gather, was, that the report of our Societies taking rise from a bull granted by the Pope in the reign of Henry VI. to some Italian architects to travel over all Europe to erect chapels, were ill-founded. Such a bull there was, and those architects were Masons. But this bull, in the opinion of the learned Mr. Ashmole, was confirmative only, and did not by any means create our Fraternity, or even establish them in his kingdom. But as to the time and manner of that establishment, something I shall relate from the same collections:

"St. Alban, the protomartyr, established Masonry here, and from his time, it flourished, more or less, according as the world went, down to the days of King Athelstane, who, for the sake of his brother Edwin, granted the Masons a charter. Under our Norman princes, they frequently received extraordinary marks of royal favor; there is no doubt to be made, that the skill of Masons, which was always transcendantly great, even in the most barbarous times; their wonderful kindness and attachment to each other, how different soever in condition; and their inviolable fidelity in keeping religiously their secrets, must expose them, in ignorant, troublesome, and superstitious times, to a vast variety of adventures, according to the different fate of parties, and other alterations in government. By the way, it may be noted, that the Masons were always loyal, which exposed them to great severities when power wore the appearance of justice, and those who committed treason punished true men as traitors. Thus, in the third year of Henry VI. an act passed to abolish the Society of Masons, and to hinder, under grievous penalties, the holding Chapters, Lodges, or other regular assemblies; yet this act was afterwards [virtually] repealed, and even before that, King Henry, and several Lords of his court, became Fellows of the Craft."

Some Lodges in the reign of Charles II. were constituted by *leave* of the several noble Grand Masters, and many gentlemen and famous scholars requested at that time to be admitted of the Fraternity.

X.

The experienced Mason of the present day, will, at one glance, perceive that the following regulations, with but little variation, are still in full force:

Extract from the Regulations made in General Assembly, Dec. 27, 1663. Henry Jermyn, Earl of St. Albans, Grand Master:

"1. That no person, of what degree soever, be made or accepted a Free Mason unless in a regular Lodge, whereof one to be a Master or a Warden in that limit or division where such Lodge is kept, and another to be a Craftsman in the trade of Free Masonry.

"2. That no person hereafter shall be accepted a Free Mason, but such as are of able body, honest parentage, good reputation, and an observer of the laws of the land.

"3. That no person hereafter who shall be accepted a Free Mason, shall be admitted into any Lodge or Assembly, until he has brought a certificate of the time and place of his acceptation from the Lodge that accepted him, unto the Master of that limit or division where such Lodge is kept: And the said Master shall enroll the same in a roll of parchment to be kept for that purpose, and shall give an account of all such acceptations at every General Assembly.

"4. That every person who is now a Free Mason shall bring to the Master a note of the time of his acceptation, to the end the same may be enrolled in such priority of place as the Brother deserves; and that the whole company and Fellows may the better know each other.

"5. That for the future, the said Fraternity of Free Masons shall be regulated and governed by one Grand Master, and as many Wardens as the said Society shall think fit to appoint at every annual General Assembly.

"6. That no person shall be accepted, unless he be twenty-one years old, or more."

Many of the Fraternity's records of this and the preceding reign were lost at the revolution; and not a few were too hastily burnt in our own times by some scrupulous Brothers, from a fear of making discoveries prejudicial to the interests of Masonry.

CHAPTER IV.

ANTIQUITY OF MASONRY, AS DERIVED FROM MODERN AUTHORITIES.

Free Masonry denotes the system of Mysteries and Secrets peculiar to the Society of Free and Accepted Masons. The origin of this Society is very ancient; but we have no authentic account of the time when it was first instituted, or even what was the reason of such an association of people under the title of *Masons*, more than of any other mechanical profession. In Dr. Henry's History, we find the origin of the Free Mason's Society in Britain attributed to the difficulty found in former times, of procuring a sufficient number of workmen to build the multitude of churches, monasteries, and other religious edifices, which the superstition of those ages prompted the people to raise. Hence the Masons were greatly favored by the Popes, and many indulgences were granted, in order to augment their numbers. In times like these we speak of, it may well be supposed that such encouragement from the supreme pastors of the church must have been productive of the most beneficial effects to the Fraternity; and hence the increase of the Society may naturally be deduced. The Doctor quotes, in confirmation of this, the words of an author who was well acquainted with their history and constitution: "The Italians, (says he,) with some Greek refugees, and with them French, Germans, and Flemings, joined into a fraternity of architects, procuring papal bulls for their encouragement and their particular privileges; they styled themselves *Free Masons*, and ranged from one nation to another, as they found churches to be built; their government was regular; and where they fixed near the building in hand, they made a camp of huts. A surveyor governed in chief; every tenth man was called a *Warden*, and overlooked each nine. The gentlemen in the neighborhood, either out of charity or commutation of penance, gave the materials and carriages. Those who have seen the accounts in records of the charge of the fabrics of some of our cathedrals near 400 years old, cannot but have a great esteem for their economy, and admire how soon they erected such lofty structures."

By other accounts, however, the antiquity of Masonry is carried up much higher, even as early as the building of Solomon's temple. In Britain the introduction of Masonry has been fixed at the year 674, when glass-making was first introduced; and it appears, indeed, that from this time many buildings in the Gothic style were erected by men in companies, who are said to have called themselves *free*, because they were at liberty to work in any part of the kingdom. Others have derived the institution of Free Masons from a combination among the people of that profession not to work without an advance of wages, when they were summoned from several counties, by writs of Edward III. directed to the sheriffs, to assist in rebuilding and enlarging the castle, together with the church and castle of St. George, at Windsor. At this time, it is said, the Masons agreed on certain tokens by which they might know and assist each other against being impressed, and not to work unless free, and on their own terms.

In a Treatise on Masonry, published in 1792, by William Preston, Master of the Lodge of Antiquity, the origin of Masonry is traced from the creation. "Ever since symmetry began, and harmony displayed her charms, (says he,) our Order has had a being." Its introduction into England, he likewise supposes to have been prior to the Roman invasion. There are, according to him, the remains yet existing of some stupendous works executed by the Britons, much earlier than the time of the Romans; even these display no small share of ingenuity of invention: so that we can have no doubt of the existence of Masonry in Britain even during these early periods. The Druids are likewise said to have had among them many customs similar to those of the Masons, and to have derived their government from Pythagoras; but the resemblance betwixt their usages and those of the Free Masons Societies now existing, cannot be accurately traced even by the Masons themselves.

Masonry is said to have been encouraged by Cæsar, and many of the Roman generals who were appointed governors of Britain; but though we know, that at this period the Fraternity were employed in erecting many magnificent fabrics, nothing is recorded concerning their Lodges and Conventions; and we have but a very imperfect account of the customs which prevailed in their assemblies.

For a long time the progress of Masonry in Britain was obstructed by the frequent wars which took place; and it did not revive till the time of Carausius, by whom it was patronized. This general, who hoped to be the founder of a British empire, encouraged learning and learned men; collecting also the best artificers from many different countries, particularly Masons, whom he held in great veneration, and appointing Albanus, his steward, the principal superintendent of their assemblies. Lodges or Conventions of the Fraternity, began now to be introduced, and the business of Masonry to be regularly carried on. The Masons, through the influence of Albanus, obtained a charter from Carausius to hold a general council, at which Albanus himself sat president, and assisted at the reception of many new members. This Albanus was the celebrated St. Alban, the first who suffered martyrdom in Britain for the Christian faith. Mr. Preston quotes an old MS. destroyed with many others, said to have been in the possession of Nicholas Stone, a curious sculptor under Inigo Jones; from which we learn that St. Alban was a great friend to Masons, and gave them two shillings per week, besides three pence for their cheer; while, before that time, they had no more than one penny per day, and their meat. He likewise obtained "a charter from the King and his Council, for them to hold a general council, which was named an *Assembly*." The same circumstances are mentioned in a MS. written in the time of James II., only this increases the weekly salary of the Masons to 3s. 6d. and 3d. per day for the bearers of burthens.

The progress of Masonry was greatly obstructed by the departure of the Romans from Britain; and in a short time fell into absolute neglect. This was occasioned first by the furious irruptions of the Scots and Picts, which left no time for the cultivation of the arts; and afterwards by the ignorance of the Saxons, whom the ill-advised Britons called in as allies, but who soon became their masters. After the introduction of Christianity, however, the barbarity of these conquerors began to wear off, the arts received some encouragement, and Masonry particularly began to flourish. Lodges were now formed; but these being under the direction of foreigners, were seldom convened, and never attained to any degree of consideration or importance. In this situation it continued till the year 557, when St. Austin, with forty more monks, among whom the sciences had been preserved, came into England. By these the principles of Christianity were propagated with such zeal, that all the Kings of the heptarchy were converted; after which Masonry was taken under the patronage of St. Austin, and the Gothic style of building was introduced into England by the numerous foreigners who resorted at this time to the kingdom. Austin himself appeared at the head of the Fraternity in founding the old cathedral of Canterbury in 600; that of Rochester in 602; St. Paul's in London in 604; St. Peter's in Westminster in 605, as well as many others. The number of Masons in England was thus greatly increased, as well as by his other buildings of castles &c., throughout the kingdom.

In 640 a few expert brethren arrived from France, and formed themselves into a Lodge under the direction of Bennet, Abbot of Wirral, whom Kenred, King of Mercia, soon after appointed Inspector of the Lodges, and General Superintendent of the Masons. During the whole time of the heptarchy, however, Masonry was in a low state, but began to revive in 856, under the patronage of St. Swithin, whom Ethelwolf employed to repair some religious houses; and from that time the art gradually improved till the year 872, when it found a zealous protector in Alfred the Great. This Prince was a most eminent patron of all kinds of arts and manufactures; and, with regard to Masonry in particular, he appropriated a seventh part of his revenue for maintaining a number of workmen, whom he constantly employed in rebuilding the cities, castles, &c., ruined by the Danes. During the reign of his successor, Edward, the Masons continued to hold their Lodges under the sanction of Ethred, husband to the King's sister, and Ethelward, his brother, to whom the care of the Fraternity was intrusted. The latter was a great architect, and founded the University of Cambridge.

The true reëstablishment of Masonry in England, however, is dated from the reign of King Athelstane; and there is still extant a Grand Lodge of Masons at York, who trace their existence from this period. This Lodge, the most ancient in England, was founded in 926, under the patronage of Edwin, the King's brother, who obtained for them a charter from Athelstane, and became Grand Master himself. By virtue of this charter, it is said that all the Masons in the kingdom were convened at a General Assembly in that city, where they established a General or Grand Lodge for their future government. Under the patronage and jurisdiction of this Lodge, it is also alleged that the Fraternity increased very considerably, and that Kings, Princes, and other eminent persons who had been initiated into the mysteries, paid due allegiance to the Assembly. But as the times were yet turbulent and barbarous, the art of Masonry was sometimes more, sometimes less patronized, and of course the Assembly more or less respected, according to the respect which the art itself met with. The appellation of *Ancient York Masons* is well known both in Ireland and Scotland; and the general tradition is, that they originated at Auldby, near York; and as Auldby was a seat of Edwin, this tradition gives considerable confirmation to the above account. There is, indeed, great reason to believe that York was the original seat of Masonic government, no other place having claimed it, and the whole Fraternity having at various times owned allegiance to the authority there established; though we know not whether that allegiance be now given or not. Certain it is, that if such a Lodge was once established there, of which there is no reason to doubt, we have no account of its being regularly moved from that place to any other part of the kingdom, with consent of its members. Many respectable meetings have, indeed, been held at different times in other parts of the kingdom, but there is no account of any other general meeting being held in another place than York till very lately.

While Prince Edwin lived, the Masons were employed as formerly in building churches, monasteries, &c., and repairing those which had suffered by the ravages of the Danes; and after his death the Order was patronized by King Athelstane himself; but, on his decease, the Masons were dispersed, and remained in an unsettled state till the reign of Edgar, in 960. They were now collected by St. Dunstan, who employed them in works of the same kind: but as no permanent encouragement was given them, their Lodges soon declined, and Masonry remained in a low state for upwards of 50 years. It revived, however, in 1041, under Edward the Confessor, who superintended the execution of several great works. By the assistance of Leofrick, Earl of Coventry, he rebuilt Westminster Abbey, the Earl being appointed Superintendent of the Masons; and by this architect many other magnificent structures were likewise erected. After the Conquest, in 1066, Gundulph, Bishop of Rochester, and Roger de Montgomery, Earl of Shrewsbury, both of them excellent architects, became joint patrons of the Masons; and under their auspices the Tower of London was begun, though finished only in the reign of William Rufus, who likewise rebuilt London bridge with wood, and, in 1087, first constructed the Palace and Hall of Westminster.

The Masons now continued to be patronized by the Sovereigns of England in succession. The Lodges assembled during the reign of Henry I., and during that of Stephen the Society were employed in building a chapel at Westminster, now the House of Commons, and several other works; the President of the Lodges being now Gilbert de Clare, the Marquis of Pembroke. During the reign of Henry II. the Lodges were superintended by the Grand Master of the Knights Templar, who employed them in building their temple in Fleet street, in the year 1155. Masonry continued under the patronage of this Order till the year 1199, when John succeeded Richard I. in the throne of England, and Peter de Colechurch was then appointed Grand Master. He began to rebuild London bridge with stone, which was afterwards finished by William Alcmain, in 1209. Peter de Rupibus succeeded Peter de Colechurch in the office of Grand Master, and Geoffrey Fitz-Peter, chief surveyor of the King's works, acted as deputy under him; Masonry continued also to flourish under the auspices of these two artists during this and the following reign. On the accession of Edward I., in 1272, the superintendence of the Masons was intrusted to Walter Giffard, Archbishop of York, Gilbert de

Clare, Earl of Gloucester, and Ralph, Lord of Mount Hermer, the progenitor of the family of the Montagues; and by these architects the Abbey of Westminster was finished, after having been begun in 1220, during the minority of Henry II. During the reign of Edward II., the Fraternity were employed in building Exeter and Oriel Colleges in Oxford, Clare Hall in Cambridge, &c., under the auspices of Walter Stapleton, Bishop of Exeter, who had been appointed Grand Master of the Masons in 1307.

Edward III. was a great encourager of learning in general, and not only patronized the Masons, but applied very assiduously to the constitutions of the Order, revised and meliorated the ancient charges, and added several useful regulations to the original code by which the Fraternity had been governed. He patronized the Lodges, and appointed five deputies under him to inspect their proceedings; and at this period it appears from some old records that the Lodges were numerous, and that the Fraternity held communications under the protection of the civil magistrates. William â Wykeham was continued Grand Master on the accession of Richard II., and by him both the new College in Oxford and Winchester College were founded at his own expense. After the accession of Henry IV. Thomas Fitz-Allan, Earl of Surrey, was appointed Grand Master, who, after the engagement of Shrewsbury, founded Battle Abbey and Fotheringay; the Guildhall at London being also built in this reign. On the accession of Henry V. the Fraternity were directed by Henry Chicheley, Archbishop of Canterbury, under whom the Lodges and communications of the Fraternity were frequent. In 1425, however, during the reign of Henry VI., an act was made against the meeting of the Chapters and Congregations of Masons, because it was said that by such meetings "the good course and effect of the statutes of laborers were openly violated and broken, in subversion of the law, and to the great damage of all the commons." But this act was not put in force, nor did the Fraternity cease to meet, as usual, under the protection of Archbishop Chichely, who still continued to preside over them. The reason of this extraordinary edict is said to have been as follows: The Duke of Bedford, at that time Regent of the kingdom, being in France, the regal power was vested in his brother Humphrey, Duke of Gloucester, who was styled Protector and Guardian of the Kingdom. The care of the young King's person and education was intrusted to Henry Beaufort, Bishop of Winchester, the Duke's uncle. This Prelate being of an ambitious disposition, and aspiring at the sole government, had continual disputes with his nephew, the Protector; and, by reason of the violent temper of that prince, gained frequent advantages over him. This animosity increased to such a degree, that the Parliament was at length obliged to interpose. On the meeting of that assembly, in the month of April, 1425, however, the servants and followers of the Peers came thither, armed with clubs and staves; on which account it received the name of the *Bat Parliament*, and at this time the act against Masons was made. This was owing to the influence of the Bishop, who wished to destroy the meetings of the Fraternity, on account of the secrecy observed in them. Dr. Anderson, in the first edition of the Book of Constitutions, makes the following observation upon this act: "It was made in ignorant times, when true learning was a crime, and geometry condemned for conjuration; but it cannot derogate from the honor of the ancient Fraternity, who, to be sure, would never encourage any such confederacy of their working brethren. By tradition, it is believed that the Parliament were then too much influenced by the illiterate clergy, who were not Accepted Masons, nor understood architecture, (as the clergy of some former ages,) and were generally thought unworthy of this Brotherhood. Thinking they had an indefeasible right to know all secrets, by virtue of auricular confession, and the Masons never confessing anything thereof, the said clergy were highly offended; and, at first suspecting them of wickedness, represented them as dangerous to the state during that minority; and soon influenced the Parliament to lay hold of such supposed arguments of the working Masons, for making an act that might seem to reflect dishonor upon even the whole Fraternity, in whose favor several acts had been made before that period, and were made after it."

The Bishop was soon after this diverted from his persecution of the Masons by an affair of a more important kind. He had formed a design of surprising the City of London on the evening of St. Simon and St. Jude's day, that on which the Lord Mayor was invested with his office. But the plot having been discovered by the Duke of Gloucester, the Mayor was sent for while at dinner, and ordered to keep a strict watch for that night. The Bishop's party accordingly made an attempt to enter by the bridge about nine the next morning, but were repulsed by the vigilance of the citizens. At this the Prelate was so much enraged, that he collected a numerous body of archers and men-at-arms, commanding them to assault the gate with shot. By the prudence of the magistrates, however, all violent measures were stopped; but no reconciliation could be procured betwixt the two parties, though it was attempted by the Archbishop of Canterbury, and Peter, Duke of Coimbra, eldest son to the King of Portugal, with several other persons of distinction. At last the Bishop wrote a letter to the Duke of Bedford, urging his return to England, and informing him of the danger there was of a civil war, and reflecting upon the Duke of Gloucester. This letter had the desired effect. The Regent returned, and held a great council at St. Albans, on the 21st of February, but adjourned it to the 15th of March, at Northampton, and to the 25th of June, at Leicester. Bats and staves were now prohibited at these meetings; but the parties assembled with weapons no less formidable, viz: with slings, stones, and leaden plummets. The Duke of Bedford employed all his authority to reconcile the differences; and at last obliged the two rivals to promise, before the Assembly, that they would bury all animosities in oblivion. During the discussion of this matter, five charges were exhibited by the Duke of Gloucester against the Bishop: one of which was, that "he had, in his letter to the Duke of Bedford, at France, plainly declared his malicious purpose of assembling the people, and stirring up a rebellion in the nation, contrary to the King's peace." To this the Bishop answered, "That he never had any intention to disturb the peace of the nation, or raise a rebellion; but that he sent to the Duke of Bedford to solicit his return to England, to settle all those differences which were so prejudicial to the peace of the kingdom; that though he had indeed written in the letter, 'that if he tarried, we should put the land in adventure by a field, such a brother you have here,' he did not mean it of any design of his own, but concerning the seditious assemblies of masons, carpenters, tylers and plaisterers; who being distressed by the late act of Parliament against the excessive wages of these trades, had given out many seditious speeches and menaces against certain great men, which tended much to rebellion," &c.

Notwithstanding this heavy charge, the Duke of Gloucester, who knew the innocence of the parties accused, took the Masons under his protection, and transferred the charge of sedition and rebellion from them to the Bishop and his followers. By the interest of the latter, however, the King granted him a pardon for all offences; and though the Duke drew up fresh articles of impeachment against him in 1442, and presented them in person to the King, the Council, being composed mostly of Ecclesiastics, proceeded so slowly in the business, that the Duke, wearied out with the tediousness of the matter, dropped the prosecution entirely.

This contest terminated in the impeachment, imprisonment and murder of the Duke of Gloucester himself. This event might have been attended with bad consequences, had not their inveterate enemy, the Prelate himself, been taken off by death, in about two months after the Duke. The Masons then continued, not only to meet in safety, but were joined by the King himself. He was, that very year, (1442,) initiated into Masonry, and from that time spared no pains to become completely master of the art. He perused the ancient charges, revised the constitutions, and, with the consent of his council, honored them with his sanction. The example of the Sovereign was followed by many of the nobility, who assiduously studied the art. The King presided over the Lodges in person, nominating William Wanefleet, Bishop of Winchester, Grand Master. This Bishop, at his own expense, built Magdalene College, Oxford, and several religious houses. Eton College, near Windsor, and King's College, at Cambridge, were also founded during this reign. Henry himself founded Christ's College, Cambridge, as his Queen, Margaret of Anjou, did Queen's College in the same University.

About this time, also, the Masons were protected and

encouraged by James I. of Scotland, who, after his return from captivity, became a zealous patron of the arts and learning of all kinds. He honored the Lodges with his royal presence, and settled an annual revenue of four pounds Scots (an English noble) to be paid by every Master Mason in Scotland, to a Grand Master chosen by the Grand Lodge, and approved by the Crown, one nobly born, or an eminent clergyman who had his deputies in cities and counties; something was likewise paid him by every new brother at his entry. His office entitled him to regulate everything in the Fraternity which could not come under the jurisdiction of the law courts; and, to prevent law suits, both mason and lord, or builder and founder, appealed to him. In his absence, they appealed to his deputy, or Grand Warden, who resided next the premises.

The flourishing state of Masonry was interrupted by the civil wars between the houses of York and Lancaster, which brought it almost totally into neglect. About 1471, however, it revived under the auspices of Robert Beauchamp, Bishop of Sarum, who had been appointed Grand Master by Edward IV. and honored with the title of *Chancellor of the Garter*, for repairing the Castle and Chapel of Windsor. It again declined during the reigns of Edward V. and Richard III., but came once more into repute on the accession of Henry VII., in 1485. It was now patronized by the Master and Fellows of the Order of St. John of Rhodes (now Malta,) who assembled their Grand Lodge in 1500, and chose Henry for their protector. On the 24th of June, 1502, a Lodge of Masters was formed in the Palace, at which the King presided as Grand Master; and having appointed John Islip, Abbot of Westminster, and Sir Reginald Bray, Knight of the Garter, his Wardens for the occasion, proceeded in great state to the east end of Westminster

Abbey, where he laid the first stone of that excellent piece of Gothic architecture, called *Henry the Seventh's Chapel*. The cape-stone of this building was celebrated in 1507. The Palace of Richmond, as well as many other noble structures, were raised under the direction of Sir Reginald Bray; and the College of Brazen Nose, in Oxford, and Jesus and St. John's, in Cambridge, were all finished in this reign.

On the accession of Henry VIII. Cardinal Wolsey was appointed Grand Master, who built Hampton Court, Whitehall, Christ Church College, Oxford, with several other noble edifices, all of which, upon the disgrace of that Prelate, were forfeited to the Crown in 1530. Wolsey was succeeded as Grand Master in 1534, by Thomas Cromwell, Earl of Essex, who employed the Fraternity in building St. James' Palace, Christ's Hospital, and Greenwich Castle. Cromwell being beheaded in 1540, John Touchet, Lord Audley, succeeded to the office of Grand Master, and built Magdalene College, in Cambridge, and many other structures. In 1547, the Duke of Somerset, guardian to the King, and Regent of the kingdom, became Superintendent of the Masons, and built Somerset House, in the Strand, which, on his being beheaded, was forfeited to the crown in 1552.

After the death of the Duke of Somerset, John Poynet, Bishop of Winchester, presided over the Lodges till the death of the King in 1553. From this time they continued without any patron till the reign of Elizabeth, when Sir Thomas Sackville áccepted of the office of Grand Master. Lodges, however, had been held during this period in different parts of England; but the General or Grand Lodge assembled in the city of York, where, it is said, the Fraternity were numerous and respectable. Of the Queen, we have the following curious anecdote with regard to the Masons: Hearing that they were in possession of many secrets which they refused to disclose, and being naturally jealous of all secret assemblies, she sent an armed force to York to break up their annual Grand Lodge. The design was prevented by the interposition of Sir Thomas Sackville, who took care to initiate some of the chief officers, whom she had sent on this duty, in the secrets of Masonry. These joined in communication with their new brethren, and made so favorable a report to the Queen on their return, that she countermanded her orders, and never afterwards attempted to disturb the meeting of the Fraternity. In 1567, Sir Thomas Sackville resigned the office of Grand Master in favor of Francis Russel, Earl of Bedford, and Sir Thomas Gresham, an eminent merchant. The former had the care of the Brethren in the northern part of the kingdom assigned to him, while the latter was appointed to superintend the meetings of the south, where the Society had considerably increased, in consequence of the honorable report which had been made to the Queen. The General Assembly, however, continued to meet at York as formerly; and here all records were kept, and appeals made, on every important occasion, to the Assembly.

Sir Thomas Gresham, above mentioned, proposed to erect a building in the city of London for the benefit of commerce, provided the citizens would purchase a spot proper for the purpose. Accordingly, some houses between Cornhill and Threadneedle street being pulled down, the foundation stone of the building was laid on the 7th of June, 1566, and with such expedition was the work carried on, that the whole was finished in November, 1567. This building, which was constructed on the plan of the Exchange of Antwerp, was called at first, simply *the Bourse;* but in January, 1570, the Queen having dined with Sir Thomas, returned through Cornhill, entered the Bourse on the south side, and having viewed every part of the building, particularly the gallery which extended round the whole structure, and which was furnished with shops filled with all sorts of the finest merchandise in the city, she caused the edifice to be proclaimed in her presence, by herald and trumpet, the *Royal Exchange;* and on this occasion, it is said, Sir Thomas appeared publicly in the character of Grand Master.

The Queen being now thoroughly convinced that the Fraternity of Masons did not interfere in state affairs, became quite reconciled to their assemblies, and from this time Masonry made a considerable progress; Lodges were held in different parts of the kingdom, particularly in London and its neighborhood, where the number of the brethren increased considerably. Several great works were carried on there under the auspices of Sir Thomas Gresham, from whom the Fraternity received every encouragement. Sir Thomas was succeeded in the office of Grand Master by Charles Howard, Earl of Effingham, who continued to preside over the Lodges in the south, till the year 1588, when George Hastings, Earl of Huntingdon, was chosen Grand Master, and remained in the office till the decease of the Queen, in 1603.

On the accession of James I. to the Crown of England, Masonry flourished in both kingdoms, and Lodges were held in both kingdoms. A number of gentlemen returned from their travels, with curious drawings of the old Greek and Roman architecture, as well as strong inclinations to revive a knowledge of it. Among these was the celebrated Inigo Jones, who was appointed general surveyor to the King. He was named Grand Master of England, and was deputed by the King to preside over the Lodges.* Several learned men were now initiated into the mysteries of Masonry, and the Society increased considerably in reputation and consequence. Ingenious artists resorted to England in great numbers; Lodges were constituted as seminaries of instruction in the sciences and polite arts, after the model of the Italian schools; the communications of the Fraternity were established, and the annual festivals regularly observed. Under the direction of this accomplished architect, many magnificent structures were raised, and, among the rest, he was employed, by command of the Sovereign, to plan a new Palace at Whitehall, worthy of the residence of the Kings of England. This was executed, but for want of a parliamentary fund, no more of the plan was ever finished than the banqueting-house. Inigo Jones continued in the office of Grand Master till the year 1618, when he was succeeded by the Earl of Pembroke, under whose auspices many eminent and wealthy men were initiated, and the mysteries of the Order held in high estimation.

After Charles I. ascended the throne, Earl Pembroke continued in his office till the year 1630, when he resigned in favor of Henry Danvers, Earl of Danby. This nobleman was succeeded in 1663 by Thomas Howard, Earl of Arundel, the ancestor of the Norfolk family. In 1635, Francis Russel, Earl of Bedford, accepted the government of the Society; but Inigo Jones having continued to patronize the Lodges during his lordship's administration, he was reëlected the following year, and continued in office till the year of his death, 1646. The progress of Masonry, however, was for some time obstructed by the breaking out of the civil wars; but it

* Mr. Preston observes, that the Grand Master of the north bears the title of *Grand Master of all England*, which (says he) may probably have been occasioned by the title of *Grand Master*.

began to revive under the patronage of Charles II., who had been received into the Order during his exile. Some Lodges, during this reign, were constituted by *leave* of the *several* noble Grand Masters, and many gentlemen and famous scholars requested at that time to be admitted into the Fraternity. On the 27th of December, 1663, a General Assembly was held, where Henry Jermyn, Earl of St. Albans, was elected Grand Master, who appointed Sir John Denham his deputy, and Mr. Christopher Wren, afterwards the celebrated Sir Christopher Wren, and John Webb, his Wardens. At this assembly several useful regulations were made, for the better government of the Lodges, and the greatest harmony prevailed among the whole Fraternity. The Earl of St. Albans was succeeded in his office of Grand Master by Earl Rivers, in the year 1666, when Sir Christopher Wren was appointed deputy, and distinguished himself beyond any of his predecessors in promoting the prosperity of the Lodges which remained at that time, particularly that of St. Paul's, now the Lodge of Antiquity, which he patronized upwards of eighteen years. At this time he attended the meetings regularly, and during his presidency made a present to the Lodge of three mahogany candlesticks, which at that time were very valuable. They are still preserved, and highly valued as a testimony of the esteem of the donor.

The fire which, in 1666, destroyed such a great part of London, afforded ample opportunity for the Masons to exert their abilities. After a calamity so sudden and extensive, however, it became necessary to adopt some regulations to prevent such a catastrophe in time to come. It was now determined, that in all the new buildings to be erected, stone should be used instead of timber. Wren was ordered by the King and Grand Master, to draw up the plan of a city with broad and regular streets.

Sir Christopher Wren was appointed surveyor general, and principal architect, for rebuilding the city, the Cathedral of St. Paul, and all the parochial churches enacted by Parliament, in lieu of those that were destroyed, with other public structures. This gentleman, however, conceiving the charge to be too important for a single person, reëlected for his assistant Mr. Robert Hook, Professor of Geometry in Gresham College. The latter was immediately employed in measuring, adjusting and setting out the ground of the private streets to the several proprietors. The model and plan were laid before the King and House of Commons, and the practicability of the whole scheme, without any infringement of private property; but unfortunately it happened, that the greater part of the citizens were totally averse to leaving their old habitations, and building houses in other places; and so obstinate were they in their determinations, that they chose rather to have their old city again, under all its disadvantages, than a new one upon the improved plan. Thus an opportunity was lost of making the new city the most magnificent, as well as the most convenient for health and commerce, of any in Europe. Hence the architect, being cramped in the execution of his plan, was obliged to alter and abridge it, and to model the city after the manner in which it has since appeared. In 1673, the foundation stone of the Cathedral of St. Paul was laid with great solemnity, by the King in person, and the Mallet which he used on this occasion, is still preserved in the Lodge of Antiquity, as a great curiosity.

During the time that the city was rebuilding, Lodges were held by the Fraternity in different places, and many new ones constituted, to which the best architects resorted. In 1674, Earl Rivers resigned the office of Grand Master, in favor of George Villiers, Duke of

Buckingham, who left the care of the Fraterity to his Wardens, and Sir Christopher Wren, who still continued to act as deputy. In 1679, the Duke resigned in favor of Henry Bennet, Earl of Arlington; but this nobleman was too deeply engaged in state affairs to attend to his duty as a Mason, though the Lodges continued to meet under his sanction, and many respectable gentlemen joined the Fraternity. During the short reign of James II. the Masons were much neglected. In 1685, Sir Christopher Wren was elected to the office of Grand Master, who appointed Gabriel Cibber and Mr. Edward Strong, his Wardens; yet, notwithstanding the great reputation and abilities of this celebrated architect, Masonry continued in a declining way for many years, and only a few Lodges were held occasionally in different parts of the kingdom.

At the revolution, the Society was in such a low state in the south of England, that only seven regular Lodges were held in London and its suburbs; and of these only two, viz: that of St. Paul's, and one at St. Thomas' hospital, Southwark, were of any consequence. But, in 1695, King William having been initiated into the mysteries, honored the Lodges with his presence, particularly one at Hampton Court, at which he is said to have frequently presided during the time that the new part of his palace was building. Many of the nobility also were present at a general assembly and feast, held in 1697, particularly Charles, Duke of Richmond and Lenox, who was elected Grand Master for that year; but in 1698, resigned his office to Sir Christopher Wren, who continued at the head of the Fraternity till King William's death in 1702.

During the reign of Queen Anne, Masonry made no considerable progress. Sir Christopher's age and infirmities drew off his attention from the duties of his office; the annual festivals were entirely neglected, and the number of Masons considerably diminished. It was therefore determined that the privileges of Masonry should not be confined to operative Masons, but that people of all professions should be admitted to participate in them, provided they were regularly approved and initiated into the Order.

Thus the Society once more rose into esteem; and on the accession of George I. the Masons, now deprived of Sir Christopher Wren, resolved to unite again under a Grand Master, and revive the annual festivals. With this view, the members of the only four Lodges at that time existing in London, met at the Apple-tree Tavern, in Charles street, Convent Garden; and having voted the oldest Master Mason then present, into the chair, constituted themselves a Grand Lodge *pro tempore.* It was now resolved to renew the quarterly communications among the brethren; and at an annual meeting held on the 24th of June, the same year, Mr. Anthony Sayer was elected Grand Master, invested by the oldest Master Mason there present, installed by the Master of the oldest Lodge, and had due homage paid him by the Fraternity. *Before this time, a sufficient number of Masons met together within a certain district, had ample power to make Masons without a Warrant of Constitution;* but it was now determined that the privilege of assembling as Masons should be vested in certain Lodges or Assemblies of Masons convened in certain places, and that every Lodge to be afterwards convened, excepting the four old Lodges then existing, should be authorized to act by a warrant from the Grand Master for the time, granted by petition from certain individuals, with the consent and approbation of the Grand Lodge in communication; and that without such warrant, no Lodge should hereafter be deemed regular or constitutional.

The former privileges, however, were still allowed to remain to the four old Lodges then extant. In consequence of this, the old Masons in the metropolis vested all their inherent privileges, as individuals, in the four old Lodges, in trust that they never would suffer the ancient charges and landmarks to be infringed. The four old Lodges, on their part, agreed to extend their patronage to every new Lodge which should hereafter be constituted according to the new regulations of the Society; and while they acted in conformity to the ancient Constitutions of the Order, to admit their Masters and Wardens to share with them all the privileges of the Grand Lodge, that of precedence only excepted.

Matters being thus settled, the brethren of the four old Lodges considered their attendance on the future communications of the Society as unnecessary; and, therefore, trusted implicitly to their Masters and Wardens, satisfied that no measure of importance would be adopted without their approbation. It was, however, soon discovered that the new Lodges being equally represented with the old ones at the communications, would at length so far out number them, that by a majority they might subvert the privileges of the original Masons of England which had been centred in the four old Lodges; on which account a Code of Laws was, with the consent of the brethren at large, drawn up for the future government of the Society. To this the following was annexed, binding the Grand Master for the time being, his successors, and the Master of every Lodge to be hereafter constituted, to preserve it inviolably: "Every annual Grand Lodge has an inherent power and authority to make new regulations, or to alter these for the real benefit of this ancient Fraternity—provided always that the old landmarks be carefully preserved; and that such alterations and new regulations be proposed and agreed to, at the third quarterly communication preceding the annual grand feast; and that they be offered also to the perusal of all the brethren before dinner, in writing, even of the youngest apprentice; the approbation and consent of the majority of all the brethren present being absolutely necessary to make the same binding and obligatory." To commemorate this circumstance, it has been customary, ever since that time, for the Master of the oldest Lodge to attend every grand installation; and, taking precedence of all present, the Grand Master only excepted, to deliver the books of the Original Constitutions to the new installed Grand Master, on his promising obedience to the ancient charges and general regulations.

By this precaution, the Original Constitutions were established as the basis of all succeeding Masonic jurisdiction in the south of England; and the ancient *landmarks*, as they are called, or the boundaries set up as checks against innovation, were carefully secured from the attacks of any future invaders. No great progress, however, was made during the administration of Mr. Sayer, only two Lodges being constituted, though several brethren joined the old ones. In 1718, Mr. Sayer was succeeded by Mr. George Payne, who collected many valuable manuscripts on the subject of Masonry, and earnestly requested that the Fraternity would bring to the Grand Lodge any old writings or records concerning the Fraternity, to show the usages of ancient times; and in consequence of this invitation, several old copies of the Gothic Constitutions were produced, arranged and digested. Another Assembly and Feast was held on the 24th of June, 1719, when Dr. Desaguliers was unanimously elected Grand Master. At this feast the old, regular and peculiar toasts were introduced; and from this time we may date the rise of

Free Masonry on its present plan, in the south of England. Many new Lodges were established, the old ones visited by many Masons who had long neglected the Craft, and several noblemen initiated into the mysteries. In 1720, however, the Fraternity sustained an irreparable loss by the burning of several manuscripts, concerning the Lodges, regulations, charges, secrets, &c., (particularly one written by Mr. Nicholas Stone, the Warden under Inigo Jones.) This was done by some scrupulous brethren, who were alarmed at the publication of the Masonic Constitutions. At a quarterly communication, it was this year agreed that, for the future, the new Grand Master shall be named and proposed to the Grand Lodge some time before the Feast; and if approved and present, he shall be saluted as Grand Master elect; and that every Grand Master, when he is installed, shall have the sole power of appointing his Deputy and Wardens according to ancient custom.

In the mean time Masonry continued to spread in the north as well as the south of England. The General Assembly, or Grand Lodge at York, continued to meet as usual. Several Lodges met in 1705, under the direction of Sir John Tempest, Baronet, then Grand Master; and many persons of worth and character were initiated into the mysteries of the Fraternity. The greatest harmony subsisted between the two Grand Lodges, and private Lodges were formed in both parts of the kingdom under their separate jurisdiction. The only distinction which the Grand Lodge in the north appears to have retained, is in the title of the *Grand Lodge of all England;* while the other was only called the *Grand Lodge of England.* The latter, however, being encouraged by some of the principal nobility, soon acquired consequence and reputation, while the other seemed gradually to decline; but, till within these few years, the authority of the Grand Lodge at York was never challenged; on the other hand, every Mason in the kingdom held that Assembly in the highest veneration, and considered himself bound by the charges which originated from that Assembly. It was the glory and boast of the brethren, in almost every country where Masonry was established, to be accounted descendants of the original York Masons: and from the universality of the idea that Masonry was first established at York, by charter, the Masons of England have received tribute from the first States in Europe. At present, however, this social intercourse is abolished, and the Lodges in the north and south are almost entirely unknown to one another; and neither the Lodges of Scotland nor Ireland court the correspondence of the Grand Lodge at London. This is said to have been owing to the introduction of some innovations among the Lodges in the south; but for the coolness which subsists between the two Grand Lodges another reason is assigned. A few brethren at York, having, on some trivial occasion, seceded from their ancient Lodge, they applied to London for a Warrant of Constitution. Their application was honored without any enquiry into the merits of the case; and thus, instead of being recommended to the Mother Lodge to be restored to favor, these brethren were encouraged to revolt, and permitted, under the sanction of the Grand Lodge in London, to open a new Lodge in the city of York itself. This illegal extension of power justly offended the Grand Lodge at York, and occasioned a breach which has never yet been made up.

The Duke of Buccleugh, who, in 1723, succeeded the Duke of Wharton as Grand Master, first proposed the scheme of raising a general fund for distressed Masons. The Duke's motion was supported by Lord Paisley, Colonel Houghton, and a few other brethren; and the

Grand Lodge appointed a committee to consider of the most effectual means of carrying the scheme into execution. The disposal of the charity was first vested in several brethren; but this number being found too small, nine more were added. It was afterwards resolved that twelve Masters of contributing Lodges, in rotation with the Grand Officers, should form the committee; and by another regulation since made, it has been determined that all past and present Grand Officers, with the Masters of all regular Lodges which shall have contributed within twelve months to the charity, shall be members of the committee. This committee meets four times in the year, by virtue of a summons from the Grand Master or his deputy. The petitions of the distressed brethren are considered at these meetings; and if the petitioner be considered as a deserving object, he is immediately relieved with five pounds. If the circumstances of the case are of a peculiar nature, his petition is referred to the next communication, where he is relieved with any sum the committee may have specified, not exceeding 20 guineas at one time. Thus the distressed have always found relief from this general charity, which is supported by the voluntary contributions of different Lodges out of their private funds, without being burdensome to any member in the Society. Thus has the committee of charity for Free Masons been established; and so liberal have the contributions been, that though the sums annually expended for the relief of the distressed brethren have, for several years past, amounted to many thousand pounds, there still remains a considerable sum.

The most remarkable events which of late have taken place in the affairs of Masonry, are the initiation of Omitul Omrah Bahauder, eldest son of the Nabob of the Carnatic, who was received by the Lodge of Trichinopoly, in the year 1779. The news being officially transmitted to England, the Grand Lodge determined to send a congratulatory letter to his Highness on the occasion, accompanied with an Apron elegantly decorated, and a copy of the Book of Constitutions superbly bound. The execution of this commission was entrusted to Sir John Duy, Advocate General of Bengal; and in the beginning of 1780, an answer was received from his Highness, acknowledging the receipt of the present, and expressing the warmest attachment and benevolence to his brethren in England. The letter was written in the Persian language, and enclosed in an elegant cover of cloth of gold, and addressed to the Grand Master and Grand Lodge of England. A proper reply was made; and a translation of his Highness' letter was ordered to be copied on vellum, and, with the original, elegantly framed and glazed, and hung up in the Hall at every public meeting of the Society.

After such a long history of the rise and progress of Masonry, it must be natural to enquire into the uses of the Institution, and for what purpose it has been patronized by so many great and illustrious personages. The profound secrecy however, in which everything relating to Masonry is involved, prevents us from being very particular on this head. The Masons themselves say, in general, that it affords relief to the poor and needy, promotes philanthropy, friendship and morality; and that in proportion as Masonry has been cultivated, the countries have been civilized. How far this can be depended upon, the Fraternity themselves best know. Another advantage however, seems less equivocal, viz: that its signs serve as a kind of universal language, so that by means of them, people of the most distant nations may become acquainted, and enter into friendship with one another. This certainly must be accounted a very important circumstance; and considering the great number which have been, and daily are, admitted to the Society, and their inviolable attachment to the art, we must in candor conclude, that it contains something of great importance to mankind at large.

CHAPTER V.

HISTORY OF GRAND LODGES.

For this chapter, I am indebted to our talented Brother A. G. Mackey.—See his *Lexicon*, article on "Grand Lodges."

The present *Organization* of Grand Lodges is by no means coeval with the origin of our Institution. Every Lodge was originally independent, and a sufficient number of brethren meeting together, were empowered to practise all the rites of Masonry without a Warrant of Constitution. This privilege, as Preston remarks, was inherent in them as individuals. The brethren were in the custom of meeting annually, at least as many as conveniently could, for the purpose of conference on the general concerns of the Order, and on this occasion a Grand Master or Superintendent of the whole Fraternity was usually chosen. These meetings were not, however, called Grand Lodges, but "Assemblies." This name and organization are as old as the fourth century of the Christian era; for in a MS.* once in the possession of Nicholas Stone, a sculptor under the celebrated Inigo Jones, it is stated that "St. Albans, (who was martyred in 306,) loved Masons well, and cherish them much. * * * * And he got them a charter from the King and his counsell, for to holde a generall counsell and gave itt to name Assemblie." The privilege of attending these annual Assemblies, was not restricted, as it now is, to the Grand Officers, and Masters, and Wardens of subordinate Lodges, but constituted one of the obligatory duties of every Mason. Thus among the ancient Masonic charges in possession of the Lodge of Antiquity at London is one which declares

* Quoted by Preston.

that "every Master and Fellow shall come to the Assemblie, if itt be within fifty miles of him, and if he have any warning. And if he have trespassed the Craft, to abide the award of Masters and Fellows."

ENGLAND. The next* charter granted in England to the Masons as a body, was bestowed by King Athelstane in 926 upon the application of his brother Prince Edwin. "Accordingly, Prince Edwin summoned all the Masons in the realm to meet him in a congregation at York, who came and composed a General Lodge, of which he was Grand Master; and having brought with them all the writings and records extant, some in Greek, some in Latin, some in French, and other languages, from the contents thereof, that Assembly did frame the Constitution and charges of an English Lodge."†

From this Assembly at York, the true rise of Masonry in England is generally dated; from the statutes there enacted, are derived the English Masonic Constitutions; and from the place of meeting, the ritual of the English Lodges is designated as the "Ancient York Rite."

For a long time the York Assembly exercised the Masonic jurisdiction over all England; but in 1567, the Masons of the southern part of the island elected Sir Thomas Gresham, the celebrated merchant, their Grand Master. He was succeeded by the illustrious architect, Inigo Jones. There were now two Grand Masters in England, who assumed distinctive titles, the Grand Master of the north being called Grand Master of all England, while he who presided in the south, was called Grand Master of England.

In the beginning of the 18th century, Masonry in the south of England had fallen into decay. The disturbances of the revolution which placed William the Third on the Throne, and the subsequent warmth of political feelings, which agitated the two parties of the state, had given this peaceful society a wound fatal to its success. Sir Christopher Wren, the Grand Master in the reign of Queen Anne, had become aged, infirm and inactive, and hence the General Assemblies of the Grand Lodge had ceased to take place. There were, in the year 1715, but four Lodges in the south of England, all working in the city of London. These four Lodges, desirous of reviving the prosperity of the Order, determined to unite themselves under a Grand Master, Sir Christopher Wren being now dead, and none having as yet been appointed in his place. They, therefore, "met

* And if the anecdote of St. Albans be not authentic, the first.

† Elias Ashmole's MS.

at the Apple-tree tavern, and having put into the chair the oldest Master Mason, (being the Master of a Lodge,) they constituted themselves a Grand Lodge *pro tempore*, in due form, and forthwith revived the quarterly communication of the officers of the Lodges, (called the Grand Lodge,) resolved to hold the Annual Assembly and Feast, and then to choose a Grand Master from among themselves, till they should have the honor of a noble brother at their head."*

Accordingly, on St. John the Baptist's day, 1717, the Annual Assembly and Feast were held, and Mr. Anthony Sayer, duly proposed and elected Grand Master. The Grand Lodge adopted, among its regulations, the following: "That the privilege of assembling as Masons, which had hitherto been unlimited, should be vested in certain Lodges or Assemblies of Masons convened in certain places, and that every Lodge to be hereafter convened, except the four old Lodges, at this time existing, should be legally authorized to act by a warrant from the Grand Master for the time being, granted to certain individuals by petition, with the consent and approbation of the Grand Lodge in communication, and that without such warrant, no Lodge should be hereafter deemed regular or constitutional."

In compliment, however, to the four old Lodges, the privileges which they had always possessed under the old organization, were particularly reserved to them, and it was enacted that "no law, rule or regulation, to be hereafter made or passed in Grand Lodge, should ever deprive them of such privilege,† or encroach on any landmark which was at that time established as the standard of Masonic government."

The Grand Lodges of York and of London, kept up a friendly intercourse, and mutual interchange of recognition, until the latter body, in 1725, granted a Warrant of Constitution to some Masons, who had seceded from the former. This unmasonic act was severely reprobated by the York Grand Lodge, and produced the first interruption to the harmony that had long subsisted between them. It was, however, followed some years after by another unjustifiable act of interference. In 1735, the Earl of Crawford, Grand Master of England, constituted two Lodges within the jurisdiction of the Grand Lodge of York, and granted, without their consent, deputa-

* Anderson's Constitutions, p. 197.

† Among these privileges, were those of assembling without a Warrant of Constitution, and raising Masons to the Master's degree, a power for a long time exercised only by the Grand Lodge.

tions for Lancashire, Durham and Northumberland. "This circumstance," says Preston, "the Grand Lodge at York highly resented, and ever afterwards viewed the proceedings of the brethren in the south, with a jealous eye. All friendly intercourse ceased, and the York Masons from that moment considered their interests distinct from the Masons under the Grand Lodge in London.*

Three years after, in 1738, several brethren, dissatisfied with the conduct of the Grand Lodge of England, seceded from it, and held unauthorized meetings for the purposes of initiation. Taking advantage of the breach between the Grand Lodges of York and London, they assumed the character of York Masons. On the Grand Lodge's determination to put strictly in execution the laws against such seceders, they still further separated from its jurisdiction, and assumed the appellation of "*Ancient York Masons.*" They announced that the ancient landmarks were alone preserved by them, and declaring that the regular Lodges had adopted new plans, and sanctioned innovations, they branded them with the name of "*Modern Masons.*" In 1739, they established a new Grand Lodge in London, under the name of the "Grand Lodge of Ancient York Masons," and persevering in the measures they had adopted, held communications and appointed annual feasts. They were soon afterwards recognized by the Masons of Scotland and Ireland, and were encouraged and fostered by many of the nobility. The two Grand Lodges continued to exist, and to act in opposition to each other, extending their schisms into other countries,† until the year 1813, when under the Grand Mastership of the Duke of Sussex, they were happily united, and discord, we trust, forever banished from English Masonry.‡

SCOTLAND. Free Masonry was introduced into Scotland by the architects who built the Abbey of Kilwinning, and the village of that name bears the same relation to Scottish Masonry that the city of York does to English. Assemblies for the general government of the Craft were frequently held at Kilwinning. In the reign of James II., the office of Grand Master of Scotland was granted to William St. Clair, Earl of Orkney and Caithness and Baron of Ros-

* Preston, p. 184.

† For instance, there were originally in Massachusetts and South Carolina two Grand Lodges, claiming their authority from these discordant bodies. In the former state, however, they were united in 1792, and in the latter in 1817.

‡ We may as well mention here, that the rites and ceremonies of these bodies were essentially the same, and that the landmarks were equally preserved by them.

lin, "his heirs and successors," by the King's charter.* But in 1736, the St. Clair who then exercised the Grand Mastership, "taking into consideration that his holding or claiming any such jurisdiction, right or privilege, might be prejudicial to the Craft and vocation of Masonry,"† renounced his claims, and empowered the Free Masons to choose their Grand Master. The consequence of this act of resignation, was the immediate organization of the Grand Lodge of Scotland, over whom, for obvious reasons, the late hereditary Grand Master was unanimously called to preside.

Ireland. In 1729, the Free Masons of Dublin held an Assembly and organized the "Grand Lodge of Ireland." The Earl of Kingston was elected the first Grand Master.

France. In the beginning of the 18th century, Free Masonry in France was in a state of great disorder. Every Lodge acted independently of all others; the Masters were elected for life, and exercised the privileges and powers which are now confined to Grand Lodges; there was no Masonic centre, and consequently no Masonic union.

In 1735, there were six Lodges in Paris, and several others in the different provincial towns. The Earl of Derwentwater, the celebrated Jacobite, who afterwards was beheaded at London, for his adherence to the house of Stuart, excercised the functions of Grand Master by a tacit consent, although not by a formal election. In the following year, Lord Harnouster was elected by the Parisian Lodges, Grand Master; and in 1738, he was succeeded by the Duc d'Antin. On his death, in 1743, the Count de Clermont was elected to supply his place.

Organized Free Masonry in France, dates its existence from this latter year. In 1735, the Lodges of Paris had petitioned the Grand Lodge of England for the establishment of a Provincial Grand Lodge, which, on political grounds, had been refused. In 1743, however, it was granted, and the Provincial Grand Lodge of France, was constituted under the name of the "Grand Loge Anglaise de France." The Grand Master Clermont was, however, an inefficient officer. Anarchy and confusion once more invaded the Fraternity; the authority of the Grand Lodge was prostrated; and the establishment of Mother Lodges in the provinces, with the original intention of superintending the proceedings of the distant Provincial Lodges, instead of restoring harmony, as was vainly expected, widened still

* See the MSS. in the Edinburg Advocate's Library quoted by Lawrie.
† See the deed of resignation in Lawrie's Hist. Masonry.

more the breach. For assuming the rank and exercising the functions of Grand Lodges, they ceased all correspondence with the metropolitan body, and became in fact its rivals.

Under these circumstances, the Grand Lodge declared itself independent of England in 1756, and assumed the title of the "Grand Lodge of France." It recognized only the three degrees of Apprentice, Fellow Craft and Master Mason, and was composed of the Grand Officers to be elected out of the body of the Fraternity, and of the Masters for life of the Parisian Lodges. Thus formally excluding the Provincial Lodges from any participation in the government of the Craft.

But the proceedings of this body were not less stormy than those of its predecessor. We have stated, that the Count de Clermont proved an inefficient Grand Master. He had appointed in succession two Deputies, both of whom had been displeasing to the Fraternity. The last, Lacorne, was a man of such low origin and rude manners, that the Grand Lodge refused to meet him as their presiding officer. Irritated at this pointed disrespect, he sought in the taverns of Paris those Masters who had made a traffic of initiations, but who heretofore had submitted to the control, and been checked by the authority, of the Grand Lodge. From among them, he selected officers devoted to his service, and undertook a complete reorganization of the Grand Lodge.

The retired members, however, protested against these illegal proceedings; and in the subsequent year, the Grand Master consented to revoke the authority he had bestowed upon Lacorne, and appointed as his deputy M. Chaillon de Joinville. The respectable members now returned to their seats in the Grand Lodge, and in the triennial election, which took place in June, 1765, the officers who had been elected during the Deputy Grand Mastership of Lacorne, were all removed. The displaced officers protested, and published a defamatory memoir on the subject, and were in consequence expelled from Masonry by the Grand Lodge. Ill feeling on both sides was thus engendered, and carried to such a height, that at one of the communications of the Grand Lodge, the expelled brethren attempting to force their way in, were resisted with violence. The next day the lieutenant of police issued an edict, forbidding the future meetings of the Grand Lodge.

The expelled party, however, still continued their meetings. The Count de Clermont died in 1771; and the excluded brethren having invited the Duke of Chartres, (afterwards Duke of Orleans,) to the

Grand Mastership, he accepted the appointment. They now offered to unite with the Grand Lodge, on condition that the latter would revoke the decree of expulsion. The proposal was accepted, and the Grand Lodge went once more into operation.

Another union took place, which has since considerably influenced the character of French Masonry. During the troubles of the preceding years, Masonic bodies were instituted in various parts of the kingdom, which professed to confer degrees of a higher nature than those belonging to Craft Masonry, and which have since been known by the name of the Ineffable degrees. These Chapters assumed a right to organize and control Symbolic or Blue Lodges, and this assumption had been a fertile source of controversy between them and the Grand Lodge. By the latter body, they had never been recognized, but the Lodges under their direction had often been declared irregular, and their members expelled. They now, however, demanded a recognition, and proposed, if their request was complied with, to bestow the government of the "Hauts Grades," upon the same person who was at the head of the Grand Lodge. The compromise was made, their recognition was decreed, and the Duke of Chartres was elected Grand Master of all the Councils, Chapters, and Scotch Lodges of France.

But peace was not yet restored. The party who had been expelled, moved by a spirit of revenge for the disgrace formerly inflicted on them, succeeded in obtaining the appointment of a committee, which was empowered to prepare a new Constitution. All the Lodges of Paris and the provinces, were requested to appoint deputies, who were to form a Convention to take the new Constitution into consideration. This Convention, or as they called it, National Assembly, met at Paris, in December 1771. The Duke of Luxembourg presided, and on the 24th of that month, the Ancient Grand Lodge of France was declared extinct, and in its place another substituted, with the title of *Grand Orient de France.*

Notwithstanding the declaration of extinction by the National Assembly, the Grand Lodge continued to meet and to exercise its functions. Thus, the Fraternity of France continued to be harassed by the bitter contentions of these rival bodies, until the commencement of the revolution compelled both the Grand Orient and the Grand Lodge to suspend their labors.

On the restoration of civil order, both bodies resumed their operations, but the Grand Lodge had been weakened by the death of many of the perpetual Masters, who had originally been attached to it: and a better spirit arising, the Grand Lodge was by a solemn and mutual declaration, united to the Grand Orient on the 28th of June, 1799.

Dissensions, however, continued to arise between the Grand Orient and the different Chapters of the higher degrees. Several of these bodies had at various periods given in their adhesion to the Grand Orient, and again violated the compact of peace. Finally, the Grand Orient perceiving that the pretentions of the Scotch Rite Masons would be a perpetual source of disorder, decreed on the 16th of September, 1805, that the Supreme Council of the 33d degree should thenceforth become an independent body, with the power to confer Warrants of Constitution for all the degrees superior to the 18th, or Rose Croix; while the chapters of that and the inferior degrees, were placed under the exclusive control of the Grand Orient.

But a further detail of the dissensions which obscured Masonry in France, would be painful as well as tedious. They were renewed in 1821, by the reorganization of the Supreme Council, which had been dormant since 1815. But in 1842, an advance towards a reconciliation was made by the Supreme Council, which has at length been met by the Grand Orient. The friendship was consummated in 1842, and peace now reigns, at last, among the Masons of France.

Germany. The first German Lodge was established at Cologne, in 1716, but it died almost as soon as it was born. Seventeen years afterwards, (in 1733,) according to Preston,* a charter was granted by the Grand Lodge of England, to eleven German Masons in Hamburg. In 1738, another Lodge was established in Brunswick, under the authority of the Grand Lodge of Scotland. This Lodge, which was called "The Three Globes," united with the Lodges of "The Three White Eagles," and "The Three Swans," to organize in 1741, a Grand Lodge, the first established in Germany. This Grand Lodge still exists, and has under its jurisdiction eighty-eight subordinate Lodges. There is another Grand Lodge at Brunswick, which was established in 1768, by the Grand Lodge of England, and which is considered as the Metropolitan Grand Lodge of Germany. It has under its jurisdiction fifty-three subordinate Lodges. Masonry is not, however, in a very flourishing condition in Germany.

Prussia. The Grand Lodge of Prussia is situated at Berlin. It was established as a subordinate Lodge in 1752. In 1765 it initiated the Duke of York, and then assumed the name of "Royal York in

* Illustrations, p. 183, edi. 1804.

Friendship." It had under its jurisdiction in 1840, twenty-seven Lodges. The "Grand Lodge of the Three Globes" was founded in 1740, and has under its jurisdiction one hundred and seventy-seven Lodges.

Belgium. In 1721, the Grand Lodge of England constituted the Lodge of "Perfect Union," at Mons, and in 1730, another at Ghent. The former was afterwards erected into a Grand Lodge. The present Grand Orient of Belgium has its seat at Brussels.

Holland. The first Lodge established in Holland, was at the Hague, in 1731, under the warrant of the Grand Lodge of England. The present Grand Lodge of Holland has seventy Lodges on its register. It was established on the 18th December, 1757.

Denmark. The Grand Lodge of Denmark was instituted in 1743. It derived its existence from the Grand Lodge of Scotland. It is situated at Copenhagen. Masonry in this country is in a flourishing condition; it is recognized by the state, and the reigning King is Grand Master.*

Sweden. In no country has the progress of Masonry been more prosperous than in Sweden. It arose there in 1654, under the charter of the Grand Lodge of Scotland. The seat of the Grand Lodge is at Stockholm.

Russia. An English Lodge was constituted at St. Petersburg, in 1740, under a warrant from the Grand Lodge of England. Masonry soon afterwards began to increase with great rapidity throughout the empire. In 1772, the Grand Lodge of England established a Provincial Grand Mastership, and Lodges were constituted successively at Moscow, Riga, Jassy and in various parts of Courland. The Order was patronized by the Throne, and of course by the nobility. But, unfortunately, politics began to poison with its pollutions, the pure atmosphere of Masonry, and the Order rapidly declined. Lodges are, however, still privately held in various parts of the empire.

Poland. In 1739, Free Masonry was suppressed in this kingdom by an edict of King Augustus II. In 1781, however, it was revived under the auspices of the Grand Orient of France, who, upon the application of three Lodges at Warsaw, established Lodges at Wilna, Dubno, Posen, Grodno and Warsaw. These united, in 1784, to form a Grand Orient, whose seat is at the last named city. Masonry in Poland is now in a flourishing condition.

Bohemia. Free Masonry was instituted in Bohemia in 1749 by

* I state this on the authority of Clavel.

the Grand Lodge of Scotland. In 1776, it was highly prosperous, and continued so until the commencement of the French revolution, when it was suppressed by the Austrian Government. Its present condition I have no means of ascertaining.

SWITZERLAND. In 1737, the Grand Lodge of England granted a patent to Sir George Hamilton, by authority of which he instituted a Provincial Grand Lodge at Geneva. Two years afterwards, the same body bestowed a Warrant of Constitution on a Lodge situated at Lausanne. Masonry continued to flourish in Switzerland until 1745, when it was prohibited by an edict of the Council of Berne. From this attack, however, it recovered in 1764. The Lodges resumed their labors, and a Grand Lodge was organized at Geneva. But Switzerland, like France, has been sorely visited with Masonic dissensions. At one time there existed not less than three conflicting Masonic authorities in the Republic. Peace has, however, been restored, and the National Grand Lodge of Switzerland, seated at Berne, now exercises sole Masonic jurisdiction.

ITALY. The enmity of the Roman Church towards Free Masonry, has ever kept the latter Institution in a depressed state in Italy. A Lodge existed at Florence as early as 1733, and Lodges still are to be found at Leghorn, Turin, Genoa and the other principal cities, but their meetings are held with great secrecy.

SPAIN. The first Lodge established in Spain was in 1726, at Gibraltar. Another was constituted the year following, at Madrid. A third was formed at Andalusia, in 1731. The persecutions of the priests and Government were always obstacles to the successful propagation of Masonry in this kingdom. Lodges, however, still exist and work in various parts of Spain, but their meetings are in private.

PORTUGAL. What has been said of Free Masonry in Italy and Spain, is equally applicable to Portugal. Though Lodges were established as early as 1727, they always were, and continue to be, holden with great secresy.

TURKEY. Of the state of Masonry in the Ottoman empire, we know but little. Clavel says, that Lodges were established at Constantinople, Smyrna and Aleppo, in 1738, but of their present existence we have no information.

ASIA. Free Masonry was introduced into India in 1728, by Sir George Pomfret, who established a Lodge at Calcutta. Another was formed in 1740, and in 1779 there was scarcely a town in Hindostan in which there was not a Lodge. In that year Omdit ul

Omrah Bahauder, the eldest son of the Nabob of the Carnatic, was initiated at Trinchinopoly. Masonry still exists in a prosperous condition in Asia Minor and all the English settlements. The Lodges are under the jurisdiction generally of the Grand Lodge of England.

Africa. Free Masonry was introduced into Africa in 1736, by the establishment of Lodges at Cape Coast on the Gambia river. Lodges have since been constituted at the Cape of Good Hope; in the islands of Mauritius, Madagascar, and St. Helena; and at Algiers, Tunis, Morocco, Cairo and Alexandria.

Oceanica. Into these remote regions has the institution of Free Masonry extended. Lodges have existed since 1828, at Sidney, Paramatta, Melbourne, and in many other of the English colonies.

America. The first Lodge established in Canada, was at Cape Breton, in the year 1745. Lodges existed from as early a period in the West India Islands. On the establishment of the Brazilian empire, a Grand Lodge was instituted, and in 1825 Don Pedro the First was elected its Grand Master. In 1825, the Grand Lodge of Mexico was organized; and in 1837, that of Texas was instituted. Long before these periods, however, Lodges had been constituted in both these countries, under charters from different Grand Lodges in the United States.

United States. The organization of Free Masonry in the United States is to be dated from the 30th July, 1733, at which time "St. John's Grand Lodge" was opened in Boston, in consequence of a charter granted on the application of several brethren residing in that city, by Lord Viscount Montague, Grand Master of England. This charter is dated on the 30th of April in the same year, and appointed the R. W. Henry Price, Grand Master in North America, with power to appoint his Deputy, and the other officers necessary for forming a Grand Lodge, and also to constitute Lodges of Free and Accepted Masons as often as occasion should require. The first charter granted by this body was to "St. John's Lodge in Boston," which Lodge is still in existence. In the succeeding year, it granted a charter for the constitution of a Lodge in Philadelphia, of which the venerable Benjamin Franklin was the first Master. This Grand Lodge, however, descending from the Grand Lodge of England, was, of course, composed of Modern Masons. A number of brethren, therefore, residing in Boston, who were Ancient Masons, applied to, and received a dispensation from Lord Aberdour, Grand Master of Scotland, constituting them a regular Lodge, under the designation of St. Andrew's Lodge No. 82, and the Massachusetts Grand Lodge, descending from the Grand Lodge of Scotland, was established on the 27th December, 1769. On the 19th June, 1792, the two Grand Lodges were united, and all the distinctions of Ancient and Modern Masons abolished.

In 1735, Free Masonry was introduced into South Carolina by the constitution of "Solomon's Lodge No. 1," under a Warrant from Lord Montague, Grand Master of Free and Accepted Masons of England. This was, therefore, the fourth Lodge organized in the United States.* Three other Lodges were soon afterwards constituted. In 1754, on the 30th of March, the Marquis of Carnarvon, Grand Master of England, issued his Warrant constituting a Provincial Grand Lodge in the province, and appointing Chief Justice Leigh, Provincial Grand Master. On the 24th of December in the same year, the Grand Lodge was solemnly constituted at Charleston. In 1787, a Grand Lodge of Ancient York Masons was also established at Charleston, and in the course of the succeeding years, many disagreeable dissensions occurred between this and the Grand Lodge of Free and Accepted Masons which had been organized in 1754. These, however, at length happily terminated, and an indissoluble union took place between the bodies in December, 1817, which resulted in the formation of the present "Grand Lodge of Ancient Free Masons."

In 1764, the Grand Lodge of Pennsylvania was established by a Warrant issued from the Grand Lodge of England. Subsequently, the Grand Lodge of North Carolina was constituted in 1771; that of Virginia in 1778; and that of New York in 1781.

These Grand Lodges were, until the close of the revolutionary war, held under the authority of Charters granted either by the Grand Lodge of England, or that of Scotland. But on the confirmation of our political independence, the brethren, desirous of a like relief from the thraldom of a foreign power, began to organize Grand Lodges in their respective limits, and there now exists such bodies in every state and territory in the Union, the last formed being those of Wisconsin and Iowa in 1844.

* It ranked as No. 45, on the Register of England, while Solomon's Lodge in Savannah, which preceded it in time of constitution, held the number 46. See Hutchinson's List.

The following is a list of the Grand Lodges of the United States, and the dates of their organization:

Alabama	December	11, 1821.
Arkansas	November	25, 1838.
California	April	19, 1850.
Colorado	November	— 1861.
Connecticut	July	8, 1789.
Delaware	June	7, 1806.
District of Columbia	February	19, 1811.
Florida	July	5, 1830.
Georgia	December	16, 1786.
Illinois	———	1823.
Indiana	January	13, 1818.
Iowa	"	8, 1844.
Kansas	March	17, 1856.
Kentucky	October	16, 1800.
Louisiana	July	11, 1812.
Maine	June	24, 1820.
Maryland	July	31, 1783.
Massachusetts	March	8, 1777.
Michigan	July	31, 1826.
Minnesota	February	23, 1853.
Mississippi	August	25, 1818.
Missouri	May	4, 1821.
Nebraska	September	23, 1857.
Nevada	January	— 1865.
New Hampshire	July	16, 1789.
New Jersey	December	18, 1786.
New York	———	1787.
North Carolina	December	16, 1787.
Ohio	January	2, 1809.
Oregon	September	15, 1851.
Pennsylvania	"	25, 1786.
Rhode Island	June	25, 1791.
South Carolina	March	24, 1787.
Tennessee	December	27, 1813.
Texas	April	16, 1838.
Vermont	October	19, 1794.
Virginia	"	30, 1778.
Wisconsin	December	18, 1843.
Washington Territory	"	— 1858.

CHAPTER VI.

The Constitution of Masonry,

COMMONLY CALLED THE

"BOOK OF CONSTITUTIONS,"

AS ADOPTED BY

THE GRAND LODGE OF VIRGINIA,

IN 1792.

CHAPTER I.

THE CONSTITUTION OF MASONRY, OR AHIMAN REZON.*

When during the reign of Athelstane, his brother Prince Edwin, of glorious memory, obtained from the King a Free Patent or Charter to Masons, imparting a "power to regulate themselves, to amend what might happen amiss, and to hold a yearly communication in General Assembly," he accordingly summoned all the

* This is the Masonic title for the Book of Constitutions. It is derived from three Hebrew words *ahim*, brothers, *manah*, to prepare, and *ratzon*, the will or law; and signifies therefore literally "the law of prepared brothers." It contains the rules and regulations of the Order, an exposition of the duties of officers, the rights of members, the detail of ceremonies to be used on various occasions, such as consecrations, installations, funerals, etc.; and in fine, a summary of all the fundamental principles of Masonry. To this book, reference is to be made in all cases, where the by-laws of the Grand Lodge are silent, or not sufficiently explicit.—*Mackey's Lexicon of Free Masonry.*

Free and Accepted Masons in the realm to meet him in congregation at York, who came and formed the Grand Lodge under him as their first Grand Master, Anno Domini 926. At this congregation Edwin required them to produce as far as practicable all old writings and records of the Craft containing the ancient Gothic Constitutions, and we have authentic record for the fact that they brought many old writings, some in Greek, some in Latin, some in French, and other languages, and from the contents thereof they framed the Constitutions of the English Lodges, and made a law for themselves, to *preserve* and *observe* the same for all time to come.

This Constitution, we have good reason to believe, continued the supreme law among the Fraternity, wheresoever dispersed, down to the year 1721, September 29, at which time, as the records show, his Grace John Montagu, Duke of Montagu, being Grand Master, and with the Grand Lodge, finding fault with all the copies of the old Gothic Constitutions, ordered Brother James Anderson, A. M., Grand Senior Warden, to digest the same in a new and better form and method; and at a session of the Grand Lodge on 27th December, 1721, said Grand Master Montagu presiding, at the desire of the Grand Lodge, appointed fourteen learned brothers to examine Brother Anderson's manuscript of the Constitution Book, and to make report. And this communication was made very interesting by the lectures of some *old* Masons.

In Grand Lodge at the Fountain tavern in the Strand, in Ample Form, 25th March, 1722, his Grace the Duke of Montagu presiding, Right Worshipful John Beal, M. D., Deputy Grand Master, Josiah Villeneau, Grand Senior Warden, and John Morrice as Junior Grand Warden, and the representatives of twenty-four Lodges.

The said committee of fourteen reported that they

had perused Brother Anderson's manuscript of the history, charges, regulations and Master's songs, and after some amendments, had approved of the same; upon which the Grand Lodge desired the Most Worshipful Grand Master to order the following to be printed, which was accordingly done, and has, with very slight modifications, continued to this day as the Constitution and Regulations of Ancient Free and Accepted Masonry, and under which the Grand Lodge of Virginia was instituted, and is emphatically *The Book of Constitutions*, now in force throughout the civilized world, and being thus of universal application to the interests of Masonry, should be well studied and understood by every Mason. Worshipful Brother Albert G. Mackey, in his truly valuable Lexicon, gives the following impressive meaning to the Book of Constitutions:

> "The book containing the system of laws and customs of the Fraternity; it is the same as the Ahiman Rezon. It is among the charges to a newly installed Master of a Lodge, that he is to search the Book of Constitutions at all times, and cause it to be read in his Lodge, that none may pretend ignorance of the excellent precepts it contains. This book, guarded by the Tiler's sword, constitutes the emblem in the Master's degree intended to admonish the Mason that he should be guarded in all his words and actions, preserving unsullied the Masonic virtues of silence and circumspection which are inculcated in that book."

And he might have added, with advantage to Masters of Lodges, that it is *emblematic* of the great HOUSEHOLD of Masonry in which the Initiates of the four quarters of the globe have an abiding and immediate interest by the selection of its members, and, therefore, have entrusted every Master of a Lodge with an officer called a Tiler, and armed him with a drawn sword to prevent the ingress of any unworthy member into the Institution of Masonry.

OF THE TEMPER AND QUALITIES REQUISITE IN THOSE WHO WOULD BE FREE AND ACCEPTED MASONS.

Before we enter upon the duties of a Free Mason, in the various offices and stations to which he may be called in the Lodge, it is proper to give some account of the temper and qualities which are absolutely requisite, in all who aspire to partake of the sublime honors and advantages belonging to those who are initiated into the mysteries, and instructed in the art of Ancient Masonry.

SECTION I.

CONCERNING GOD AND RELIGION.

Whosoever from love of knowledge, interest or curiosity, desires to be a Mason, is to know, that as his foundation and great corner stone, he is to believe firmly in the Eternal God, and to pay that worship which is due to Him as the great Architect and Governor of the Universe. A Mason is also obliged by his tenure to observe the moral law, as a true *Noachida**; and if he rightly understands the Royal Art, he cannot tread in the irreligious paths of the unhappy libertine, or stupid atheist; nor, in any case, act against the great inward light of his own conscience.

He will likewise shun the gross errors of bigotry and superstition; making a due use of his own reason, according to that liberty wherewith a Mason is made free. For although in ancient times, the Christian Masons were charged to comply with the usages of the countries where they sojourned or worked, (being found in all nations, and of divers religions and persuasions,) yet it is now thought most expedient, that the brethren

* Sons of Noah, the first name for Free Masons.

in general, should only be charged to adhere to the essentials of religion, in which all men agree; leaving each brother to his own private judgment, as to particular modes and forms. Whence it follows that all Masons are to be good men and true—men of honor and honesty, by whatever religious names or persuasions distinguished; always following that golden precept, of "doing unto all men as (upon a change of conditions) they would that all men should do unto them."

Thus, since Masons, by their tenure, must agree in the three great articles of *Noah*,* Masonry becomes the centre of union among the brethren, and the happy means of conciliating and cementing into one body, those who might otherwise have remained at a perpetual distance; thereby strengthening the divine obligations of religion and love.

SECTION II.

CONCERNING GOVERNMENT AND THE CIVIL MAGISTRATE.

Whoever will be a true Mason, is further to know, that by the rules of this art, his obligations as a subject and citizen will not be relaxed but enforced. He is to be a lover of quiet, peaceable and obedient to the civil powers, which yield him protection, and are set over him where he resides or works, so far as they infringe not the limited bounds of reason and of religion. Nor can a real Craftsman ever be concerned in plots against the state, or be disrespectful to the magistracy; because the welfare of his country is his peculiar care.

But if any brother by forgetting for a time the rules of his Craft, and listening to evil counsels, should unhappily fall into a contrary conduct, he is not to be countenanced in his crimes or rebellion against the state; but

* Brotherly Love, Relief, and Truth.

he forfeits all benefits of the Lodge, and his fellows would refuse to associate or converse with him in private, while he continues in his crimes; that neither offence nor umbrage may be given to lawful government. But such a person is still considered as a Mason, his character as such being indefeasible; and hopes are to be entertained, that the rules of the Craft may again prevail with him, over every evil counsel and device that may have led him astray.

From this quiet and meek temper of true Masons, and their constant desire to adorn the countries where they reside with all useful arts, crafts, and improvements, they have been from the earliest ages, encouraged and protected by the wisest rulers of states and commonwealths; who have likewise thought it an honor to have their names enrolled among the Fraternity. And thus Masonry having always flourished most in the most flourishing and peaceable times of every country, and having often suffered in a particular manner through the calamitous effects of war, bloodshed, and devastation, the Craftsmen are therefore the more strongly engaged to act agreeably to the rules of their art, in practising peace and love, as far as possible, with all men.

SECTION III.

CONCERNING PRIVATE QUALITIES AND DUTIES.

In regard to himself, whoever would be a Mason, should know how to practise all the private virtues. He should avoid all manner of intemperance or excess, which might obstruct his performance of the laudable duties of his Craft, or lead him into crimes which would reflect dishonor on the Ancient Fraternity. He is to be industrious in his profession, and true to the lord and master he serves. He is to labor justly and not to eat any man's bread for nought, but to pay truly for his meat and drink. What leisure his labor allows, he is to employ in studying the arts and sciences with a diligent mind, that he may the better perform all his duties (as aforesaid) to his Creator, his country, his neighbor and himself. For, in a few words, "to walk humbly in the sight of God, to do justice, and love mercy," are the truly indispensable characteristics of a real Free and Accepted Mason.

For the better attainment of these shining qualities, he is to seek and acquire, as far as possible, the virtues of patience, meekness, self-denial, forbearance and the like, which give him the command over himself, and enable him to govern his own family with affection, dignity and prudence; at the same time checking every disposition injurious to the world, and promoting that love and service which brethren of the same Lodge or household owe to each other. Therefore to afford succor to the distressed, to divide our bread with the industrious poor, and to put the misguided traveller into the way, are qualities inherent in the Craft, and suitable to its dignity. But though a Mason is never to shut his ear unkindly to the complaints of any of the human species, yet when a brother is oppressed or suffers, he is in a more peculiar manner called to open his whole soul in love and compassion to him, and to relieve without prejudice, according to his capacity.

It is further necessary, that all who would be true Masons, should learn to abstain from malice and slander, evil-speaking, backbiting, unmannerly, scornful, provoking, reproachful and ungodly language; and that he should know how to obey those that are set over him, on account of their superior qualifications as Masons, however they may be in worldly rank or station. For although Masonry divests no man of his temporal honors or titles, but on the contrary, highly respects them, yet in the Lodge, preëminence of virtue and knowledge in the Royal Art, is considered as the true fountain of all nobility, rule and government.

The last quality and virtue which I shall mention as absolutely requisite in all those who would be Masons, is that of SECRESY, which, indeed, from its importance, ought to have held the first place in this chapter, if it had not been intended to treat of it more fully, as a conclusion of the whole.

So great stress is laid upon this particular virtue, that it is enforced among Masons under the strongest penalties and obligations, nor, in their esteem, is any man to be counted wise who is void of intellectual strength and ability to cover and conceal such honest secrets as are committed to him, as well as his own more serious affairs. Both sacred and profane history teach us, that numerous virtuous attempts have failed of their intended scope and end through defect of secret concealment.

The ancient philosophers and wise men (the princes of whom were Masons) were so fully persuaded of the great virtue of secresy, that it was the first lesson which they taught their pupils and followers. Thus in the school of Pythagoras we find it was a rule that every novitiate was to be silent for a time, and refrain from speaking, unless when a question was asked, to the end that the valuable secrets which he had to communicate might be the better preserved and valued. Lycurgus made a perpetual law, obliging every man to keep secret whatever was committed to him, unless it were to the injury of the state. And Cato, the Roman Censor, told his friends, that of three things (if ever he happened to be guilty) he always repented, viz: 1st. If he divulged a secret; 2d. If he went on water when he might stay on dry land; and, 3d. If he suffered a day to pass without doing (or endeavoring to do) some good. We also read that the Persian law punished the betraying of a secret more grievously than any other common crime.

Nor is the virtue of secresy recommended only by the wisest heathen philosophers and law-givers, but likewise by the fathers of the church and by inspired writers.

St. Ambrose places the patient gift of silence among the principal foundations of virtue, and the wise King Solomon deems the man unworthy to reign, or have any rule over others, who cannot command himself and keep his own secrets. A discoverer of secrets, he deems infamous and a traitor; but him that conceals them, he accounts a faithful brother. "A tale bearer," says he, "revealeth secrets; but he that is of a faithful spirit concealeth them. Discover not a secret to another, lest he that heareth it put thee to shame, and thine infamy turn not away. He that keepeth his tongue, keepeth his own soul." To the same purpose in the Book of Ecclesiasticus, (chap. xxvii.) we meet with the following beautiful passages, worthy to be forever recorded in the hearts of all Masons:

"Whosoever discovereth secrets, loseth his credit, and shall never find a friend to his mind. Love thy friend, and be faithful unto him; but if thou bewrayest his secrets, follow no more after him: for as a man hath destroyed his enemy, so hast thou lost the love of thy neighbor. As one that letteth a bird go out of his hand, so hast thou let thy neighbor go, and shall not get him again. Follow after him no more, for he is too far off; he is as a roe escaped out of the snare. As for a wound, it may be bound up; and after reviling, there may be reconcilement; but he that bewrayeth secrets is without hope."

Thus far hath been spoken of the internal qualities and virtues required in all who aspire to the sublime honor and advantage of becoming Free and Accepted Masons. We speak next of the external qualities, and the steps to be pursued, in order to obtain initiation and admission into a duly warranted Lodge of Ancient York Masons.

Be it known to you, then, in the first place, that no person is capable of becoming a member of such Lodge, unless, in addition to the qualities and virtues mentioned above, or at least a disposition and capacity to seek and acquire them, he is also "free born, of mature and discreet age; of good report; of sufficient natural endowments, and the senses of a man; with an estate, office, trade, occupation, or some visible way of acquiring an honest livelihood, and of working in his Craft, as becomes the members of this most ancient and honorable Fraternity, who ought not only to earn what is sufficient for themselves and families, but likewise something to spare for works of charity and for supporting the ancient grandeur and dignity of the Royal Craft. Every person desiring admission, must also be upright in body, not deformed or dismembered at the time of making, but of hale and entire limbs, as a man ought to be."

Thus, you see, a strict, though private and impartial inquiry, will be made into your character and ability before you can be admitted into any Lodge; and by the rules of Masonry, no friend who may wish to propose you can show you any favor in this respect. But if you have a friend who is a Mason, and is every way satisfied in these points, his duty is described as follows, viz:

SECTION IV.

CONCERNING THE PROPOSING OF NEW MEMBERS IN A LODGE.

Every person desirous of being made a Free Mason in any Lodge, shall be proposed by a member thereof, who shall give an account of the candidate's name, age, quality, title, trade, place of residence, description of his person, and other requisites as mentioned in the foregoing sections. And it is generally required that such proposal be also seconded by some one or more members, who likewise know something of the candidate. Such proposal shall also be made in Lodge hours,* at least one Lodge night before initiation, in order that the brethren may have sufficient time and opportunity to make a strict inquiry into the morals, character, circumstances and connections of the candidate, for which purpose a special committee is sometimes appointed.

The brother who proposes a candidate, shall at the same time deposit such a sum of money for him as the rules or by-laws of the Lodge may require, which is forfeited to the Lodge, if the candidate should not attend according to his proposal; but is to be returned to him, if he should not be approved or elected. In case he is elected, he is to pay (in addition to his deposit) such further sum as the laws of the Lodge may require, and clothe the Lodge, or make some other present, if his circumstances will admit, and the brethren agree to accept the same for the benefit of the Craft, and of distressed members.

Having shown that a strict enquiry will be made into your character, justice requires that you should also be advised to be alike circumspect on your side, and to make enquiry into the character of the Lodge into which you desire admission; for there is no excellence without its opposite, and no true coin without counterfeits.

In the first place, then, you have a right before admission, to desire your friend to show you the warrant or

* That is, from March 25th to September 25th, between the hours of seven and ten; and from September 25th to March 25th, between the hours of six and nine.

dispensation by which the Lodge is held; which, if genuine, you will find to be an instrument printed or written upon parchment, and signed by some noble Grand Master, his Deputy and Grand Wardens, and Grand Secretary, sealed with the Grand Lodge seal, constituting particular persons (therein named) as Master and Wardens, with full power to congregate and hold a Lodge at such place, and therein "make and admit Free Masons, according to the most ancient and honorable custom of the Royal Craft, in all ages and nations, throughout the known world; with full power and authority to nominate and chuse their successors," &c.

You may request the perusal of the by-laws, which, being short, you may read in the presence of your friend, or he will read to you, and show you also a list of the members of the Lodge, by all which, you will be the better able to judge whether you would choose to associate with them, and submit to be conformable to their rules. Being thus free to judge for yourself, you will not be liable to the dangers of deception, nor of having your pocket picked by impostors, and of perhaps being afterwards laughed at into the bargain; but, on the contrary, you will be admitted into a Society, where you will converse with men of honor and honesty, be exercised in all the offices of brotherly love, and be made acquainted with mysteries of which it is not lawful to speak further, or to reveal out of the Lodge.

CHAPTER II.

Having in the foregoing chapter treated as briefly as possible "of the temper and qualities required in those who wish to become Free and Accepted Masons," I now proceed (according to our proposed method) to collect and digest, under proper heads, those general regulations (old as well as new,) which more immediately concern operative Masons, avoiding prolixity and the insertion of such old regulations as are explained or supplied by subsequent ones, universally received and now in force in all the Lodges.

SECTION I.

CONCERNING A LODGE AND ITS GOVERNMENT.

1. A Lodge is a place in which Masons meet to work. The assembly or organized body of Masons is also called a Lodge, (just as the word church is expressive both of the congregation of people and of the place in which they meet to worship,) and is officered by a Master, Senior and Junior Warden, Secretary, Treasurer, Senior and Junior Deacon, Steward and Tiler.

2. The qualities of those who are to be admitted as members of a Lodge have been fully mentioned in the foregoing chapter, and it is only necessary to repeat here in general, that they are to be "men of good report, free born, of mature age,* hale and sound, not deformed or dismembered at the time of their making, and no woman or eunuch."

3. A Lodge ought to assemble for work at least once in each calendar month, and must consist of one Master, two Wardens—Senior and Junior, one Secretary, one Treasurer, and as many members as the Master and a majority of the Lodge shall, from time to time, think proper; although more than forty or fifty (when they can attend regularly, as the wholesome rules of the Craft require,) are generally found inconvenient for working

* In this country they are not supposed to be mature before they are twenty-one years of age.

to advantage; and, therefore, when a Lodge comes to be thus numerous, some of the ablest master workmen, and others under their direction, will obtain leave to separate and apply to the Grand Lodge for a warrant to work by themselves, in order to the further advancement of the Craft, as the laws hereafter to be delivered will more particularly show. But such warrant cannot be granted to any number of Masons, nor can a new Lodge be formed unless there he among them three Master Masons, to be nominated and installed officers for governing and instructing the brethren of such Lodge, and promoting them in due time according to their merit.

4. When men of eminent quality, learning, rank or wealth apply to be made and admitted into the Lodge, they are to be accepted with proper respect after due examination, for among such are often found those who afterwards prove good Lords or Founders of work, excellent officers and the ablest designers, to the great honor and strength of the Lodge. From among them also the Fraternity can generally have some honorable or learned Grand Master and other Grand Officers. But still these brethren are equally subject to all the charges and regulations, except in what more immediately concerns operative Masons and their preferment, as well as the preferment of all other Masons, must be governed by the general rule; that is to say, founded upon real worth and personal merit, and not upon mere seniority, or any other particular rank or quality.

5. In order that due decorum may be observed while the Lodge is engaged in what is serious and solemn, and for the better preservation of secresy and good harmony, a brother well skilled in the Master's part, shall be appointed and paid for tiling the Lodge door during the time of communication.

6. Every Lodge shall keep a book containing their by-

laws, the names of their members, with a list of all the Lodges under the same Grand Lodge, and united in general communication, with the usual times and places of meeting in such Lodges, and such other necessary parts of their transactions as are proper to be written.

7. No Lodge shall make more than five new brethren at one time, unless by dispensation from the Grand Master, or Deputy in his absence; nor shall any person be made or admitted a member of the Lodge without being proposed one month before, (unless in particular cases,) that due notice may be given to all the members, to make the necessary enquiries into the candidate's character and connections, and that there may be such unanimity in the election and admission of members as the by-laws require, because unanimity is essential to the being of every Lodge: and, therefore, no member can be imposed on any Lodge, by any power whatever, without their consent; nor would it be proper to admit any brother to work among them who has openly violated the sacred principles of Masonry, until undoubted proof of his reformation has been given, least the harmony of the Lodge might be thereby disturbed, and not then, till a certificate is produced of his having paid all arrearages to that Lodge of which he was last a member; for should any Lodge admit a brother, who is in arrears to any other Lodge, the Lodge where he is admitted make the debt their own.

8. As every Lodge has a right to keep itself an entire body, they ought never to interfere in the business of another Lodge. Therefore it would be highly improper in any Lodge to confer a degree on a brother who is not of their household; for every Lodge ought to be competent to their own business, and are indubitably the best judges of the qualifications of their own members;

and it does not follow as of course, that a brother admitted among the household as an Apprentice, to learn the Royal Art, is capable of taking charge of that household, however skilled he may be in his apprenticeship; for there are many very necessary qualifications essential in those who are promoted to the higher orders.

9. As the officers of every Lodge are the proper representatives of their own Lodge in Grand Lodge, still for the sake of equal representation, the officers are allowed deputies, when unable to attend themselves, which deputies must be appointed by the majority of every particular Lodge when duly congregated, and their appointment shall be attested by the Secretary, with the seal of their Lodge. And every Lodge has the privilege of instructing their Master and Wardens, or their deputies, for their conduct in the Grand Lodge and quarterly communication.

10. Every brother ought to be a member of some Lodge, nor is it proper that any number of brethren should withdraw or separate themselves from the Lodge in which they were made, or were afterwards admitted members, without a sufficient cause, although the right is an inherent one, and can never be restrained by any power whatever; still, such separation would be improper, unless the Lodge becomes too numerous for working; in which case a sufficient number may withdraw with the approbation of their Lodge, in order to form a new one. But before application can be made to the Grand Lodge, they shall pay all dues to their Lodge, and give them notice in writing that they intend to apply to the Grand Lodge for a warrant to form a new one. The Lodge then shall certify to the Grand Lodge the cause of the application, and at the same time shall recommend the most fitten brethren as Master and Wardens, before they can obtain the warrant. And no set

of Masons, without such warrant, shall ever take upon themselves to work together or form a new Lodge.

SECTION II.

OF THE ANCIENT MANNER OF CONSTITUTING A LODGE.

A new Lodge, for avoiding many irregularities, should be solemnly Constituted by the Grand Master, with his Deputy and Wardens; or in the Grand Master's absence, the Deputy acts for his Worship, the Senior Grand Warden as Deputy, the Junior Grand Warden as the Senior, and the present Master of a Lodge as the Junior: or if the Deputy is also absent, the Grand Master may depute either of his Grand Wardens, who can appoint others to act as Grand Wardens *pro tempore.**

The Lodge being opened, and the candidates or new Master and Wardens being yet among the fellow crafts, the Grand Master shall ask his deputy if he has examined them, and whether he finds the Master well skilled in the noble science and the Royal Art, and duly instructed in our mysteries, &c. The deputy answering in the affirmative, shall (by the Grand Master's order) take the candidate from amongst his fellows, and present him to the Grand Master, saying: "Right Worshipful Grand Master, the brethren here desire to be formed into a regular Lodge, and I present my worthy Brother A. B. to be installed their Master, whom I

* When institutions are required, where the distance is so great as to render it impossible for the Grand Officers to attend, the Grand Master, or his Deputy, issues a written instrument, under his hand and private seal, to some worthy brother, who has been properly installed Master of a Lodge, with full power to congregate, install, and constitute the petitioners.

If the Grand Master and Deputy be absent, or (through sickness) rendered incapable of acting, the Grand Wardens and Grand Secretary, jointly, may issue a like power under their hands and seal of the Grand Lodge, provided the Grand Master has first signed a Warrant for holding such new Lodge: but the Grand Wardens must never issue any Masonical writings under their private seal or seals.

know to be of good morals and great skill, true and trusty, and a lover of the whole Fraternity, wheresoever dispersed over the face of the earth."

Then the Grand Master, placing the candidate on his left hand and having asked and obtained the unanimous consent of the brethren, shall say, (after some other ceremonies and expressions, that cannot be written,) "I constitute and form these good brethren into a new regular Lodge, and appoint you, Brother A. B. the Master of it, not doubting of your capacity and care to preserve the cement of the Lodge," &c.

Upon this the Deputy, or some other brother for him, shall rehearse the charge of a Master, and the Grand Master shall ask the candidate, saying: "Do you submit to these charges as Masters have done in all ages:" and the new Master signifying his cordial submission thereto, the Grand Master shall by certain significant ceremonies and ancient usages, install him and present him with his warrant, the Book of Constitutions, the Lodge book, and the instruments of his office, one after another, and after each of them, the Grand Master, his deputy, or some brother for him, shall rehearse the short and pithy charge, that is suitable to the thing presented.

Next, the members of this new Lodge, bowing altogether to the Grand Master, shall return his worship their thanks, (according to the custom of Masters,) and shall immediately do homage to their Master, and (as faithful Craftsmen) signify their promise of subjection and obedience to him, by usual congratulations.

The Deputy and Grand Wardens, and any other brethren that are not members of this new Lodge, shall next congratulate the new Master; and he shall return his becoming acknowledgments, first to the Grand Master and Grand Officers, and to the rest in their order.

Then the Grand Master orders the new Master to enter immediately upon the exercise of his office, and calling forth his Senior Warden, a Fellow Craft,* (Master Mason,) presents him to the Grand Master for his worship's approbation, and to the new Lodge for their consent; upon which the Senior or Junior Grand Warden, or some brother for him, shall rehearse the charge of a Warden, &c., of a private Lodge, and he signifying his cordial submission thereto, the new Master shall present him singly, with the several instruments of his office, and in ancient manner and due form install him in his proper† place.

In like manner the new Master shall call forth his Junior Warden, who shall be a Master Mason, and present him (as above) to the Junior Grand Warden, or some other brother in his stead; and he shall in the above manner be installed in his proper place; and the brethren of this new Lodge shall signify their obedience to their new Wardens, by the usual congratulations due to Wardens.

The Grand Master then gives all the brethren joy of the Master and Wardens, &c., and recommends harmony, &c., hoping their only contention will be a laudable emulation in cultivating the Royal Art, and the social virtues.

Then the Grand Secretary or some brother for him, (by the Grand Master's order) in the name of the Grand Lodge, declares and proclaims this new Lodge duly constituted No.—, &c. Upon which all the new Lodge together, (after the custom of Masters,) return their hearty and sincere thanks for the honor of his constitution.

The Grand Master also orders the Grand Secretary to

* They were called Fellow Crafts, because the Masons of old times never gave any man the title of Master Mason, until he had first passed the chair.

† The Grand Wardens generally install the Wardens at new Constitutions, as being best qualified for transacting such business.

register this new Lodge in the Grand Lodge book, and to notify the same to the other particular Lodges; and after some other ancient customs and demonstrations of joy and satisfaction, he orders the Senior Grand Warden to close the Lodge.

SECTION III.

CONCERNING THE BEHAVIOR OF MASONS AS MEMBERS OF A LODGE.

1. *Of Attendance.*

Every brother ought to belong to some regular Lodge, and should always appear therein properly clothed, and in clean and decent apparel, truly subjecting himself to all its by-laws and general regulations. He must attend all meetings, whether stated or emergent, when duly summoned, unless he can offer to the Master and Wardens such plea of necessity for his absence as the said laws and regulations admit.

By the ancient rules and usages of Masonry, (which are generally adopted among the by-laws of every Lodge,) no plea was judged sufficient to excuse any absentee, unless he could satisfy the Lodge that he was sick, lame, in confinement, upwards of three miles from the place of meeting, or detained by some extraordinary and unforeseen necessity.

2. *Of Working.*

All Masons should work hard and honestly on working days, that they may live reputably, and appear in a decent and becoming manner on holidays. All the working hours appointed by law, or confirmed by custom, are to be strictly observed under the penalties and fines hereafter to be laid down. The hours of work are "from seven o'clock in the evening till ten, between the 25th of March and the 25th of September, and from six till nine, between the 25th of September and the 25th of March."

The Master and Masons shall faithfully finish the Lord's work, whether task or journey; nor shall they take the work at task, which have been accustomed to journey.

None shall envy a brother's prosperity, nor supplant or put him out of his work, if capable to finish it.

All Masons shall meekly receive their wages without murmuring or mutiny, nor desert the matter till the Lord's work is finished. They must avoid all unbecoming modes of expression, calling each other Brother and Fellow, both within and without the Lodge, with much courtesy as beseemeth. They shall instruct the younger brothers to become bright and expert workmen, that the Lord's materials be not spoiled. But as Free and Accepted Masons, they must not allow cowans to work with them, nor even be themselves employed by cowans, without an urgent necessity. And when such necessity happens, they shall have a separate communication, and not suffer cowans to learn from them, nor any laborer to be employed in the proper work of Free Masons.

3. *Of Behavior in the Lodge while open.*

While the Lodge is open for work, Masons must hold no private conversation or committees, without leave from the Master; nor talk of anything foreign or impertinent to the work in hand; nor interrupt the Master or Wardens, or any other brother addressing himself to the chair; nor act ludicrously while the Lodge is engaged in what is serious and solemn; but every brother shall pay due reverence to the Master, the Wardens, and all his Fellows, and put them to worship.

Every brother found guilty of a fault, shall stand to the award of the Lodge, unless he appeals to the Grand Lodge; but if the Lord's work be hindered in the mean while, a particular reference may be made.

No private piques, or quarrels about nations, families, religions or politics, must be brought within the doors of the Lodge, as being directly contrary to the rules already laid down—Masons being declared of the oldest Catholic religion, universally acknowledged as such, and of all nations, bound to live upon the square, level and plumb with each other, following the steps of their predecessors, in cultivating the peace and harmony of the Lodge, without distinction of sect or political party.

4. *Of Behavior after the Lodge is closed, and before the Brethren depart home.*

When the Lodge is closed, and the labors of the day finished, the brethren before they depart home to their rest, may enjoy themselves with innocent mirth, enlivened and exalted with their own peculiar songs, and sublime pieces of music, treating one another according to ability, but avoiding all excess and compulsion, both in eating and drinking; considering each other in the hours both of labor and festivity as always free. And, therefore, no brother is to be hindered from going home when he pleases; for although after Lodge hours, Masons are as other men, yet if they should fall into excess, the blame, though unjustly, may be cast upon the Fraternity by the ignorant or envious world.

SECTION IV.

CONCERNING THE BEHAVIOR OF MASONS IN THEIR PRIVATE CHARACTER.

1. *When a number of Brethren happen to meet, without any Strangers among them, and not in a formal Lodge.*

In such a case you are to salute each other in a courteous manner, as you are or may be instructed in the Lodge, calling each other brother, and freely communicating hints of knowledge, but without disclosing secrets, unless those who have given long proof of their taciturnity and honor; and taking care in all your actions and conversations, that you are neither overseen or overheard of stranges. In this friendly intercourse, no brother shall derogate from the respect due to another, were he not a Mason. For though all Masons, as brothers, are upon the level, yet Masonry (as was said in a former section) divests no man of the honors due to him before, or that may become due after he was made a Mason. On the contrary, it increases his respect, teaching us to add to all his other honors those which, as Masons, we cheerfully pay to an eminent brother, distinguishing him above all of his rank and station, and serving him readily according to our ability.

2. *When in presence of Strangers, who are not Masons.*

Before those who are not Masons, you must be cautious in your words, carriage and motions; so that the most penetrating stranger shall not be able to discover what is not proper to be intimated. The impertinent and ensnaring questions, or ignorant and idle discourse of those who seek to pry into the secrets and mysteries committed to you, must be prudently answered and managed, or the discourse wisely diverted to another subject, as your discretion and duty shall direct.

3. *When at Home and in your Neighborhood.*

Masons ought to be moral men, and fully qualified as is required in the foregoing sections and charges. Consequently they should be good husbands, good parents, good sons and good neighbors, not staying too long from home, avoiding all excess injurious to themselves or families, and wise as to all affairs, both of their own household and of the Lodge, for certain reasons known to themselves.

4. *Of behavior towards a Foreign Brother, or Stranger.*

You are cautiously to examine a stranger or foreign brother, as prudence and the rules of the Craft direct, that you may not be imposed upon by a pretender; and if you discover any one to be such, you are to reject him with scorn and shame, taking care to give him no hints; but such as are found to be true and faithful you are to respect as brothers, according to what is directed above; relieving them, if in want, to your utmost power; or directing them how to find relief, and employing them, if you can, or else recommending them to employment.

5. *Of Behavior behind a Brother's back as well as before his face.*

Free and Accepted Masons have ever been charged to avoid all manner of slandering and backbiting of true and faithful brethren, with all malice and unjust resentment, or talking disrespectfully of a brother's person or performance. Nor must they suffer any others to spread unjust reproaches or calumnies against a brother behind his back, nor to injure him in his fortune, occupation or character; but they shall defend such a brother, and give him notice of any danger or injury wherewith he may be threatened, to enable him to escape the same, as far as is consistent with honor, prudence, and the safety of religion, morality and the state, but no further.

6. *Concerning Differences and Law Suits, if any should unhappily arise among Brethren.*

If a brother do you an injury, or if you have any difference with him about any worldly or temporal business or interest, apply first to your own or his Lodge to have the matter in dispute adjusted by the brethren. And if either party be not satisfied with the determination of the Lodge, an appeal may be carried to the Grand Lodge, and you are never to enter into a law suit, till the matter cannot be decided as above. And if it be a matter that wholly concerns Masonry, law suits are to be entirely avoided, and the good advice of prudent brethren is to be followed, as they are the best referees of such differences.

But where references are either impracticable or unsuccessful, and courts of law or equity must at last decide, you must still follow the general rules of Masonry already laid down, avoiding all wrath, malice, rancor and personal ill-will in carrying on a suit with a brother, neither saying or doing anything to hinder the continuance or renewal of that brotherly love and friendship which are the glory and cement of this Ancient Fraternity.

Thus shall we show to all the world the benign influence of Masonry, as wise, true and faithful brethren before us have done from the beginning of time; and as all who shall follow us and would be thought worthy of that name will do, till architecture shall be dissolved, with the great fabric of the world, in the last general conflagration!

These charges, and such others as shall be given to you, in a way that cannot be written, you are strictly and conscientiously to observe; and that they may be the better observed, they should be read or made known to new brethren at their making, and at other times, as the Master shall direct. Amen! So mote it be!

SECTION V.

OF THE MASTER OF A LODGE, HIS ELECTION, OFFICE AND DUTY.

No brother can be Master of a Lodge till he has first served the office of Warden somewhere, unless in extraordinary cases, or when a new Lodge is to be formed, and no past or former Warden is to be found among the members. In such cases, three Master Masons, although they have served in no former offices, (if they be well learned,) may be constituted Master and Wardens of such new Lodge, or any Lodge in the like emergency.

The Master of every Lodge shall be chosen by ballot on the stated Lodge night each St. John's day; and the present Wardens (where they regularly are) shall be put up among the number of candidates for the chair, but shall then withdraw, while every free member (viz: all who have paid up their fines and dues, or have been excused payment according to law) gives his vote in favor of him whom he deems most worthy. Each free member hath one vote, and the Master two votes, where the number of votes happens to be equal, otherwise he has but one vote.

When the ballot is closed, and before it be examined, the former Master shall order the candidates to be brought back before him, and to take their seats again as Wardens. He shall then carefully examine the poll, and audibly declare him that hath the majority of votes duly elected.

The Master elect shall then nominate one for the Senior Warden's chair, and the present Master and brethren shall nominate one in opposition; both of whom shall withdraw till the ballot is closed as aforesaid, after which they shall be called before the Master, and the poll shall be examined and declared by him as above directed; in like manner shall the Lodge proceed in the choice of all the inferior officers, great care being taken that none be put in nomination for favor or affection, birth or fortune, exclusive of the consideration of real merit and ability, to fill his office for the honor and advancement of Masonry. No Mason chosen into any office can refuse to serve without incurring the penalties laid down in the chapter of fines, unless he has served in the same office before. The Master of every regular Lodge, thus duly elected and installed, has it in his special charge (as appurtenant to his office, duty and dignity) to see that the by-laws of his Lodge, as well as the general regulations from the Grand Lodge, be duly observed; that his Wardens discharge their office faithfully, and be examples of diligence and sobriety to the Craft; that true and exact minutes and entries of all proceedings be made and kept by the Secretary; that the Treasurer keep and render exact and just accounts at the stated times, according to the by-laws and orders of the Lodge; and in general, that all the goods and moneys belonging to the body be truly managed and dispensed, as if they were those of his own private household, according to the vote and direction of the majority, whether in charity or in working; and that no more wages than are just be given to any Fellow or Apprentice.

The Master shall further take care that no Apprentice or Fellow be taken into his house or Lodge, unless he has sufficient employment for him, and finds him to be the son of honest parents, a perfect youth, without maim or defect in body, of full age,* and otherwise duly qualified (according to the rules before laid down) for learning and understanding the sublime mysteries of the Art. Thus shall the Lords or Founders be well served, and the Craft not despised. Thus also shall such Apprentices, when expert in the business of their apprenticeship, be admitted, upon further improvement, as Fellow Crafts; and in due time, be raised to the sublime degree of Master Masons, capable themselves to undertake the Lord's work; animated with the prospect of passing in future through all the higher honors of Masonry, viz: those of Wardens and Masters of their Lodges, and perhaps, at length, of Grand Wardens and Grand Masters of all the Lodges, according to their merit.

The Master of a particular Lodge has the right and authority of calling his Lodge, or congregating the members into a Chapter at pleasure, upon the application of any of the brethren, and upon any emergency and occurrence, which in his judgment may require their meeting; and he is to fill the chair when present. It is likewise his duty, together with his Wardens, to attend the Grand Lodge at the quarterly communications, and also the Steward's Lodge, and such occasional or special Grand Communications as the good of the Craft may require, when duly summoned by the Grand Secretary, and within such reasonable distance of the place of holding the Grand Lodge as the laws of the same may have ascertained on that head. When in the Grand or Steward's Lodge, and at General as well as

* See note, page 87.

Special Communications, the Master and Wardens, or either of them, have full power and authority to represent their Lodge, and to transact all matters relative thereto, as well and as truly as if the whole body were there present.

The Master has the right of appointing some Brother (who is most commonly the Secretary of the Lodge) to keep the book of by-laws and other laws given to the Lodge by the proper authority; and in this book shall also be kept the names of all the members of the Lodge, and a list of all the Lodges within the said Grand Communication, with the usual times and places of their meeting.

The Master has also the particular right of preventing the removal of his Lodge from one house to another; and whereas several disputes have arisen on this head, and it hath been made a question in whom the power of removing a Lodge to any new place is invested, when the old place of meeting appears to be inconvenient, the following rule for this purpose hath been finally agreed upon and settled by lawful authority, viz:

"That no Lodge be removed without the Master's knowledge, nor any motion made for that purpose in the Lodge when he is absent. But if the Master be present, and a motion be made for moving the Lodge to some other more convenient place, (within the district assigned in the warrant of such Lodge,) and if the said motion be seconded and thirded, the Master shall order summonses to every individual member of the Lodge, specifying the business and appointing a day for hearing and determining the affair, at least ten days before, and the determination shall be made by the majority. But if the Master is not of the majority, the Lodge shall not be removed, unless full two-thirds of the members present have voted for such removal.

"But if the Master refuse to direct such summons to be issued, (upon a motion duly made as aforesaid,) then either of the Wardens may direct the same; and if the Master neglects to attend on the day fixed, the Warden may preside in determining the affair in the manner above prescribed. But the Lodge shall not, in the Master's absence, (on such special call,) enter upon any other cause or business but what is particularly mentioned in the said summons.

"If the Lodge is thus regularly ordered to be removed, the Master or Warden shall send notice to the Grand Secretary that such removal may be notified and duly entered in the Grand Lodge books at the next Grand Lodge.

"N. B. It is also a good method to have a certificate from the Grand Lodge that such removal hath been allowed, confirmed and duly registered in their books; which will be a business of course, unless an appeal be lodged against such removal by the minority, and then a hearing will be given to both parties in the Grand Lodge, before such removal be confirmed or registered in their books."

The Master's duty in making and admitting new brethren, and some other particular duties of his office, being such as cannot be written, save on the tablet of his heart, are, therefore, not to be looked for in this place, and, moreover, such duties as more particularly belong to the Master and other officers of Lodges, when they sit as members of the Grand Lodge, are to be learned from the chapter which treats of the Grand Lodge.

SECTION VI.

OF THE WARDENS OF A LODGE.

1. None but Master Masons can be Wardens of a Lodge. The manner of their election, and several of their duties being connected with the election and duties of the Master, have been mentioned in the former section.

2. The Senior Warden succeeds to all the duties of the Master, and fills the chair when he is absent. Or if the Master goes abroad on business, resigns, demits or is deposed, the Senior Warden shall forthwith fill his place till the next stated time of election. And although it was formerly held, that in such cases the Master's authority ought to revert to the last Past Master who is present, yet it is now the settled rule that the authority devolves upon the Senior Warden, and in his absence upon the Junior Warden, even although a former Master be present. But the Wardens will generally waive this privilege in honor of any Past Master that may be present, and will call on him to take the chair, upon the presumption of his experience and skill in conducting the business of the Lodge. Nevertheless, such Past Master still derives his authority under the Senior Warden, and cannot act till he congregates the Lodge. If none of the officers be present, nor any former Master, to take the chair, the members according to seniority and merit, shall fill the places of the absent officers.

The business of the Wardens in the Lodge is, generally to assist the Master in conducting the business thereof, and managing the Craft, in due order and form, when the Master is present, and in doing his duties (as above set forth) when he is necessarily absent; all which is to be learned from the foregoing section. Particular

Lodges do likewise by their by-laws assign particular duties to their Wardens for their own better government; which such Lodges have a right to do—provided they transgress not the old land marks, nor in any degree violate the true genius and spirit of Masonry.

SECTION VII.

OF THE SECRETARY OF A LODGE.

The Secretary shall keep a regular register or record of all transactions and proceedings of the Lodge that are fit to be committed to writing, which shall be faithfully entered in the Lodge books, from the minutes taken in open Lodge, after being duly read, amended (if necessary) and approved of before the close of every meeting, in order that the said transactions, or authentic copies thereof, may be ready to be laid before the Grand Lodge once in every quarter if required.

In particular, the Secretary shall keep exact lists of all the members of the Lodge, with the times of admission of new members; and upon or near every St. John's day, shall prepare and send to the Secretary of the Grand Lodge the list of members for the time being, which shall be signed not only by the newly installed officers of each Lodge, but also by the last past officers; to the intent that the Grand Secretary, and consequently the members of the Grand Lodge, may be at all times enabled to know the names and number of members in each Lodge under their jurisdiction, with the handwriting of the different officers, and to pay all due respect to the brethren recommended or certified by them from time to time.

SECTION VIII.

OF THE TREASURER OF A LODGE.

The Treasurer is to receive and keep exact accounts of all moneys raised or paid in, according to the rule for the advancement of the Lodge and benefit of the brethren, and to pay all orders duly drawn upon him by the authority of the Lodge. He is to keep regular entries, both of his receipts and disbursements, and to have his books and vouchers always ready for examination at such stated times as the by-laws require, or when specially called upon by order of the Master and brethren.

The Treasurer is likewise to have the charge and custody of the chest, jewels and furniture of the Lodge, unless when the Master and majority may judge it more convenient to appoint some other responsible brother for that particular duty, or when the officers of the Lodge may take the charge immediately upon themselves. The warrant in particular is in the charge and custody of the Master.

SECTION IX.

OF THE DEACONS OF A LODGE.

To the Senior and Junior Deacons, with such assistants as may be necessary, is entrusted the examination of visitors. It is their province also to attend on the Master and Wardens, and to act as their proxies in the active duties of the Lodge, such as the reception of candidates into the different degrees of Masonry, and in the immediate practice of our rites.

SECTION X.

OF THE TILER OF A LODGE.

The Tiler shall be a Master Mason, of knowledge and experience, and generally a brother is to be prefered, to whom the fees of the office may be necessary and serviceable, on account of his particular circumstances. His duty is fixed by custom, and known to every brother; and his chief charge is, not to admit any person, (not even a member, while the Lodge is sitting,) without the knowledge and consent of the presiding officer; neither shall he admit any visitor (that is not a member of a warranted Lodge) a second time, sojourners producing certificates excepted.

CHAPTER III.

SECTION I.

OF A GRAND LODGE.

1. A Grand Lodge consists of the Masters and Wardens of all the regular Lodges in its jurisdiction, who, when duly assembled, have the inherent power to elect the Grand Officers, which are a Grand Master, Deputy Grand Master, Grand Senior Warden, Grand Junior Warden, Grand Secretary, Grand Treasurer, Grand Senior Deacon, Grand Junior Deacon, Grand Pursuivant and Grand Tiler.

2. The Present Grand Officers, and all Past Grand Masters, and Past Grand Wardens and Past Masters of Regular Lodges under the same Grand jurisdiction, are members of the Grand Lodge, and to constitute a quorum for business it is necessary there should be the representatives of five Regular Lodges.

3. The Grand Lodge thus organized should meet at least once a year, and this meeting to be considered and denominated the Grand Annual Communication, or Convention of Deputies from each Lodge within its jurisdiction. The Grand Communication thus convened,

shall have a right at all times, and possess an inherent power and authority to make local ordinances and new regulations, as well as to amend old ones, for their own particular benefit, and the good of Masonry in general: provided always, that the ancient landmarks be carefully preserved, and that such regulations be first duly proposed in writing, for the consideration of all the members, and be finally regularly enacted by the consent of the majority. This has never been disputed, for the members of every Grand Lodge are the representatives of all the Fraternity in Communications, and are an absolute and independent body, with legislative authority: provided, as before observed, that the Grand Masonic Constitution be preserved inviolate; nor any of the landmarks removed. And at this Grand Lodge the different Lodges by their officers or deputies, shall attend with or without notice.

4. No brother whatever can be admitted into the Grand Lodge, unless he is a member of some regular Lodge; nor does the appointment of a brother to an office in the Grand Lodge prevent his holding an office in the private Lodge whereof he is a member.

5. A brother of the rank of Master, having business, or whose attendance may be necessary in point of evidence or intelligence, or a brother of eminence, upon motion, or leave asked and obtained, may be admitted into the Grand Lodge; but such brother, being admitted, shall not be allowed to vote, nor have a right to speak to any question or matter in debate, without leave, or unless desired to give his opinion, and then he is to confine himself to matters that concern Masonry only.

6. No Master or Warden of private Lodges, or other members of the Grand Lodge, shall ever attend the same, without the jewels which he ought to wear in his

own private Lodge, except for some good and sufficient reason to be allowed of in the Grand Lodge. And when any officer of a private Lodge, from such urgent business as may necessarily plead his excuse, cannot personally attend the Grand Lodge, his own Lodge may nominate and appoint any one of their members (being a Master Mason) with his jewels and clothing, to supply his place, and support the honor of his Lodge in the Grand Lodge: provided such deputy has a certificate of his appointment, with the seal of the Lodge, and attested by the Secretary.

SECTION II.

IN CASE OF THE ABSENCE OF ANY OF THE GRAND OFFICERS.

1. If the Grand Master is absent at any meeting of the Grand Lodge, either stated or occasional, the Deputy Grand Master is to supply his place; if the Deputy Grand Master be likewise absent, the Senior Grand Warden takes the chair; and in his absence, the Junior Grand Warden: and although by old regulations, the Master or Past Master of any private Lodge, who has been longest a Mason, had the preference of the chair, in the absence of the Grand Officers, yet now the rule is, that the Master of the senior private Lodge who may be present, is to take the chair. Nevertheless, any of them may waive the privilege, to do honor to a Past Grand Officer, or any eminent brother and Past Master. In all cases, the brother filling the chair may nominate his deputy, and call on any eminent brethren to fill the vacancies of the Grand Lodge *pro tem.*

2. The Grand Master at all times, when he finds he must necessarily be absent from any Lodge, still has the privilege of giving a special commission, under his hand and seal of office, to any eminent brother, being a mem-

ber of the Grand Lodge, to supply his place, if the Deputy Grand Master should not attend, or be necessarily absent.

3. In case of the death of a Grand Master, or any other Grand Officer, the same order of succession and precedency shall take place, as is above set forth, till the next election; when they shall be regularly chosen, and duly installed.

SECTION III.

OF THE PARTICULAR BUSINESS.

1. The business of the Grand Lodge at their stated Annual Communications, is seriously to discourse of, and sedately to consider, transact and settle all matters that concern the prosperity of the Craft, and the Fraternity in general, or private Lodges, and single brothers in particular. Here, therefore, are all differences to be seriously considered and decided, that cannot be made up and accommodated privately, nor by particular Lodges. And if any brother thinks himself aggrieved by the decision of any private Lodge, he may, by lodging an appeal in writing with the Grand Secretary, (who shall summon the parties and their witnesses to appear at the next ensuing Grand Communication,) have the matter reheard, and finally determined upon; and the Grand Lodge may adjourn from day to day, until the business is finished. And the Grand Master, or presiding officer, when the Lodge is regularly opened, shall communicate to the Lodge the nature of whatever business is to come before them; and for the sake of admitting witnesses, it is esteemed most proper to try all matters of controversy in a committee of the Lodge; and in order thereto, the presiding officer shall direct a committee of the whole Lodge, to meet in the Lodge room on the succeeding day for the aforesaid purposes;

who shall examine and determine upon all and every kind of business that may be referred to them, and make a report of their proceedings to the Grand Lodge on the same evening, for their ratification.

2. In hearing all complaints and punishing delinquents, according to the laws of the Craft, they are instructed to adhere most religiously to the old Hebrew regulation, viz: "If a complaint be made against a brother, by another brother, and he be found guilty, he shall stand to the determination of the Lodge; but if the accuser or complainant cannot support his charge, and it should appear to the Lodge to be groundless, being the result of hatred, malice or some unwarrantable passion, he shall incur such penalty as the accused would have done, had he been duly convicted."

3. All matters of controversy before the Grand Lodge shall be determined by a majority of votes; that is to say, the Grand Master or presiding officer having one vote, (unless in case of an equal division, and then two,) the Deputy Grand Master one vote; the other Grand Officers for the time being, collectively, one vote; the Past Grand Officers and Past Masters, collectively, one vote; and the officers, or their deputies, of each purticular Lodge, collectively, one vote.

4. The Grand Master, or presiding officer, shall for the sake of conveniency in voting, direct every collective body to sit together, that when a question is before the Lodge, they may consult among themselves how the vote shall be given, and when the question is put, either by holding up of hands, or otherwise, one of those collective bodies shall vote for the whole, and that duty should fall on the senior Mason.

SECTION IV.

OF PARTICULAR REGULATIONS.

1. The election of the officers of the Grand Lodge shall be annual. The Grand Master shall be elected by a majority of ballots, who shall have the privilege of appointing his Deputy. The other Grand Officers shall also be elected by a majority of ballots agreeably to the manner of voting laid down in the succeeding section; all of which elections shall be for one year, and until a new election shall take place.

2. Whenever application is made to the Grand Lodge, by a sufficient number of brethren, for a Charter to form a new Lodge, the Grand Lodge shall not grant the Charter, unless the skill of the petitioners as Masons, and their good conduct as men, will justify it. Great regard should always be had to the morals of such brethren as are entrusted with this important charge; therefore it is highly essential, that when the petitioners are not sufficiently known to the members of the Grand Lodge, that a certificate of their Masonic and moral characters, from two or more eminent brethren, showing them to be Master Masons regularly made, should accompany the petition; this being done, the Grand Lodge shall then issue a Charter, authorizing the petitioners, with such other brethren as they may call to their assistance, to enter Apprentices, pass Fellow Crafts, and raise Master Masons, agreeably to the ancient customs.

3. When a Lodge becomes too numerous for working together, and application is made by some of the members for leave to separate, and form a new Lodge, the cause of their separation should be certified by their Lodge, to the annual stated Grand Communication, at the same time recommending the most proper and fit-

ting brethren as officers of the new Lodge, before a Charter shall issue.

4. The Grand Master, or in his absence out of the state, his Deputy, or either of the intermediate Grand Officers, may grant a dispensation for forming a new Lodge, to continue in force until the next stated Grand Communication, provided the petitioners comply with the requisition in the preceding article; which dispensation shall have the seal of the Grand Lodge, attested by the Grand Secretary, and entered by him in the book of proceedings—the fee for which shall be one guinea to the Grand Secretary. Still it shall rest with the Grand Lodge at their next Grand Communication, whether a Charter shall issue.

5. Whenever a Charter shall issue from the Grand Lodge, which can be done at no other time than in Grand Communication, they shall direct a dispensation to issue, signed by the presiding officer, with the seal of the Grand Lodge, and attested by the Grand Secretary, directed to some Past Master, with powers to appoint his Wardens, to install the officers of the new Lodge, and set them to work agreeably to ancient customs and usages; but the Master of this new Lodge shall receive his degree in the presence of three Past Masters at least—all of which must be done before that Lodge can be entitled to a representation in the Grand Lodge.

6. Every Charter issued from the Grand Lodge, shall be signed by the Grand Master for the time being, or in case of his death or absence out of the state, by the Deputy Grand Master and Wardens, sealed with the seal of the Grand Lodge, and attested by the Grand Secretary, directed to three reputable brethren, authorizing them to call in other brethren to their assistance, and to enter Apprentices, pass Fellow Crafts, and raise Master Masons, agreeably to ancient customs and usages;

the fee for which shall be ——, for the purpose of Grand Charity and other contingencies; and —— to the Grand Secretary for providing parchment and affixing the seal, to be paid previous to the delivery of the Charter.

7. The members of the Grand Lodge, and of all Warranted Lodges within their jurisdiction, so far as they have abilities and numbers, have an undoubted right to exercise all degrees of the Ancient Craft, and consequently the Royal Arch; but no Masons of any denomination can hold any Lodge, without a warrant for the place where held. Nevertheless, Royal Arch Masons must not at processions, nor in any other place, except in the Royal Arch Lodge, be distinguished by any garment or badge, different from what belongs to them as officers or members of the Grand, or their own private Lodges.

8. That each person admitted to any degree of Masonry in the Grand Lodge, shall pay a fee of —— for the purpose of the Grand Charity.

9. Each Lodge on record, shall annually on the stated Grand Communication, pay to the Grand Treasurer for the time being, as a support to the Grand Lodge, the sum of ——; or a sum of money equal to ——, for each and every member belonging to such Lodge.

10. The several Lodges on record shall transmit to the Grand Lodge annually, a list of all the officers and members composing each Lodge, distinguishing their rank and degree; together with such other matters relating to the Craft in general, as may be deemed proper to communicate; and that the said list be recorded by the Grand Secretary in a book to be set apart for that purpose; to the end that the Grand Lodge may at all times know the number of laborers engaged in this great work.

11. Every brother requiring a Grand Lodge certifi-

cate or diploma, which is impressed on parchment, and signed by the proper officers, and signed also opposite the seal by the member himself, shall pay to the Treasurer the sum of ——, towards the Grand Charity Fund. Nor is any brother to be entitled to such certificate, without a previous certificate from the Lodge of which he is a member, setting forth his regular behavior, and that he has discharged regularly all Lodge dues.

CHAPTER IV.

OF THE ELECTION, OFFICE AND DUTY OF THE GRAND OFFICERS.

The election of Grand Officers shall be at the Stated Communication annually, and shall be the first business that comes properly before the Grand Lodge, after receiving the reports of the subordinate Lodges represented. And the Grand Lodge being opened in ample form, the Most Worshipful Grand Master shall direct the Grand Lodge to proceed to the choice of Grand Officers for the ensuing year.

SECTION I.

OF THE ELECTION OF THE GRAND MASTER.

The Most Worshipful Grand Master in the chair, shall call on the Grand Lodge to nominate some eminent and skilful brother or brethren for the office of Grand Master. Should there be but one in the nomination, it shall be the indispensable duty of the Most Worshipful to nominate one other in the opposition; but if the present Grand Master is again eligible, and is then in the chair, and willing to serve another year, he shall direct his Deputy to nominate the one in opposition. The Grand

Master shall, if eligible, be at all times in the nomination. The members shall then be directed to prepare their ballots for one of the brethren in the nomination, and when done, shall be collected by one of the Grand Deacons. The Worshipful Grand Master shall then call on two of the members to examine the ballots, and deliver to him in writing, the number of votes each candidate shall have; when the Worshipful Grand Master shall cause the brother having the greatest number of votes, to be thrice proclaimed aloud by the Grand Secretary, GRAND MASTER OF MASONS! The Most Worshipful shall then cause the Grand Master elect to be conducted to the chair, and, after introducing him to the members as a brother skilled in the Royal Art, and a lover of the Craft, he shall be clothed with the badges of the office, and installed in due form.

All the members shall then salute him according to the ancient and laudable customs of Masonry.

SECTION II.

OF THE ELECTION OR APPOINTMENT OF THE DEPUTY GRAND MASTER.

The Grand Master elect shall then nominate and appoint the Deputy Grand Master as being his inherent right; because as the Grand Master is generally a brother of the first eminence and abilities, and long experience, and cannot be supposed to give his attendance on every emergency, it hath always been adjudged needful, not only to allow him a Deputy, but that such Deputy should be a person in whom he can perfectly confide, and with whom he can have full harmony—for which reason it is proper that the Grand Master should have the nomination of his Deputy. Although cases may arise when the Grand Lodge may exercise the right of rejecting the

Grand Master's nomination, and of choosing for themselves, of which case (although they seldom happen) the majority of the Lodge can only be judges.

The Deputy Grand Master being thus chosen, or appointed as above, he shall be introduced, installed, congratulated and saluted in due form as before.

SECTION III.

OF THE ELECTION OF GRAND SENIOR WARDEN.

The Grand Master elect shall then nominate some skilful brother as Grand Senior Warden, and the Grand Lodge have the inalienable right of nominating one or more in opposition; (for an opposition is essentially necessary in the choice of all the officers,) and the person having the greatest majority of votes, or ballots, (still preserving due harmony) is declared, as before, duly elected.

The Grand Senior Warden being thus elected, he shall be introduced, installed and saluted in due form as before.

SECTION IV.

OF THE ELECTION OF THE GRAND JUNIOR WARDEN.

The election of the Grand Junior Warden is precisely in the same manner as the Grand Senior Warden; but sometimes, for the sake of dispatch, both the Grand Wardens are elected together in balloting, by writing Senior opposite the name of one of the candidates, and Junior opposite the name of another.

SECTION V.

OF THE APPOINTMENT AND OFFICE OF GRAND SECRETARY.

The office of Grand Secretary hath always been of very great importance in the Grand Lodge, from the multiplicity of matters committed to his care, and from the abilities and learning requisite in the management of them. All the transactions of the Grand Lodge are to be drawn into form, and duly recorded by him. All petitions, applications and appeals, are to pass through his hands. No warrant, certificate or instrument of writing from the Grand Lodge, is authentic, without his attestation or signature, and his affixing the Grand Seal as the laws require. The general correspondence with Lodges and brethren over the whole world, is to be managed by him agreeably to the voice of the Grand Lodge, and directions of the Grand Master or his Deputy; and he must, therefore, be ready to attend with his Assistant or Clerk, and the books of his Grand Lodge, in order to give all necessary information concerning the general state of matters, and what is proper to be done upon an emergency.

For this reason, at every annual election of Grand Officers, the nomination or appointment of the Grand Secretary is considered as the inherent right of the Grand Master, being properly his amanumensis, and an officer as necessary to him as his Deputy. It is, therefore, held under the old regulations, which yet stand unrepealed, that if the Grand Lodge should disapprove either of the Deputy Grand Master or Grand Secretary, they cannot disannul their appointment, without choosing a new Grand Master, by which all his appointments are rendered void. But this is a case which hath but very seldom happened, and which all true Masons hope there never will be any occasion to make a provision against.

The Grand Secretary, by virtue of his office, is a member of the Grand Lodge, and hath a right to vote in common with the Grand Wardens in everything, except in choosing Grand Officers; he also hath the right of appointing his own Deputy, or Assistant Grand Secretary or Clerk—but such Deputy or Clerk must be a Master Mason, yet shall not by virtue of that appointment be a member of the Grand Lodge, nor speak without being allowed or asked, unless he hath otherwise a right, by being either a Past Grand Officer, or Past Master, or Deputy of some regular private Lodge within the jurisdiction.

SECTION VI.

OF THE ELECTION AND OFFICE OF GRAND TREASURER.

The Grand Treasurer is elected by the body of the Grand Lodge in the same manner as the Grand Wardens, he being considered as an officer peculiarly responsible to all the members in due form assembled, as having the charge of their common stock and property. For to him is committed the care of all money raised for the General Charity and other uses of the Grand Lodge; an account of which, he is regularly to enter into a book, with the respective ends and uses for which the several sums are intended. He is likewise to pay out or disburse the same upon such orders, signed, as the rules of the Grand Lodge in this respect shall allow valid.

The Grand Treasurer, by virtue of his office, is a member of the Grand Lodge, and hath power to move the same in any matter that concerns his office, and may vote in common with the Grand Wardens; he hath a right to appoint an Assistant or Clerk, who must be a Master Mason, but shall have no vote, nor be a member of the Grand Lodge, nor allowed to speak without permission, unless otherwise entitled to a seat, as having been a Past Officer of the Grand Lodge, or Past Master or Deputy of some regular private Lodge within the jurisdiction.

The Grand Treasurer, or his Assistant, shall always be present in the Grand Lodge, and ready to attend the Grand Master and other Grand Officers with his books for inspection when required; and likewise any Grand Committee that may be appointed for examining and adjusting the accounts.

SECTION VII.

OF THE GRAND DEACONS.

The Grand Deacons, whose duty is well known in the Grand Lodge, as particular Assistants to the Grand Master and Wardens, in conducting the business of the Grand Lodge, are always members of the same, so long as they continue in their office, and are most commonly elected by the Grand Lodge as other Grand Officers, though the appointment of right belongs to the Grand Master and Grand Senior Warden, and may be appointed annually, or on every Grand Lodge night.

SECTION VIII.

OF THE GRAND TILER AND GRAND PURSUIVANT.

These officers must be Master Masons, but none of them are members of the Grand Lodge, nor allowed to speak to any matter before the Grand Lodge, without permission.

The Grand Tiler's duty is to look after the door on the outward side, to see that none but members enter in; and not even them, if the Grand Lodge is opened, without first informing the Grand Master (through the channel of the Grand Pursuivant) of their being at the door, and wishing to enter. The Grand Tiler is also to summon the members on any special occasion or emergency, by order of the Grand Master or his Deputy, signified to him under the hand of the Grand Secretary or his Clerk.

The business of the Grand Pursuivant is to stand at the inward door of the Grand Lodge, and to report the names and titles of all that want admission, as reported to him by the Grand Tiler. He is also to go upon messages while the Grand Lodge is open, and perform sundry other services known only in the Grand Lodge.

SECTION IX.

RULES TO BE OBSERVED DURING THE TIME OF PUBLIC BUSINESS.

1. At the third stroke of the Master's gravel, there shall be a general silence, and he who breaks silence without leave from the Chair, shall be publicly reprimanded.

2. Under the same penalty, every brother shall keep his seat and be perfectly silent whenever the Most Worshipful, his Deputy, or Warden shall think proper to call to order.

3. In the Grand Lodge every member shall take his seat according to the number of his Lodge, and not move about from place to place during the Communication, except the Grand Wardens, as having more immediately the care of the Grand Lodge, and such other officers whose immediate business may call them to different parts of the Lodge room.

4. No brother is to speak more than twice on the same subject, unless to explain himself, or when called upon by the Chair to speak.

5. Every one who speaks shall rise and keep standing, addressing himself in a proper manner to the Chair; nor shall any one presume to interrupt him under the aforesaid penalty, unless he is wandering from the point, and the Grand Master shall think proper to reduce him to order, and then the said speaker shall sit down. But after he has been set right, he may again proceed if he pleases.

6. If any member be twice called to order at any one Grand Lodge, for transgressing these rules, and is guilty

of a third offence of the same nature, the Chair shall peremptorily order him to quit the Grand Lodge room for that night.

7. Whoever shall be so rude as to hiss or laugh at any brother or what he may have advanced, shall be forthwith solemnly excluded the Communication, and declard incapable of ever being a member of the Grand Lodge in future, until another time he publicly owns his fault, and his grace be granted.

8. No motion for a new regulation, or for the alteration of an old one, shall be made until it be first handed up in writing to the Chair; and after it has been perused by the Grand Master, the thing may be moved publicly, and then audibly read by the Grand Secretary; and if it is then seconded and thirded, it must immediately be submitted to the consideration of the whole Assembly, that the sense of the Lodge may be fully heard upon it; after which the question shall be put, *pro* or *con*.

9. In order to preserve harmony, it was thought necessary to use counters and a balloting box when occasion requires; at other times by holding up of hands, or by putting the question aye or no.

CHAPTER V.

REGULATIONS FOR CHARITY TO BE OBSERVED IN THE GRAND LODGE.

1. The Committee of Charity, commonly called the Grand Steward's Lodge, consists of all the present Grand Officers, all Past Grand Masters and Wardens, and all Past Masters of regular private Lodges within its jurisdiction, the Grand Secretary and Treasurer, and such other members as the Grand Lodge may on the day of

annual election appoint; any five of whom, for the sake of expedition, shall be a quorum, whose business shall be to meet four stated times in the year, viz: April 1st, July 1st, October 1st, and January 1st, (except those days happen on a Sunday, in which case the next day,) and as often at other times as may be deemed necessary, to hear all petitions, &c., and to order such relief to distressed brethren, as their case may require, and prudence may direct. It shall also be the duty of this Lodge to examine the Grand Treasurer's accounts, and report at every Grand Communication the state of the funds.

2. None but registered Masons who have themselves contributed to the Grand Lodge charity fund, and were members of a Warranted Lodge during that time, can be considered and relieved. Sojourners and traveling Masons, if duly certified and recommended, are to be relieved by private contributions, made for them on the occasion, or out of the general fund, as the majority shall think proper.

3. The petitioners for relief, (if within any convenient distance, or unless detained by sickness, or some other reasonable cause,) must attend the Grand Steward's Lodge or committee in person, and prove to their satisfaction, that he or they had been formerly in reputable, or at least in tolerable circumstances, and that they have not from any cause forfeited their privileges as Masons. And although any brother may send in a petition or recommendation, yet none can be admitted to see and hear the debates, except the members of the Grand Steward's Lodge or committee.

4. It is the inherent right of this committee to dispose of the Grand Charity under the aforesaid restrictions, and to such as appear really necessitous and deserving, either by weekly support or otherwise, as to them shall seem meet: provided always, that no brother made

in a clandestine manner, nor any brother who has ever assisted in any clandestine making, can ever be qualified to receive any assistance out of the said fund.

5. All the transactions of this Committee of Charity or Steward's Lodge, are to be regularly entered of record, and audibly read by the Grand Secretary before all the members of the Grand Lodge, at their Annual Grand Communication.

CHAPTER VI.

OF GRAND VISITATIONS AND COMMUNICATIONS.

All the different Lodges in the same General Communication should, as much as possible, observe the same rules and usages. "Solomon, my son, forget not my law, but let thine heart keep my commandments, and remove not the ancient landmark which thy fathers have set."

And to this end it shall be the duty of the Grand Master, or in his absence the presiding officer, on the Grand Lodge of annual election, to appoint some of the Grand Officers, or other skilful Past Grand Officers or Past Masters, to visit all the Lodges within the Communication, and see that the ancient customs and usages are strictly observed. And as this laudable duty has become impracticable, from the extent of their jurisdiction and large number of Lodges, for the brethren before mentioned, to perform the whole of this duty collectively, the Grand Master shall cause the Lodges to be laid off in convenient districts, and allot one or more visitors to each district, with such other assistants as may be thought proper, who shall make faithful report of their proceedings to the Grand Communication annually, according to the instructions given them.

The brethren so appointed, shall have a dispensation signed by the Grand Master or his Deputy, and attested by the Grand Secretary, with the seal of the Grand Lodge, explaining the nature of their business, whose duty then shall be to visit every Lodge of his district at one of their stated meetings—previously notifying to the Lodge the intended time of visiting them.

[The foregoing is the Constitution of Masonry, as compiled and adopted by the Grand Lodge of England in 1721.]

CHAPTER VII.

History of the Organization

OF THE

GRAND LODGE OF VIRGINIA.

At a Convention of Delegates from the Lodges below mentioned, met in the city of Williamsburg, on Tuesday, the 6th of May, 1777, in consequence of a petition of the Williamsburg Lodge, recommending that the Worshipful Masters and Wardens of the different Lodges, or their Deputies, should meet in Williamsburg, for the purpose of choosing a Grand Master for the state of Virginia:

Matthew Phripp, Esq., Deputy from the Norfolk Lodge; James Kemp, from the Kilwinning Port Royal Cross Lodge; Duncan Rose, from the Blandford Lodge; William Waddill and John Rowsay, from the Williamsburg Lodge; and William Simmons and John Crawford, from the Cabin Point Royal Arch Lodge.

Matthew Phripp, Esq., being elected President, and James Kemp, Clerk.

Brother Waddill laid the following letters before the Convention, which were directed to the Williamsburg Lodge, viz: a letter from the Fredericksburg Lodge, enclosing an order of that Lodge; a letter from the Botetourt Lodge; also a letter from Brother James Taylor, as Master of the Norfolk Lodge; which were severally read, and referred to the Williamsburg Lodge for proper answers.

A motion being made, and it being the unanimous opinion of this Convention that a Grand Master ought to be chosen to preside over the Craft in this commonwealth:

Resolved, That a committee be appointed for drawing up reasons why a Grand Master should be chosen, consisting of Duncan Rose, William Waddill, James Kemp and John Crawford, and that their proceedings be laid before this Convention, on Tuesday the 13th May next, at 6 o'clock P. M.

Resolved, That this Convention be adjourned till Tuesday the 13th May next.

TUESDAY, 13*th May*, 1777.

The Convention met agreeably to adjournment.

Brother Phripp being absent upon business, Brother Rose was elected President.

Brother Waddill reported, that the committee having met, had drawn up their reasons why they thought a Grand Master should be chosen, which he delivered to the Chair; and being read, it was agreed the same should be recorded, and are as follow:

To the Right Worshipful Master, Worshipful Wardens, and worthy Brethren of the ——— Lodge:

In consequence of a proposition of the Williamsburg Lodge, inviting all the regular Lodges in Virginia to attend at their Lodge on the 5th May, 1777, for the purpose of electing a Grand Master of Free Masons for the said commonwealth of Virginia, five regular Lodges appeared by deputation, on the 7th instant, viz: Norfolk, Kilwinning Port Royal Cross, Blandford, Williamsburg and Cabin Point Royal Arch, and thence by adjournment to the 13th instant; when taking the subject of meeting into consideration, are unanimously of opinion, that a Grand Master is requisite in this state, for the following reasons, founded on the principles of necessity, convenience and right, viz:

First. We find that the Lodges in this state hold their charters under five distinct and separate authorities, viz: the Grand Master of England, Scotland, Ireland, Pennsylvania and America; (the last at second hand;) of course all have an equal right to appoint their Deputies, who can claim no authority over those not holding this principle. Therefore any difference arising between Lodges holding differently, cannot be settled for want of a common tribunal. For the same reason, the Craft can never meet in Annual Communication, manifesting that brotherly love and affection, the distinguishing characteristic of Masonry from the beginning. Such divided and subdivided authority can never be productive to the real good of the Craft.

Secondly. We cannot discover, upon strict enquiry, that Masonry has ever derived any benefit from the foreign appointment of a Grand Master in this country, they being as little known and as little acknowledged.

Thirdly. Being at this time without a supreme, and so circumstanced as to render it impossible to have recourse to the Grand Lodge beyond sea, should any abuses creep into the Lodges, or should any body of the brotherhood be desirous of forming a new Lodge, there is no settled authority to apply to. In this case we are of opinion that a Grand Lodge is a matter of necessity.

Fourthly and Lastly. We find upon record, that the Grand Lodges of England, Scotland and Ireland, founded their original right of election upon their sole authority, by mutual consent, distinct and separate from all foreign power whatever. We therefore conclude, that we have and ought to hold the same rights and privileges that Masons in all times heretofore have confessedly enjoyed.

We, the Deputies aforesaid, for ourselves and our respective Lodges, humbly beseech and desire that you will be pleased to take the foregoing reasons into consideration, and that you will favor us with your attendance, by deputation in this Lodge, for the purpose of electing a Grand Master for this state, on the 23d June next, at 10 o'clock A. M., for the first time, and ever after at such time and place as the Grand Lodge shall determine—we having signified this our desire to all others, our regular and loving brethren, in like manner as we have done to you, hoping to see you on the day appointed; and we have caused these our proceedings to be signed by our loving Brother Duncan Rose, our President, and attested by our worthy Brother James Kemp, Secretary, this 13th May, A. L. 5777, A. D. 1777.

Resolved, That copies of the above be made out and sent to all the different regular Lodges in this state.

Resolved, That this Convention be adjourned till the 23d June next ensuing, at 10 o'clock A. M.

Signed, DUNCAN ROSE, *President.*

Attest: JAMES KEMP, *Secretary.*

Truly recorded from the minutes.

W. WADDILL, *G. Secretary.*

At a Convention of five Lodges, assembled at the Lodge Room in Williamsburg, on the 23d June, 1777, pursuant to an adjournment of deputies the 13th May last, and agreeably to the letter of invitation to the several regular Lodges of this state—present, Duncan Rose, Past Master, Blandford Lodge; James Kemp, Master's degree, Kilwinning Port Royal Cross Lodge; James Mercer, Master, and Benjamin Johnston, Secretary, Fredericksburg Lodge; William Finnie, Master, and William Waddill, P. M., Williamsburg Lodge; William Simmons, Master, and A. Campbell, Master's degree, Cabin Point Royal Arch Lodge.

James Mercer being elected President, and James Kemp Secretary of this Convention, the several deputations being inspected, and letters of other Lodges, and also several Charters, being read and considered:

This Convention are unanimously of opinion, that a Grand Master for this state is essential to the prosperity and dignity of Masonry in general: but there not being a deputation from a majority of the Lodges therein, decline the choice of a Grand Master for the present—but in order to prepare for the appointment of so essential an officer, in the amplest and most constitutional mode, by which scrupulous Masons may be reconciled to such a measure,

This Convention are unanimously of opinion, that the most unexceptionable mode of procuring such an officer in this state agreeably to the Charters constituting the several Lodges therein, will be for the respective Lodges to solicit their respective Masters for an appointment of some one worthy Mason, resident within this State, as Grand Master thereof, by which the several authorities of the different Grand Masters of England, Scotland and Ireland, from whom the several Lodges in this State hold their Charters, will be united in one and the same person; and in order to continue such an officer in this state, this Convention are of opinion that such Charter of Appointment should contain authority to such Grand Master to resign the superiority of his Principal into the hands of the respective Lodges, in order that such Lodges, by their Deputies, may form a general Convention of the Craft, to elect a Grand Master and proper officers of a Grand Lodge in time to come.

And, in order to give dispatch to this business, this Convention beg leave to recommend to their constituents, and to the members of all other Lodges in this state, His Excellency General George Washington as a proper person to fill the office of Grand Master for the same, and to whom the Charter of appointment aforementioned be made.

But should the Lodges prefer any other person to this office, it is recommended that the respective Lodges do elect some other person, and notify the same to the Williamsburg Lodge, being most convenient, who are to examine such appointment, and declare thereupon, on whom the majority falls, to be nominal Grand Master of this state, for the purpose of accepting a Charter of Resignation as aforeproposed, and notify the same to the respective Lodges in this state, in order to their solicitation aforerecommended.

But in case such an appointment is not made by the first day of June next, then this Convention are unanimously of opinion, that the several Lodges of this State should proceed to elect such Grand Master, and to that end that the President of this Convention, or in case of his death, the Master of the Williamsburg Lodge, for the time being, ought to invite a Convention of the Deputies of such Lodges, to meet at such time and place as to him shall seem most convenient.

Ordered, That these proceedings be attested by James Kemp, Secretary, and copies transmitted to the several Lodges in this state, who are requested to pay the earliest attention to the same.

Attest,

JAMES KEMP, *Secretary*.

23 *June*, *A. L.* 5777, *A. D.* 1777.

At a Convention of the Craft, agreeably to an advertisement of the Right Worshipful James Mercer, held on the 13th day of October, A. L. 5778—present, Robert Andrews, Master; James M. Fontain, S. W.; James Willison, J. W.; Duncan Rose, Tr; William Waddill, Secretary; D. Rose, Deputy, Blandford Lodge; Robert Andrews, W. Waddill, James M'Clurg and John M. Galt, Williamsburg Lodge; James M. Fontain and Christ. Pryor, Botetourt Lodge; James Willison, James Belches and John Crawford, Cabin Point R. A. Lodge.

On the question being put,

This Convention are unanimously of opinion, that there is a sufficient number of Lodges present to proceed to business.

It is the opinion of this Convention, that the power and authority of Cornelius Harnet, Esq., as Deputy Grand Master of America, does not now exist.

It is the opinion of this Convention, that it is agreeable to the Constitutions of Masonry, that all the regular chartered Lodges within this state, should be subject to the Grand Master of the said state.

The Right Worshipful Warner Lewis, Past Master of the Botetourt Lodge, being nominated to the office of Grand Master, declined the acceptance thereof—and then the Right Worshipful John Blair, Past Master of the Williamsburg Lodge, was nominated, and unanimously elected—who was pleased to accept of the office.

Signed, ROBERT ANDREWS, *M.*

Truly recorded from the minutes, by

W. WADDILL, *Secretary.*

At a Convention of the Craft, agreeably to adjournment, of the R. W. Robert Andrews, Master, held 13th October, A. L. 5778, now assembled for the purpose of installing the R. W. John Blair, Past Master of the Williamsburg Lodge, into the office of Grand Master of Free and Accepted Masons, of the state of Virginia, held in the Lodge Room in Williamsburg, the 30th October, A. L. 5778—present, Rob't Andrews, Master; Dr. James Taylor, S. W.; John Crawford, J. W.; James Galt, Treasurer; Duncan Rose, Secretary, and forty-four members.

The Lodge being opened in due form, the Right Worshipful Master Rob't Andrews, agreeably to the meeting, installed the Right Worshipful John Blair in the office of Grand Master of this commonwealth; when he was pleased to appoint the Right Worshipful and Rev. Robert Andrew, D. G. M.

At a Grand Lodge, held in the city of Richmond, on the fourth day of October, A. D. 1784, A. L. 5784—the Most Worshipful G. M. John Blair, having resigned the Chair, the R. W. James Mercer was elected Grand Master, who was pleased to appoint the R. W. Edmund Randolph, D. G. M.

At a Grand Lodge, held in the city of Richmond on the 27th October, A. D. 1786, A. L. 5786—the term of service of the present Grand Master expiring, Edmund Randolph, Esq., was unanimously elected Grand Master, installed and congratulated, according to the ancient usage, who was pleased to appoint John Marshall, Esq., D. G. M.

At a half yearly Grand Communication, holden in the Masons Hall, Richmond, 28th October, A. L. 5789—R. W. Alexander Montgomery, Esq., was elected Grand Master, who was pleased to appoint the Hon. Thomas Matthews, Esq., D. G. M.

At a half yearly Grand Communication, holden in the Masons Hall in the city of Richmond, 28th October, A. L. 5790—the Most Worshipful A. Montgomery having resigned the Chair, the Hon.

Thomas Matthews, Esq., was unanimously elected and installed Grand Master, who resigning his right of nominating his Deputy, consigned the choice to the Lodge, who unanimously elected John K. Read Deputy Grand Master. And on 28th October, 1791, in Grand Communication, the Hon. Thomas Matthews was re-elected Grand Master; J. K. Read, Esq., Deputy Grand Master; Robert Brooke and William Bentley, Esqs., Grand Wardens.

LIST OF GRAND OFFICERS

From the Organization of the Grand Lodge of Virginia, down to December, 1866, *A. L.* 5866.

GRAND MASTERS.	DATE.	DEP. G. MASTERS.
JOHN BLAIR, of Williamsburg,.	Oct. 13, 1778,....	Rev. Robert Andrews.
James Mercer,..........................	Nov. 4, 1784,....	Edmund Randolph.
Edmund Randolph,....................	Oct. 27, 1786,....	John Marshall.
Re-elected,.........................	Oct. 29, 1787,....	James Taylor.
Alexander Montgomery,..........	Oct. 28, 1789,....	Thomas Matthews.
Thomas Matthews,................	Oct. 28, 1790,....	John K. Read.
Re-elected,.........................	Oct. 29, 1792,....	John Marshall.
John Marshall,.........................	Oct. 28, 1793,....	Robert Brooke.
Robert Brooke,.......................	Nov. 23, 1795,....	William Bentley.
Benjamin Day,.........................	Nov. 27, 1797,....	Nathaniel W. Price.
Re-elected,.........................	Nov. 10, 1798,....	William Austin.
Re-elected,.........................	Dec. 8, 1800,....	Alexander M'Rae.
Alexander M'Rae,..................	Dec. 14, 1801,....	James Byrne.
James Byrne,........................	Dec. 13, 1803,....	William W. Hening.
William W. Hening,..............	Dec. 10, 1805,....	David Robertson.
David Robertson,..................	Dec. 15, 1807,....	John H. Foushee.
John H. Foushee,..................	Dec. 12, 1809,....	Robert Brough.
Solomon Jacobs,.....................	Dec. 11, 1810,....	Re-elected.
Robert Brough,......................	Dec. 14, 1813,....	Charles H. Graves.
Charles H. Graves,................	Dec. 11, 1815,....	Archibald Magill.
Archibald Magill,..................	Dec. 9, 1817,....	John H. Purdie.
John H. Purdie,....................	Dec. 14, 1819,....	Samuel Jones.
Samuel Jones,.......................	Dec. 10, 1821,....	Charles Yancey.
Charles Yancey,....................	Dec. 10, 1822,....	Mordecai Cooke.
Mordecai Cooke,....................	Dec. 14, 1824,....	D. W. Patteson.
D. W. Patteson,....................	Dec. 12, 1826,....	Robert G. Scott.
Robert G. Scott,...................	Dec. 9, 1828,....	George C. Dromgoole.
George C. Dromgoole,............	Dec. 14, 1830,....	William H. Fitzwhylsonn.
William H. Fitzwhylsonn,........	Dec. 11, 1832,....	William Mitchell, Jr.
William Mitchell, Jr..............	Dec. 9, 1834,....	Levi L. Stevenson.
Levi L. Stevenson,................	Dec. 13, 1836,....	William A Patteson.
William A. Patteson,............	Jan. 13, 1838,....	Oscar M. Crutchfield.
Oscar M. Crutchfield,............	Dec. 14, 1841,....	J. W. Smith.
J. W. Smith,..........................	Dec. 12, 1843,....	John R. Purdie.
John R. Purdie,.....................	Dec. 10, 1844,....	Sidney S. Baxter.
Sidney S. Baxter,.................	Dec. 15, 1846,....	Josiah Bigelow.

12

GRAND MASTERS.	DATE.	DEP. G. MASTERS.
James Points,..................	Dec. 12, 1848,....	James Evans.
James Evans,......................	Dec. 10, 1850,....	Edmund P. Hunter.
Edmund P. Hunter,...............	Dec. 13, 1852,....	James A. Leitch.
James A. Leitch, ...	Dec. 12, 1854,....	John S. Caldwell.
John S. Caldwell,.................	Dec. 9, 1856,....	Powhatan B. Starke.
Powhatan B. Starke,..............	Dec. 14, 1858,....	John Robin M'Daniel.
John Robin M'Daniel,............	Dec. 13, 1859,....	Lewis B. Williams.
Lewis B. Williams,...............	Dec. 10, 1861,....	William H. Harman.
William H. Harman,..............	Dec. 15, 1863,....	Edward H. Lane.
Edward H. Lane,.................	Dec. 12, 1865,....	William Terry.

CHAPTER VIII.

WORK AND ILLUSTRATIONS OF MASONRY, AS PRACTISED BY THE GRAND LODGE OF VIRGINIA.

In the Grand Lodge, December 14th, 1843, M. W. J. Worthington Smith, presiding:

Resolved, That the Grand Lodge of Virginia request Wor. Bro. John Dove, as President of the Convention of Grand Lecturers at Baltimore, and Chairman of the Committee on the Trestle Board, to draw up and submit to the next Grand Annual Communication a report embodying the designs laid down by the Convention.

In Grand Lodge, December 9th, 1844, M. Wor. John R. Purdie, M. D., presiding:

Wor. Bro. John Dove reported a Text-Book, embodying the Work and Lectures of the Convention at Baltimore in May, 1843, in obedience to an order of the last Grand Lodge: Whereupon,

Resolved, That a committee of five brethren be appointed by the M. W. G. Master, to whom shall be referred the Masonic Text-Book, together with the report submitted by Wor. Bro. John Dove, in obedience to the said resolution, and that they be required to report thereupon at the next Grand Annual Communication.

Whereupon the Chair was pleased to appoint M. W. William A. Patteson, M. W. Robert G. Scott, M. W. William Mitchell, Jr., Wor. James Evans and Wor. Jas. D. M'Cabe, to compose said committee.

In Grand Lodge, December 8th, 1845, M. W. John R. Purdie, M. D., presiding:

M. W. William A. Patteson, from the committee appointed at the last Grand Lodge to report upon the work compiled by Wor. Bro. John Dove, made the following report:

The committee appointed at the session of the Grand Lodge in December, 1844, A. L. 5844, to examine the report of Bro. John Dove, made at that time in accordance with a request of this Grand Lodge, at its session in December, 1843, A. L. 5843, that he should draw up and submit to it a report embodying the designs laid down by the Baltimore Convention, held at Baltimore in May, A. D. 1843, A. L. 5843, have duly performed the same.

They have examined the Work compiled by Brother Dove, as his report of the designs of the Trestle Board, and while it is impossible for them to say that it reflects the exact conclusions of that Convention, they believe it does, so far as memory permits. They think it presents the proper Work and Lectures, and will be found an useful Text-Book for Masons. Although not requested so to do, they find the Compilator has prefixed to this report upon the Trestle Board, the Constitution of Masonry from the Ahiman Rezon, and has also attached the Methodical Digest of the Laws of the Grand Lodge of Virginia, by our late Bro. Wor. James Henderson, heretofore adopted by the Grand Lodge, and the Laws subsequently passed.

The whole, together with the alterations and amendments advised and adopted, under the criticism desired by Bro. Dove, form an useful Book for the Craft under our jurisdiction; and the committee respectfully recommeud to the Grand Lodge, for the benefit of Masonry, that it sanction the publication of this work, as containing probably as few errors and as many recommendations as any like work known to the committee.

Signed,
Wm. A. Patteson, P. G. M.
Robert G. Scott, P. G. M.
Wm. Mitchell, Jr., P. G. M.
James Evans, P. M.
James D. M'Cabe, P. M.

Resolved, That said report, together with the Text-book, be referred to the Grand Working Committee, with instructions to report at this Grand Annual Communication.

The M. W. G. Master appointed the following brethren to compose the Grand Working Committee, to wit: M. Wor. Levi L. Stevenson, Josiah Bigelow, James Evans, Edward H. Gill and James D. M'Cabe.

In Grand Lodge, December 10th, 1845, M. Wor. John R. Purdie presiding, the Grand Working Committee made the following report upon the Text-Book, which was received and confirmed:

The Grand Working Committee respectfully report that they have critically examined the manuscript of a Text or Working-Book for the use of the Lodges under our jurisdiction—and having made a few verbal corrections, recommend its adoption as containing the designs which entirely reflect the unwritten Work and Lectures adopted by the Grand Lodge of Virginia.

They also recommend that the Methodical Digest of the Laws of this Grand Lodge be referred to Wor. Bro. John Dove to revise and correct, and that the various Regulations adopted since the publication of the last edition of that Work be digested, and the whole brought down to the present time, and published as an appendix to the Work.

They would also recommend that the work be published under the direction of the Grand Secretary at as early a period as possible. Your committee are satisfied that the immediate and pressing wants of the Craft would absorb a large edition of the work; and that so far from being an expense to the Grand Lodge, it will produce from the profits of the sale a handsome sum in aid of the Grand Charity Fund. One thousand copies for a first edition would, in the opinion of your committee, be sufficient. The expense, it is presumed, would not exceed $500, and by fixing the price to the Lodges at $1, a handsome profit would be afforded.

In view of the great labor and time bestowed upon this work by Brother Dove, they recommend the adoption of the following resolution:

Resolved, That as a compensation for the necessary labor and trouble in preparing the Text-Book, and superintending its publication, Wor. Bro. John Dove be paid the sum of one hundred and fifty dollars.

Signed, Levi L. Stevenson, P. G. M., *Chairman.*

Whereupon, the Grand Working Committee submitted the following report of Wor. Bro. John Dove, Grand Secretary, as embodying the Work and Lectures of the Grand Lodge of Virginia, compiled from the writings of Preston, Webb, Read, and others:

M. W. Sir and Brother:

In obedience to a resolution of the last Grand Lodge, in the following words: "*Resolved*, That the Grand Lodge of Virginia request Wor. Bro. John Dove, as President of the Convention of Grand Lecturers at Baltimore, and Chairman of the Committee on the Trestle Board, to draw up and submit to the next Grand Annual

Communication, a report embodying the designs laid down by the Convention," I have, after much deliberation, embodied the work as far as I thought consistent with strict Masonic prudence, and much farther than I would have gone had it been an original work on the Masonic Lectures, well knowing the great unwillingness of this Grand Lodge to commit to writing anything upon the subject of the Masonic Work and Lectures. I have, however, strictly confined myself to such illustrations as I found in print, and bearing the authority of Preston, Webb and this Grand Lodge; and having been now in use for near a century, it might be termed a species of innovation to omit them in a work professing to be a Text-Book. Nevertheless, I am satisfied from much conversation with old and well informed brethren, that if nothing had ever been committed to writing, the Fraternity generally would be much better informed by oral teaching, and a much higher estimate placed upon that information; for it is at this day literally true, that brethren will be found more rusty and uninformed in these parts of the Lectures which are written, than those which are oral.

Sincerely hoping that the Text-Book which I now submit as in every essential particular embodying the work as agreed upon by the Convention in Baltimore, may receive the sanction of this Grand Lodge, and through its influence be the means of enforcing uniformity throughout the Masonic jurisdiction of the United States, I submit it to their consideration.

Respectfully submitted.

JOHN DOVE, *G. Secretary.*

FORMS.

FORM OF A PETITION FOR A NEW LODGE.

To the Most Worshipful Grand Master of the Grand Lodge of Free and Accepted Masons of the State of Virginia:

We, the undersigned, being Master Masons of good standing, and having the prosperity of the Craft at heart, are anxious to exert our best endeavors to promote and diffuse the genuine principles of Free Masonry; and for the convenience of our respective dwellings, and other good reasons, we are desirous of forming a new Lodge at ———, in the county of ———, to be named ———. We, therefore, respectfully pray for a Dispensation, empowering us to open and hold a regular Lodge at ———, and therein discharge the duties of Ancient York Masonry in a constitutional manner, according to the Forms of the Order and the Laws of the Grand Lodge; and we have nominated and do recommend Brother A. B. to be the first Master; Brother C. D. to be the first Senior Warden; and Brother E. F. to be the first Junior Warden of the said Lodge. Should the prayer of the petitioners be granted, we promise a strict conformity to all the regulations of Masonry, and the laws, resolutions and edicts of the Grand Lodge.

[To be signed by not less than seven, and recommended by the Lodge nearest the proposed locality of the new Lodge.]

FORM OF RECOMMENDATION.

We, the officers and members of ——— Lodge, No. ———, do hereby cheerfully vouch for the Masonic and moral qualifications of the petitioners for a Charter of a Lodge at ———, in the county of ———, and recommend their petition to the favorable consideration of the M. Wor. Grand Master.

FORM OF DISPENSATION.

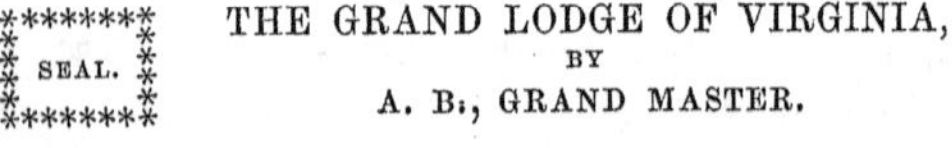

To all whom these presents may concern—greeting:

Whereas it hath been duly represented to me, that in the ———, and state of Virginia, there resides a number of brethren of the Most Ancient and Honorable Society of Free and Accepted Masons, who are desirous of being authorized to proceed forthwith to work as a regular Lodge; and it appearing to be for the benefit of the Craft in general, as well as the aforesaid brethren in particular, that they should be encouraged in their laudable endeavors and designs:

Therefore, Ye do hereby know that I, ———, Grand Master of Masons in and for the state of Virginia, by virtue of the power and authority in me vested, during the recess of the Grand Lodge, do hereby nominate and appoint our trusty and well beloved brothers ——— as Master, ——— as Senior Warden, and ——— as Junior Warden, together with all such true and lawful brethren as may be permitted to associate with them, to assemble and work as a regular Lodge in the ——— aforesaid, by the designation of ——— Lodge No. ——, and there to enter Apprentices, pass Fellow Crafts, and raise Master Masons agreeably to the customs and usages of Ancient Free and Accepted Masons, and the ordinances and regulations of the Grand Lodge of Virginia, but not otherwise. And I do hereby require and enjoin the Master and Wardens aforesaid to make due return of this Dispensation, and of a copy of all the proceedings had thereunder, to our Grand Lodge, at the next Grand Annual Communication, to be holden in the city of Richmond on the second Monday in December next ensuing, until which time this Dispensation shall continue in full force and virtue.

Given under the hand of the ———, and the seal of the Grand Lodge of Virginia, this —— day of ———, A. L. 586—, A. D. 186—.

——— ———, *G. Secretary.*

FORM OF CHARTER.

To all whom these presents may concern—greeting:

Whereas it hath been duly represented that in the ——— and state of Virginia, there resides a number of the brethren of the Most Ancient and Honorable Society of Free and Accepted Masons, who are desirous of being formed into a regular Lodge; and it appearing to be for the good increase of our excellent Craft, that the said brethren should be encouraged in their laudable endeavors and designs: Therefore,

Know ye, That I, ——— Grand Master of Masons in the state of Virginia, by and with the consent of our Grand Lodge, do hereby constitute and appoint our trusty and well beloved brethren, the Worshipful —— Master, —— Senior Warden, and —— Junior Warden, together with all such other true and lawful brethren as may be admitted to associate with them, to assemble and work as a regularly constituted Lodge of Ancient Free and Accepted Masons, ——— aforesaid; by the name, title and designation of ———, hereby requiring and enjoining all regular Lodges to hold, acknowledge and respect them as such. And we do hereby grant and commit to the Master, Wardens and brethren aforesaid, and their successors, full power and authority to receive and enter Apprentices, to pass Fellow Crafts, to raise Master Masons, and to perform all other works of the Craft, agreeably to the ancient customs and usages of Free and Accepted Masons, and the ordinances and regulations of the Grand Lodge of Virginia, and not otherwise. And also to choose a Master and Wardens and other officers annually; and to exact from their members such fees as they shall judge necessary for the support of their said Lodge, the relief of their brethren in distress, and the regular payment of their annual contribution towards the Grand Charity Fund. And we do hereby require and enjoin the Master, Wardens and brethren aforesaid, and their successors, to record in their books, along with this present Charter, their own regulations and by-laws, and their whole acts and proceedings from time to time as they occur; and also to correspond with our Grand Lodge whenever occasion may require, and to attend the meetings thereof regularly, by their proper representatives or deputies, and also to pay due respect and obedience to all such ordinances and instructions as they may from time to time receive from the Grand Lodge, or from the Grand Master for the time being. And lastly, the Master, Wardens and brethren aforesaid, in behalf of themselves and their successors, do, by accepting hereof, solemnly engage strictly to conform to all and every of the foregoing requisitions and injunctions, and at all times to acknowledge and recognize the Grand Lodge and the Grand Master of Virginia as their superiors, and to obey them, or either of them, in all things appertaining to the Craft.

Done in the Grand Lodge of Virginia, in the city of Richmond, this —— day of ——, A. L. —, A. D. —.

[SEAL.] ——— ———, *Grand Secretary.*

FORM OF DISPENSATION FOR THE CONSTITUTION OF A NEW LODGE.

To our trusty and well beloved ——— *greeting:*

Whereas a Charter hath been issued by order of our Most Worshipful Grand Lodge, dated on the — day of ———, Anno Lucis 58—, Anno Domini 18—, for the permanent establishment of a Lodge, &c., —— by the name, title and designation of —— No. —.

These are therefore to require you, or any —— of you, with the aid of such other Past Masters as you may deem it expedient to call in to your assistance, to proceed forthwith to install and set to work, agreeably to the customs and usages of Ancient York Masons, as practised by our said Most Worshipful Grand Lodge the said —— No. —; and after you have performed the duty hereby committed to you, you are to make due return of this Warrant, and of your proceedings had thereunder, to our Grand Secretary.

Given under the hand of the —— and the seal of the Grand Lodge of Virginia, this — day of ——, Anno Lucis 58—, Anno Domini 18—.

[SEAL.] —— ——, *Grand Sec'y.*

CHAPTER IX.

ON THE QUALIFICATIONS AND DUTIES OF CANDIDATES FOR FREE MASONRY.

"Whoever from love of knowledge, interest or curiosity, desires to be a Mason, is to know that as his foundation or great cornerstone, he is to believe firmly in the Eternal God, and to pay that worship which is due to Him as the great Architect and Governor of the Universe. A Mason is also obliged by his tenure to observe the moral law as a true Noachida, and if he rightly understands the Royal Art, he cannot tread in the irreligious paths of the unhappy libertine or stupid atheist; nor in any case act against the great inward light of his own conscience.

"He will likewise shun the gross errors of bigotry and superstition, making a due use of his own reason, according to that liberty wherewith a Mason is made free; for although in ancient times the Christian Masons were charged to comply with the Christian usages of the country where they sojourned or worked, (being found in all nations, and of divers religions and persuasions,) yet it is now thought most expedient that the brethren in general should only be charged to adhere to the essentials of religion, in which all men agree, leaving each brother to his own private judgment as to particular modes and forms. Whence it follows that all Masons are to be good men and true—men of honor and honesty, by whatever religious names or persuasions distinguished, always following that golden precept of 'doing unto all men as (upon a change of condition) they would that all men should do unto them.'

"No person is capable of becoming a Free Mason, unless in addition to the qualities and virtues mentioned above, or at least a disposition and capacity to seek and acquire them, he is also free born, of mature and discreet age, of good report, of sufficient natural endowments and the senses of a man, with an estate, office, trade, occupation, or some visible way of acquiring an honest livelihood, and of working in his Craft as becomes the members of this most ancient and honorable Fraternity, who ought not only to earn what is sufficient for themselves and families, but likewise something to spare for works of charity, and for supporting the ancient grandeur and dignity of the Royal Craft."

The candidate being thus shown that a strict enquiry will be made into his character and qualifications, justice and duty require that he should also be advised to be alike circumspect on his side, and to make enquiries into the character of the Lodge into which he desires admission, for there is no true excellence without its opposite, and true coin without its counterfeit.

In the first place, then, he has a right before admission to desire his friend to show him the Warrant or Dispensation by which the Lodge is held, which, if genuine, will be found written or printed on parchment, and signed by the Grand Master, with the seal of the Grand Lodge attached; he may also request a perusal of the by-laws of the Lodge, and a list of members belonging to the same, by all which he will be better able to judge whether he would choose to associate with them, and submit to be conformable to their rules.

The necessary preliminaries being thus settled by the candidate and his friend, he is required to sign the following

FORM OF PETITION.

To the Wor. Master, Wardens and Members of Lodge No. ——, of Free and Accepted Masons:

The subscriber, residing in ———, of lawful age, and by occupation a ———, begs leave to state that unbiased by friends, and uninfluenced by mercenary motives, he freely and voluntarily offers himself as a candidate for the mysteries of Masonry: And that he is prompted to solicit this privilege by a favorable opinion conceived of the Institution, a desire of knowledge, and a sincere wish of being serviceable to his fellow creatures. Should his petition be granted, he will cheerfully conform to all the established usages and customs of the Fraternity.

Signed, A. B.

Recommended and vouched for by

C. D.
E. F.

This petition, accompanied with such fee as the by-laws of the Lodge prescribe, is presented to the Lodge on a stated or regular meeting, and read aloud between Lodge hours,* and is then deposited with the Secretary for one month, at which time a ballot is taken and unanimity required for the admission of the candidate.

CHAPTER X.

ON OPENING AND CLOSING LODGES.

The ceremony of opening and closing Lodges with solemnity and decorum, is universally admitted among Masons; and though the mode in some Lodges may vary, and in every degree must in some parti-

* By Lodge hours is meant between seven and ten P. M., from 25th March to 25th September, and between six and nine P. M., from 25th September to 25th March, when their meetings are held at night; but when held in the day time, the three first hours of each session are considered technically the working hours.

culars, still an uniformity prevails in every Lodge, and the variations, if any, are only occasioned by want of method, which a little application might easily remove.

To conduct this ceremony with propriety, decorum and solemnity ought to be the study of every Mason, but more especially those who are called to officiate as officers of the Lodge; to those of our brethren who are thus honored, every eye is naturally directed for propriety of conduct and behavior, and from them our brethren who are less informed will expect an example worthy of imitation.

From a share in this ceremony no Mason present can be exempted; it is a general concern in which all must assist; the first notice of which is given by the Worshipful Master, with a request of the attention and assistance of his brethren. No sooner has it been signified, than every officer repairs to his station, duly clothes himself, and the brethren, previously clothed, repair to their seats.

The next object is to detect imposters among ourselves, and for this purpose recourse is had to our peculiar rites as Masons; this object being accomplished, our next care is directed to the external avenues of the Lodge, and the proper officers, whose province it is to discharge that duty, execute their trust with fidelity, and by certain mystic forms of no recent date, intimate that we may safely proceed.

At opening the Lodge, two purposes are wisely effected: the Master is reminded of the dignity of character he is to maintain from the elevation of his office, and the brethren of the reverence and respect due from them in their several stations. These are not the only advantages resulting from a due observauce of this truly imposing ceremony; the mind is drawn with reverential awe and adoration to the Supreme Architect of the Universe, and the eye and heart fixed on Him who is the only Author of life and immortality. Here we are taught to worship and adore the Supreme Jehovah, and to supplicate his protection and assistance in all our well-meant endeavors. After the customary salutations, the Master pronounces the Lodge to be opened in due and ancient form, and assumes the government, and under him his Wardens; the brethren with one accord unite in duty and respect, and the business of the meeting is conducted with order and harmony.

At the closing of a Lodge a similar ceremony takes place as at opening. The avenues of the Lodge are guarded; a recapitulation of the duties of the officers is rehearsed, a proper tribute of gratitude is offered up to the Author of our existence, and His blessing invoked and extended to the whole Fraternity.

PRAYER AT OPENING.

Most Holy and Glorious Lord God, the Great Architect of the Universe, the giver of all good gifts and graces, thou hast promised "where two or three are gathered together in thy name, thou will be in the midst of them and bless them;" in thy name we assemble, most humbly beseeching thee to bless us in all our undertakings, that we may know and serve thee aright, and that all our actions may tend to thy glory and to our advancement in knowledge and virtue. And we beseech thee, O Lord, to bless our present assemblage, and to illuminate our minds with the divine precepts of Free Masonry, and direct us so to walk in the light of Thy divine countenance, that when the trials of our probationary state are over, we may be admitted into the Temple not made with hands, eternal in the heavens. So mote it be—Amen!

If the Chaplain be absent, and this duty is performed by the Master, the prayer at opening is:

Supreme Architect of the Universe! We invoke Thy blessing at this time: may this meeting thus begun in order, be conducted in peace and closed in harmony. Amen!

Response—So mote it be.

PRAYER AT CLOSING.

Supreme Architect of the Universe, accept our humble praises, and hearty thanks for the many mercies and blessings which thy bounty has conferred on us, and especially for this friendly and social intercourse. Pardon, we beseech thee, whatever thou hast seen amiss in us since we have been together, and continue to us Thy presence, protection and blessing. Make us sensible of the renewed obligations we are under to love thee supremely, and to be friendly to each other. May all our irregular passions be subdued, and may we daily increase in Faith, Hope and Charity, but more especially in that Charity which is the bond of peace, and the perfection of every virtue. May we so practice Thy precepts in the rigid observance of the Tenets of Free Masonry, that we may finally obtain Thy promises, and find an entrance through the gates into the Temple and City of our God. So mote it be—Amen.

If the Chaplain be absent, and this duty is performed by the Master, the following benediction is pronounced :

BENEDICTION AT CLOSING.

May the blessing of Heaven rest upon us and all regular Masons, may brotherly love prevail, and every moral and social virtue unite and cement us. So mote it be—Amen !

CHARGE AT CLOSING.

BRETHREN :

We are now about to quit this sacred retreat of friendship and virtue, to mix again with the world. Amidst its concerns and employments, forget not the duties which you have heard so frequently inculcated, and so forcibly recommended in this Lodge. Remember that around this altar you have promised in the most solemn manner to befriend and relieve every brother who shall need your assistance. You have promised in the most friendly manner to remind him of his errors and aid a reformation. These generous principles are to extend further : every human being has a claim upon your kind offices ; do good unto all ; recommend it more especially "to the household of the faithful." Finally, brethren, be ye all of one mind ; live in peace ; and may the God of peace and love delight to dwell with and bless you.

Degree of Entered Apprentice.

SECTION I.

The first Lecture upon Masonry, is divided into three sections, which paints virtue in the most beautiful colors, and enforces the whole duty of morality. In it we are taught those useful lessons which prepare the mind for a regular progress in the principles of knowledge and philosophy. They are imprinted on the mind by lively and sensible symbols and images, to influence our conduct in the proper discharge of the duties of social life.

The first section consists of general heads, which, though short and simple, carry much weight with them, and qualify us to try and examine the rights of others to our privileges, while they prove ourselves. It also accurately elucidates the mode of initiating a candidate into our Order.

PRAYER AT THE INITIATION OF A CANDIDATE.

Vouchsafe thine aid, Almighty Father of the Universe, to this our present convention, and grant that this candidate for Masonry may dedicate and devote his life to Thy service, and become a true and faithful brother among us; endue him with a competency of Thy Divine Wisdom, that aided with the secrets of Free Masonry, he may be enabled to unfold the mysteries of godliness; and grant that we may understand and keep all the statutes of the Lord and this Holy Mystery, pure and unviolated, to the end of our days. So mote it be—Amen!

The following passage of Scripture (Psalm cxxxiii) is rehearsed:

Behold how good and how pleasant it is for brethren to dwell together in unity; it is like the precious ointment upon the head, that ran down upon the beard, even Aaron's beard; that went down to the skirts of his garments: As the dew of Hermon, and as the dew that descended upon the mountains of Zion; for there the Lord commanded the blessing, even life for evermore.

It is the duty of the Master of the Lodge, as one of the precautionary measures of initiation, to explain to the candidate the nature and design of the Institution; and while he informs him that it is founded on the purest principles of virtue; that it possesses great and invaluable privileges; and that, in order to secure those privileges to worthy men, and worthy men alone, voluntary pledges of fidelity are required; he will at the same time assure him that nothing will be expected of him incompatible with his civil, moral, or religious duties.

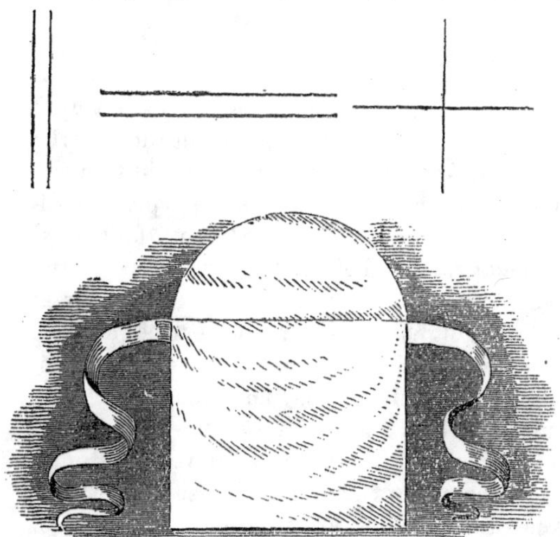

The Lamb-skin or white leather apron is an emblem of innocence and the badge of a Free Mason, more ancient than the Golden Fleece or Roman Eagle, more honorable than the Star and Garter, or any other Order that could be conferred upon the candidate at that or any future period, by King, Prince, Potentate or any other person, except he be a Mason, and which every one ought to wear without spot or blemish, with pleasure to himself and honor to the Fraternity.

This section closes with an explanation of the working tools of an Entered Apprentice, which are the Twenty-four Inch Guage and Common Gavel.

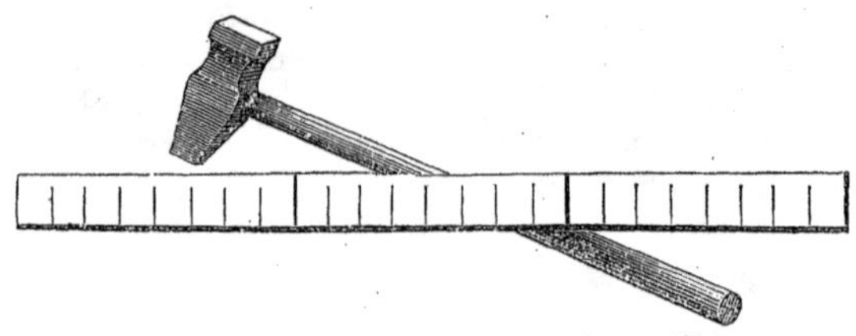

The Twenty-four Inch Guage is an instrument used by operative Masons to measure and lay out their work; but we, as Free and Accepted Masons, are taught to make use of it for the more noble and glorious purpose of dividing our time. It being divided into twenty-four equal parts, is emblematical of the twenty-four hours of the day, which we are taught to divide into three equal parts: whereby are found eight hours for the service of God and a distressed worthy brother; eight for our usual vocations; and eight for refreshment and sleep.

The Common Gavel is an instrument used by operative Masons to break off the corners of rough stones, the better to fit them for the builder's use; but we, as Free and Accepted Masons, are taught to make use of it for the more noble and glorious purpose of divesting our hearts and consciences of all the vices and superfluities of life; thereby fitting our minds, as living stones, for that spiritual building—that house not made with hands—eternal in the heavens.

SECTION II.

This section rationally and minutely accounts for the ceremony of initiating a candidate into our Ancient Institution.

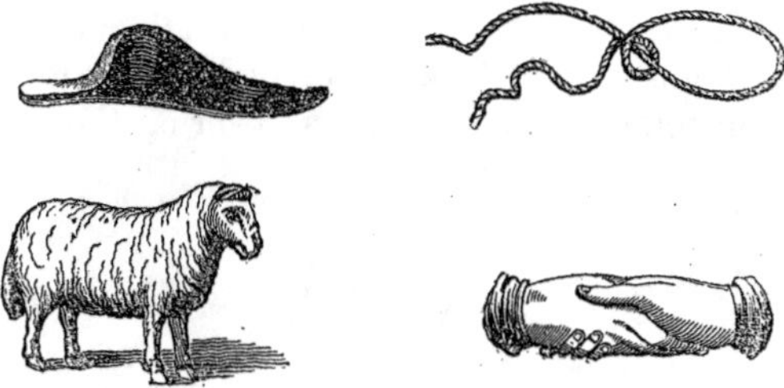

Every candidate at his initiation is presented with a Lamb-skin or white leather apron.

The Lamb has in all ages been deemed an emblem of innocence; he, therefore, who wears the Lamb-skin as the badge of a Mason, is thereby reminded of that purity of life and conduct which is so essentially necessary to his gaining admittance into the Celestial Lodge above, where the Supreme Architect of the Universe presides.

SECTION III.

This section explains the nature and principles of our Institution; in it also we receive instruction relative to the Form, Supports, Covering, Furniture, Ornaments, Lights and Jewels of the Lodge, how it should be Situated, and to whom Dedicated.

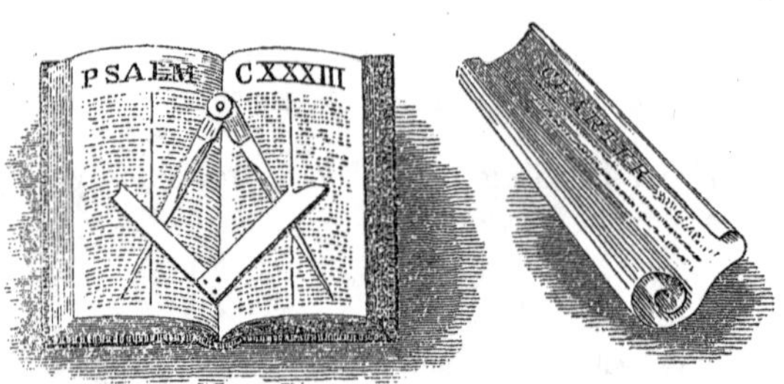

The word Lodge is used to designate a certain number of Free and Accepted Masons duly assembled, with a Holy Bible, Square and Compasses, and a Charter or Warrant from some Grand Lodge empowering them to work.

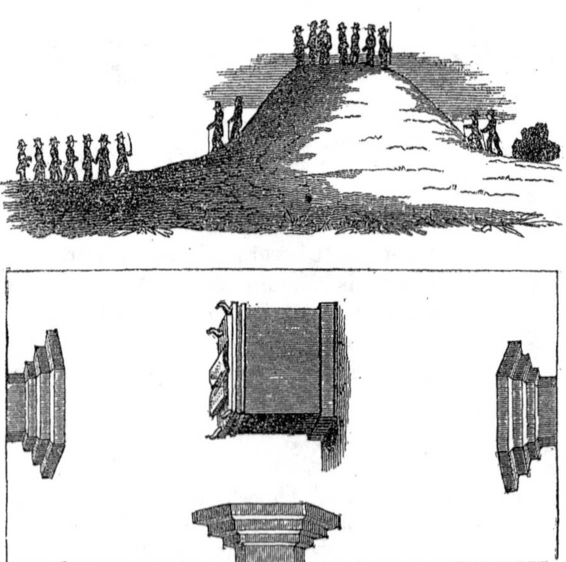

The Form of a Lodge is familiar to every Mason; from East to West, and between North and South, Free Masonry extends, and in every clime a brother may be found.

Our Institution is supported by Wisdom, Strength and Beauty; because it is necessary there should be Wisdom to contrive, Strength to support, and Beauty to adorn all great and important undertakings.

Its Covering is the clouded canopy or starry decked Heavens, where all good Masons hope at last to arrive, by the aid of that Theological ladder which Jacob in his vision saw ascending from earth to Heaven; the three principal rounds of which are denominated Faith, Hope and Charity, and which admonish us to have Faith in God; Hope in immortality; and Charity to all mankind. The greatest of these is Charity, for our Faith may be lost in sight; Hope ends in fruition; but Charity extends beyond the grave into the boundless realms of eternity.

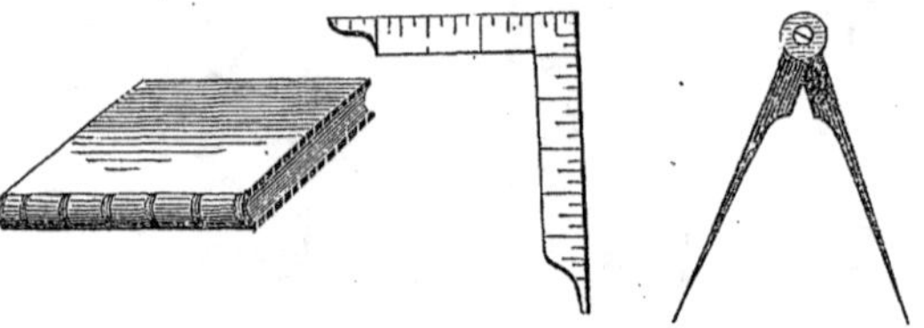

Every Lodge is furnished with a Holy Bible, Square and Compasses. The Holy Bible is dedicated to God; the Square to the Master; and the Compasses to the Craft.

The Ornaments of a Lodge are the Mosaic Pavement, Indented Tessel, and Blazing Star. The Mosaic Pavement is a representation of the ground floor of King Solomon's Temple; the Indented Tessel, of the beautiful border or skirting which surrounded it; and the Blazing Star an emblem of Deity, or an overruling Providence.

The Mosaic Pavement is emblematical of human life, chequered with good and evil; the beautiful border which surrounds it, of the manifold blessings and comforts which surround us, and which we hope to enjoy by a faithful reliance on Divine Providence, which is hieroglyphically represented by the Blazing Star in the centre.

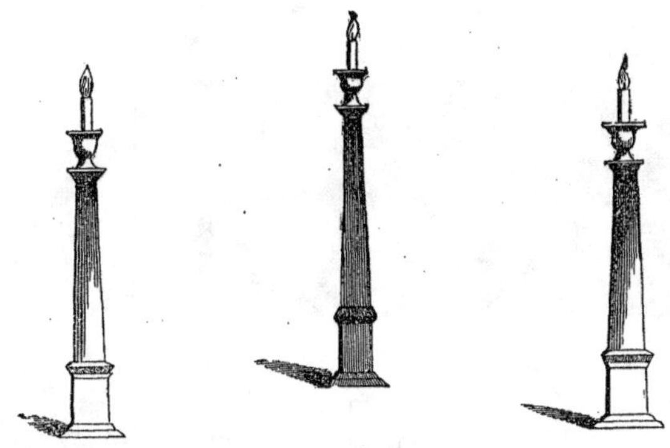

The Lights are three in number.

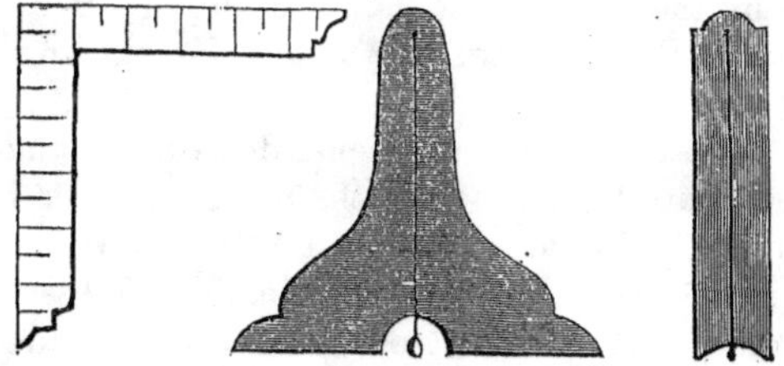

The Immoveable Jewels are the Square, Level and Plumb, worn by the three stationed officers. The Square teaches morality, the Level equality, and the Plumb rectitude of life.

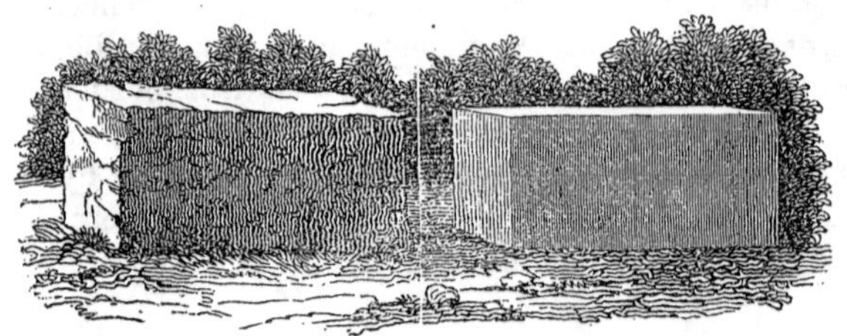

The Moveable Jewels are the Rough Ashler, the Perfect Ashler, and the Trestle Board.

The Rough Ashler is a stone as taken from the quarry in its rude and natural state; the Perfect Ashler is a stone made ready by the hands of the Apprentice, to be adjusted by the working tools of the Fellow Craft; and the Trestle Board is for the Master Workman to draw his designs upon.

By the Rough Ashler we are reminded of our rude and imperfect state by nature; by the perfect Ashler, of that state of perfection at which we hope to arrive by a virtuous education, our own endeavors, and the blessing of God; and by the Trestle Board, we are reminded that as the operative workman erects his temporal building agreeably to the rules and designs laid down by the Master on his Trestle Board, so should we, both operative and speculative, endeavor to erect our spiritual building agreeably to the rules and designs laid down by the Supreme Architect of the Universe, in the Great Book of Nature and of Revelation, which is our Spiritual, Moral and Masonic Trestle Board.

The Situation of our Lodges is sufficiently familiar, and the reasons therefor.

Lodges were anciently dedicated to King Solomon, who was our first Most Excellent Grand Master; but Masons professing Christianity, dedicate theirs to St. John the Baptist and St. John the Evangelist, who were two eminent Christian patrons in Masonry; and since their time, there is represented in every regular and well governed Lodge, a certain Point within a Circle—the point representing an individual brother; the circle, the boundary line of his duty to God and man, beyond which which he is never to suffer his passions, prejudices or interests to betray him, on any occasion. This circle is embordered by two perpendicular parallel lines, representing those Saints, who were perfect parallels in Christianity, as well as in Masonry; and upon the vertex rests the Book of Constitutions, which point out the whole duty of a Mason. In going round this Circle, we necessarily touch upon these two lines, as well as upon the Book of Constitutions; and while a Mason keeps himself thus circumscribed, it is is impossible he should materially err.

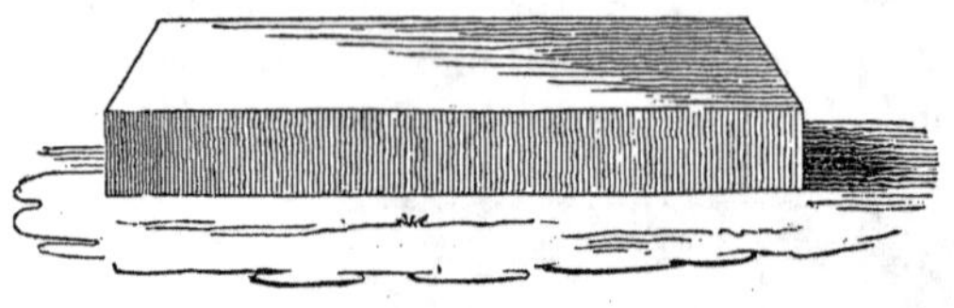

THE TENETS

Of our profession, and by the due exercise of which every worthy Free Mason may be at once distinguished, are three in number: Brotherly Love, Relief and Truth.

Brotherly Love.—By the exercise of Brotherly Love, we are taught to regard the whole human species as one common family, the high, the low, the rich and poor, who, as created by one Almighty Parent, and inhabitants of the same planet, are sent into the world to aid, support and protect each other. On this principle Free Masonry unites men of every country, sect and opinion, and conciliates true friendship among those who might otherwise remain at a perpetual distance.

Relief.—To relieve the distressed is a duty incumbent on all men, but particularly on Masons, who are linked together by an indissoluble chain of sincere affections; to soothe the unhappy, to sympathize with their misfortunes, to compassionate their miseries, and to restore peace to their troubled minds, is the grand aim we have in view. On this basis we form our friendships and establish our connections.

Truth is a divine attribute, and the foundation of every virtue; to be good men and true, is the first lesson we are taught in Masonry. On this theme we contemplate, and by its dictates endeavor to regulate our conduct;

hence, while influenced by this principle, hypocrisy and deceit are unknown among us; sincerity and plain dealing characterize us, and the heart and tongue join in promoting each others welfare, and rejoicing in each others prosperity.

THE CARDINAL VIRTUES.

There are four Perfect Points and essential Cardinal Virtues necessary to complete the lesson of instructions to every Initiate into the Philosophy of Masonry, illustrated by Temperance, Fortitude, Prudence and Justice.

Temperance is that due restraint upon our affections and passions, which renders the body tame and governable and frees the mind from the allurements of vice. This virtue should be the constant practice of every Mason, as he is thereby taught to avoid excess, or contracting any vicious or licentious habit, the indulgence of which might lead him to disclose some of those valuable secrets which he has promised to conceal and never reveal, and which would subject him to the contempt and detestation of all good Masons, * * * * *

Fortitude is that noble and steady purpose of the mind whereby we are enabled to undergo any pain, peril or danger, when prudentially deemed expedient. This virtue is equally distant from cowardice and rashness, and like the former, should be deeply impressed upon the mind of every Mason, as a safeguard or security against any illegal attack that may be made by force or otherwise to extort from him any of those valuable secrets with which he has been so solemnly entrusted, and which were emblematically represented upon his first admission into the Lodge, * * * * *

Prudence teaches us to regulate our lives agreeably to the dictates of reason, and is that habit by which we wisely judge, and prudentially determine on all things relative to our present as well as to our future happiness. This virtue should be the peculiar characteristic of every Mason, not only for the government of his conduct while in the Lodge, but also when abroad in the world. It should be particularly attended to in all strange and mixed companies, never to let fall the least expression or hint whereby the secrets of Free Masonry might be unlawfully obtained, * * * * *

Justice is that standard, or boundary of right, which enables us to render to every man his just due without distinction. This virtue is not only consistent with Divine and human laws, but is the very cement and support of all civil society; and as justice in a great measure constitutes the really good man, so should it be the invariable practice of every Mason, never to deviate from the minutest principles thereof, * * *

Thus the Lecture of the First or Entered Apprentice's degree is closed with a few appropriate remarks explanatory of the freedom, fervency and zeal necessary to be exercised during the probation of his service, and show how a due veneration was paid to our ancient Patrons in Masonry; and the whole is concluded with the following charge:

CHARGE AT INITIATION INTO THE FIRST DEGREE.

BROTHER A. B.

As you are now introduced into the first principles of Masonry, I congratulate you on being accepted into this Ancient and Honorable Order—ancient, as having subsisted from time immemorial, and honorable as tending in every particular so to render all men who will be conformable to its precepts. No Institution was ever raised on a better principle or more solid foundation; nor were ever more excellent rules and useful maxims laid down than are inculcated in the several Masonic lectures. The greatest and best of men in all ages, have been encouragers and promoters of the Art; and have never deemed it derogatory to their dignity to level themselves with the Fraternity, extend their privileges, and patronize their assemblies. There are three great duties, which in your new character, you are charged to practise and inculcate: to God, your neighbor, and yourself. To God, in never mentioning His Holy name but with that reverential awe which is due from a creature to his Creator, to implore His aid in all your laudable undertakings, and esteem Him as the chief good. To your neighbor, in acting upon the square, and doing unto him as you wish he should do unto you; and to yourself, in avoiding all irregularity and intemperance, which may impair your faculties or debase the dignity of your profession. A zealous attachment to, and practice of these duties will ensure public and private esteem.

In the state you are to be a quiet and peaceful citizen, true to your government, and just to your country; you are not to countenance disloyalty or rebellion, but patiently submit to legal authority, and conform with cheerfulness to the government of the country in which you live. In your outward demeanor be particularly careful to avoid censure or reproach. You are not to suffer your zeal for the Institution to lead you into argument with those who through ignorance may ridicule it.

At your leisure hours, that you may improve in Masonic knowledge, you are to converse with well informed brethren, who will be always as ready to give as you will be to receive instruction.

Finally, keep sacred and inviolable the mysteries of the Order, as these are to distinguish you from the rest of the community, and mark your consequence among Masons. If in the circle of your acquaintance, a person applies to you who may be desirous of being initiated into the secrets of Masonry, be particularly careful not to afford him any encouragement, unless you are convinced he will conform to our rules, in which event you may refer him to those who have authority to recommend him to the Lodge, that the honor, glory and reputation of the Institution may be firmly established, and the world at large convinced of its good effects.

Such is the arrangement of the different sections of the first Lecture, which, with the forms adopted in opening and closing the Lodge, comprehends the whole of the first degree in Masonry. This plan, while it has the advantage of regularity to recommend it, has the support of authority, and the sanction and respect which flow from antiquity. The whole is a regular system of morality, conceived in a strain of interesting allegory, which must unfold its beauties to every candid and industrious enquirer.

Degree of Fellow Craft.

Masonry is a progressive science, and is divided into different classes or degrees for the more regular advancement of its professors in the knowledge of its mysteries. According to the progress we make, we are led to limit or extend our enquiries; and in proportion to the genius or capacity with which it has pleased our Almighty Father to bless us, we attain to a greater or less degree of perfection.

The first degree of Masonry is well calculated to enforce the duties of morality, and to imprint on the memory the noblest principles which can adorn the human mind. Therefore it is the best introduction to the second degree, and not only extends the same plan, but comprehends a more diffusive system of knowledge.

SECTION I.

The first section recapitulates the ceremony of initiation into this class, and instructs the diligent Craftsman how to proceed in the proper arrangement of the ceremonies used on the occasion, and should, therefore, be well understood by every officer and member of the Lodge. Here the candidate is instructed in, and invested with those particular tests which enable him to prove his title to the privileges of this degree, and satisfactory reasons are given for the same.

The following passage of Scripture from Amos, chapter vii, verse 7, 8, is rehearsed:

Thus he showed me; and behold the Lord stood upon a wall, made by a plumb line, with a plumb line in his hand. And the Lord said unto me, Amos, what seest thou? And I said a plumb line. Then said the Lord, behold I will set a plumb line in the midst of my people Israel; I will not again pass by them any more.

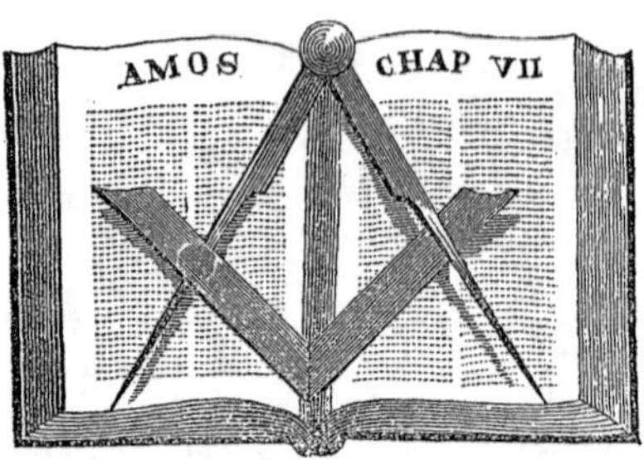

The Holy Bible, Square and Compasses, opened at Amos, chap. vii.

The working tools of a Fellow Craft are here introduced and explained, which are the Plumb, Square and Level.

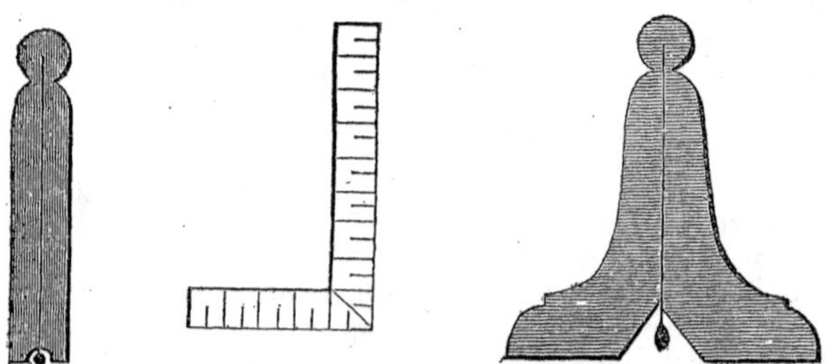

The Plumb is an instrument used by operative workmen to try perpendiculars; the Square, to square their work; and the Level, to prove horizontals; * * * * * and by the Level a King is reminded, that although a crown may adorn the head, and a sceptre the hand, yet the blood in his veins is derived from the same Almighty Parent, and is no better than the humblest citizen, and *teaches* us all that we are traveling on the broad level of time to that undiscovered country, from whose bourne no traveler returns.

SECTION II.

This section has reference to the origin of the Institution, and views Masonry under two denominations—Operative and Speculative. The period is fixed for rewarding merit, the character of that reward designated, and the inimitable moral to which that circumstance alludes is explained.

OPERATIVE MASONRY.

By Operative Masonry, we allude to a proper application of the useful rules of architecture, whence a structure will derive figure, strength and beauty, and whence will result a due proportion and just correspondence in all its parts. It furnishes us with dwellings and convenient shelters from the vicissitudes and inclemencies of the seasons; and while it displays the effect of human wisdom, as well in the choice, as the arrangement of the sundry materials of which an edifice is composed, it demonstrates that a fund of science and industry is implanted in man, for the best, most salutary, and beneficent purposes.

SPECULATIVE MASONRY.

By Speculative Masonry, we learn to subdue the passions, act upon the square, keep the tongue of good report, maintain secrecy and practise charity. It is so far interwoven with religion as to lay us under obligation to pay that rational homage to the Deity, which at once constitutes our duty, and our happiness. It leads the contemplative to view with admiration and delight, the glorious works of Creation, and inspires him with the most exalted ideas of the perfection of his Divine Creator.

* * * * * * * * *

In six days God created the Heavens and the Earth,

and all things therein contained, and rested on the seventh. The seventh, therefore, our ancient brethren consecrated as a day of rest from their labors, thereby enjoying frequent and stated opportunities to contemplate the glorious works of Creation, and to adore their great Creator.

Peace, Unity and Plenty are here introduced and explained. Next, the doctrine of the Spheres is illustrated in the Sciences of Geography and Astronomy, by the Globes Terrestrial and Celestial.

As the studious Craftsman advances, various subjects arrest his attention and engross his thoughts in the progress of the three first degrees of Masonry, over which preside the three officers of a Lodge.

As Architecture comes now under consideration, a brief description of it may not be improper.

ORDER IN ARCHITECTURE.

By Order in Architecture is meant a system of all the members, proportions and ornaments of columns and pilasters; or it is a rrgular arrangement of the projecting parts of a building, which, united with those of a column, form a beautiful, perfect and complete whole.

ITS ANTIQUITY.

From the first foundation of society, Order in Architecture may be traced. When the rigor of seasons obliged men to contrive shelters from the inclemency of the weather, we learn that they first planted trees on end, and then laid others across to support its covering. The bands which connected those trees at top and bottom are said to have given rise to the idea of base and capital of pillars; and from this simple hint originally proceeded the more improved art of Architecture.

The Five Orders of Architecture are thus classed: Tuscan, Doric, Ionic, Corinthian and Composite.

THE INVENTION OF ORDER IN ARCHITECTURE.

The ancient and original Orders of Architecture revered by Masons, are no more than three—the Doric, Ionic and Corinthian, which were invented by the Grecians. To these the Romans have added two—the Tuscan, which they made plainer than the Doric, and the Composite, which is nothing more than the Corinthian enriched with the Ionic volute. To the Greeks, therefore, and not to the Romans, are we indebted for what is great, judicious and beautiful in Architecture.

The Five Senses of Human Nature, which are Hearing, Seeing, Feeling, Smelling and Tasting, come next in order—the first three of which are most revered by Masons, for reasons which must be apparent to every enlightened Craftsman.

Next in order come the Seven Liberal Arts and Sciences, to wit: Grammar, Rhetoric, Logic, Arithmetic, Geometry, Music and Astronomy. Passing over most of these, each of which affords a large field for the accomplished Scholar and Mason to dilate upon, we are arrested by the fifth Science, or Geometry, which treats of the powers and properties of Magnitudes in general, where length, breadth and thickness are concerned, from a point to a line, from a line to a superfice, and from a superfice to a solid.

THE ADVANTAGES OF GEOMETRY.

By this Science, the Architect is enabled to construct his plans and execute his designs, the General to arrange his soldiers and mark out his lines for encampment, the Geographer to give us the dimensions of the earth, and all things therein contained, to delineate the extent of seas, and specify the divisions of empires, kingdoms and provinces. By it also the Astronomer is enabled to make his observations, and to fix the duration of times and seasons, years and cycles. In fine, Geometry is the foundation of Architecture and the root of the Mathematics.

Here an emblem of Plenty is introduced and explained.

The Jewels of a Fellow Craft and the wages of a Worthy One are here explained.

THE MORAL ADVANTAGES OF GEOMETRY.

Geometry, the first and noblest of Sciences, is the basis on which the Superstructure of Masonry is erected. By Geometry we may curiously trace Nature through her various windings, to her most concealed recesses;

by it we may discover the power, the wisdom, and the goodness of the Grand Artificer of the Universe, and view with delight the proportions which connect this vast machine.

By it we may discover how the planets move in their different orbits, and demonstrate their various revolutions; by it we account for the return of seasons, and the variety of scenes which each season displays to the discerning eye. Numberless worlds are around us, all framed by the same Divine Artist, which roll through the vast expanse, and are all conducted by the same unerring law of Nature.

A survey of Nature, and the observation of her beautiful proportions, first determined man to imitate the Divine Plan, and study symmetry and order; this gave rise to societies, and birth to every useful art; the Architect began to design, and the plans which he laid down, being improved by experience and time, have produced works which are the admiration of every age.

The lapse of time, the ruthless hand of ignorance, and the devastations of war, have laid waste and destroyed many valuable monuments of antiquity on which the utmost exertions of human genius have been employed. Even the Temple of Solomon, so spacious and magnificent, and constructed by so many celebrated Artists, escaped not the unsparing ravages of barbarous force. Free Masonry, notwithstanding, has still survived. The attentive ear receives the sound from the instructive tongue, and the mysteries of Free Masonry are safely lodged in the repository of faithful breasts. Tools and implements of Architecture, and symbolic emblems most expressive, are selected by the Fraternity to imprint on the mind wise and serious truths; and thus through a succession of ages are transmitted unimpaired the most excellent tenets of our Institution.

This Section closes with a solemn admonition to every Craftsman to pay that rational homage to the Deity which constitutes the duty of every good man.

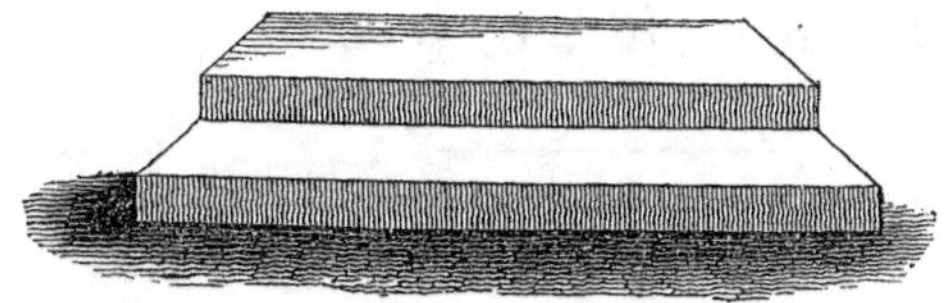

CHARGE AT PASSING TO THE DEGREE OF FELLOW CRAFT.

BROTHER A. B.

Being passed to the second degree of Masonry, we congratulate you on your preferment. The internal and not the external qualifications of a man, are what Masonry regards. As you increase in knowledge you will improve in social intercourse.

It is unnecessary to recapitulate the duties, which as a Craftsman you are bound to discharge, or to enlarge upon the necessity of a strict adherence to them, as your own experience must have established their value.

The study of the liberal arts, that valuable branch of education, which tends so effectually to polish and adorn the mind, is earnestly recommended to your consideration; especially the Science of Geometry, which is established as the basis of our Art. Geometry or Masonry, originally synonimous terms, being of a divine and moral nature, is enriched with the most useful knowledge; while it proves the wonderful properties of nature, it demonstrates the more important truths of morality.

Your past behavior and regular deportment, have merited the honor we have now conferred; and in your new character, it is expected that you will conform to the principles of the Order, by steadily persevering in the practice of every commendable virtue. Such is the nature of your engagement as a Fellow Craft, and to these duties you are bound by the most sacred ties.

Degree of Master Mason.

SECTION I.

The ceremony of raising to the Sublime Degree of Master Mason is particularly specified, and other useful instructions are given in this branch of the Lecture. To a complete knowledge of the whole Lecture, few, indeed, ever arrive; but it is an infallible truth, that he who acquires by merit, the mark of pre-eminence which this degree confers, receives a reward which amply compensates for all his past diligence and assiduity.

The following passage of Scripture, from Ecclesiastes xii: 1–7, is introduced:

Remember now thy Creator in the days of thy youth, while the evil days come not, nor the years draw nigh, when thou shalt say, I have no pleasure in them; while the sun, or the light, or the moon, or the stars be not darkened, nor the clouds return after the rain; in the day when the keepers of the house shall tremble, and the strong men shall bow themselves, and the grinders cease because they are few, and those that look out of the windows be darkened; and the doors shall be shut in the streets, when the sound of the grinding is low; and he shall rise up at the voice of the bird, and all the daughters of music shall be brought low; also when they shall be afraid of that which is high, and fears shall be in the way, and the almond tree shall flourish, and the grasshopper shall be a burden, and desire shall fail; because man goeth to his long home, and the mourners go about the streets; or ever the silver cord be loosed, or the golden bowl be broken, or the pitcher be broken at the fountain, or the wheel broken at the cistern. Then shall the dust return to the earth as it was; and the spirit shall return unto the God who gave it.

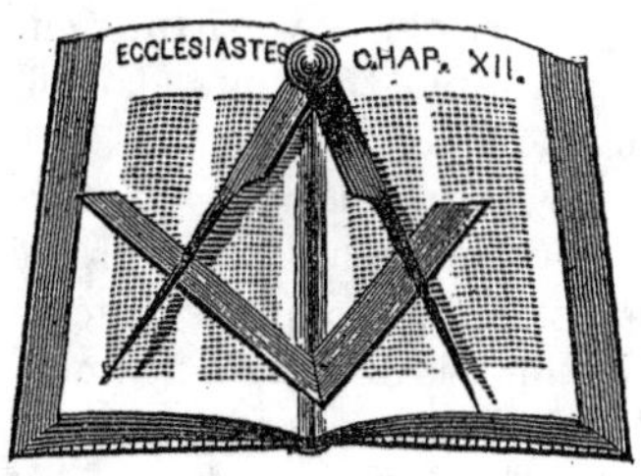

The Holy Bible, Square and Compasses, those inestimable lights of Free Masonry, are here again brought to view.

THE WORKING TOOLS

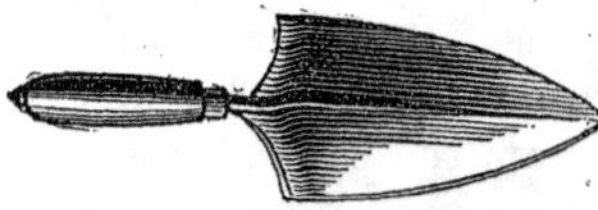

Of a Master Mason are all the implements of Masonry indiscriminately, but more especially the Trowel.

The Trowel is an instrument made use of by operative Masons to spread the cement which unites a building into one common mass or whole; but it is used symbolically for the far more noble and glorious purpose of spreading the cement of Brotherly Love and Affection, which unites us into one sacred band or society of friends and brothers, a Temple of living stones, among whom no contention should ever exist, but that noble contention or rather emulation of who can best work or best agree.

SECTION II.

This section recites the historical tradition of the Order, and presents a finished picture of the utmost consequence to the Fraternity. It exemplifies an instance of virtue, fortitude and integrity unparalleled in the history of man.

PRAYER AT RAISING A BROTHER TO THE SUBLIME DEGREE OF MASTER MASON.

Thou, O God! knowest our downsitting and our uprising, and understandest our thoughts afar off. Shield and defend us from the evil intentions of our enemies, and support us under the trials and afflictions we are destined to endure while traveling through this vale of tears. Man that is born of a woman is of few days and full of trouble. He cometh forth as a flower and is cut down, he fleeth as a shadow and continueth not. Seeing his days are determined, the number of his months is with thee, thou hast appointed his bounds that he cannot pass, turn from him that he may rest, till he shall accomplish as a hireling his day. For there is hope of a tree if it be cut down, that it will sprout again, and that the tender branch thereof will not cease. But man dieth and wasteth away; yea, man giveth up the ghost, and where is he? As the waters fail from the sea and the flood decayeth, and drieth up, so man lieth down, and riseth not up again till the Heavens shall be no more. Yet, O Lord! have compassion on the children of Thy creation, administer them comfort in the time of trouble, and save them with an everlasting salvation. So mote it be—Amen.

It has been the practice of all ages to erect monuments to the memory of exalted worth.

SECTION III.

The third section illustrates certain Hieroglyphical emblems and inculcates many useful lessons, to extend knowledge and promote virtue. In this branch of the Lecture many important particulars relative to King Solomon's Temple are noticed and explained.

* * * * * * * * *

The three Grand Masonic Pillars here introduced and explained, show the Wisdom of Solomon, the Strength and support afforded him by King Hiram, and the skill and ingenuity of Hiram Abiff.

* * * * * * * * *

This magnificent structure was founded in the fourth year of the reign of Solomon, on the second day of the month Zif, being the second month of the sacred year. It was located on Mount Moriah, near the place where Abraham was about to offer up his son Isaac, and where David met and appeased the destroying angel. Josephus informs us, that although more than seven years were occupied in its building, yet, during the whole period, it did not rain in the day-time, that the workmen might not be obstructed in their labor. From sacred history we also learn, that there was not the sound of axe, hammer, or any tool of iron, heard in the house while it was building.

It was supported by 1,453 Columns, 2,906 Pilasters, all of the finest Parian Marble.

There were employed in its erection,
Three Grand Masters,
3,300 Overseers,
80,000 Fellow Crafts, and
70,000 Entered Apprentices, all of whom were so methodically classed and arranged by the wisdom of Solomon, and the Masonic Art, that neither envy, discord, nor confusion were known among them.

The division of Lodges is next explained.

* * * * * * * * *

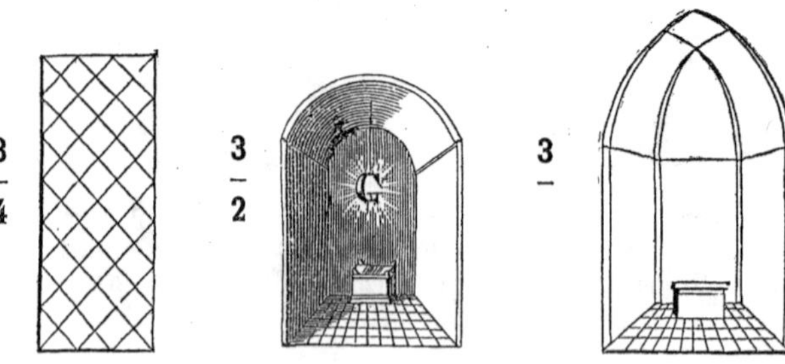

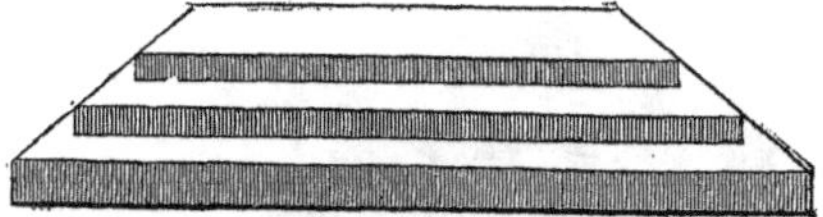

THE THREE STEPS

Are emblematic of the three stages of human life—Youth, Manhood and Old Age. In Youth, as Entered Apprentices, we ought industriously to apply our minds to the attainment of useful knowledge; in Manhood, as Fellow Crafts, we should apply our knowledge to the discharge of our respective duties to God, our neighbors and ourselves; that so in Old Age, as Master Masons, we may enjoy the happy reflections consequent on a well spent life, and die in the hope of a glorious immortality.

THE POT OF INCENSE

Is an emblem of a Pure Heart, which is always an acceptable sacrifice to Deity; and as this glows with fervent heat, so should our hearts continually glow with gratitude to the great and beneficent Author of our existence, for the manifold blessings and comforts we enjoy.

THE BEE HIVE

Is an emblem of Industry, and recommends the practice of that virtue to all created beings, from the highest Seraph in Heaven, to the lowest reptile of the dust. It teaches us that as we came into the world rational and intelligent beings, so we should ever be industrious ones, never sitting down contented while our fellow creatures around us are in want, when it is in our power to relieve them without inconvenience to ourselves.

When we take a survey of nature, we view man in his infancy—more helpless and indigent than the brute creation; he lies languishing for days, months and years, totally incapable of providing sustenance for himself, of guarding against the attacks of the wild beasts of the field, or sheltering himself from the inclemencies of the weather. It might have pleased the Great Creator of Heaven and Earth to have made man independent of his fellow man and all other beings, but as dependence is one of the strongest bonds of society, mankind were made dependent on each other for protection and security, as they thereby enjoy better opportunities of fulfilling the duties of reciprocal love and friendship. Thus was man formed for social and active life, the noblest part of the work of God; and he that will so demean himself as not to be endeavoring to add to the common stock of knowledge and practical philanthropy, may be deemed a Drone in the Hive of Nature, a useless member of society, and unworthy of our protection and respect as Masons.

THE BOOK OF CONSTITUTIONS GUARDED BY THE TYLER'S SWORD,

Reminds us that we should ever be watchful and guarded in our words and actions, particularly when before the enemies of Masonry, ever bearing in remembrance those truly Masonic virtues, silence and circumspection.

THE SWORD POINTING TO A NAKED HEART,

Demonstrates that justice will sooner or later overtake us; and although our thoughts, words and actions may be hidden from the eyes of men, yet that

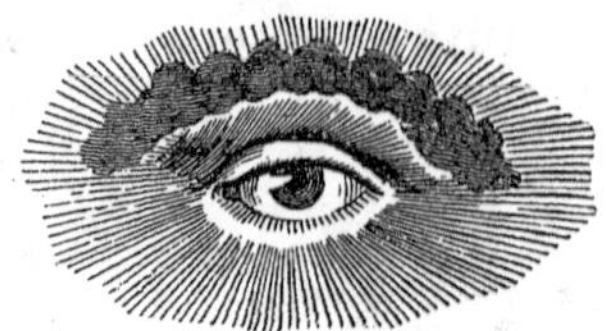

ALL-SEEING EYE,

Whose all pervading intelligence

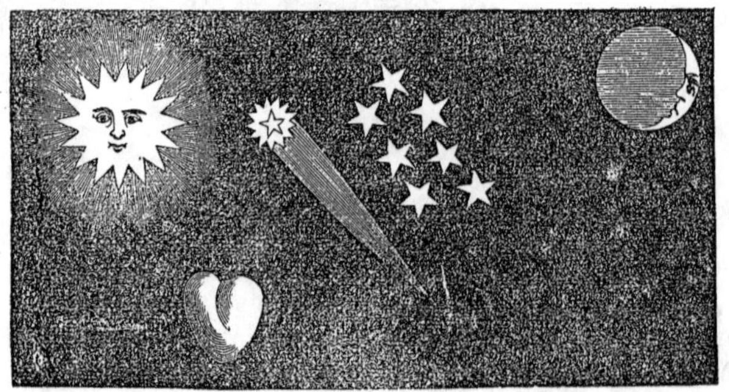

THE SUN, MOON AND STARS

Obey; and under whose watchful care even the Comets perform their stupendous revolutions, pervades the inmost recesses of the human heart, and will reward us according to our merits.

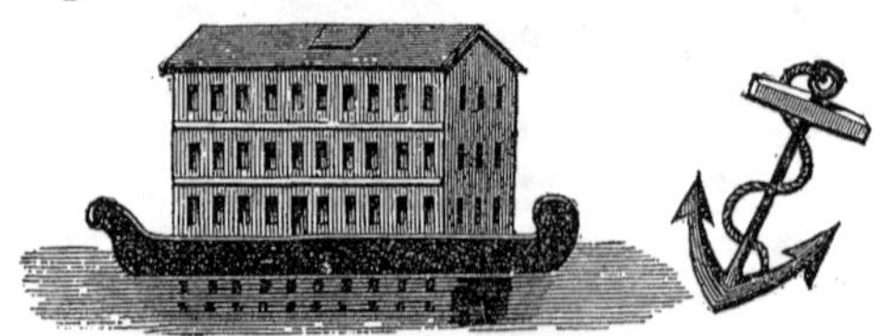

THE ANCHOR AND ARK

Are emblems of a well grounded hope and a well spent life. They are emblematic of that Divine Ark which safely wafts us over this tempestuous sea of troubles, and that Anchor which shall safely moor us in a peaceful harbor, where the wicked cease from troubling, and where the weary shall find rest.

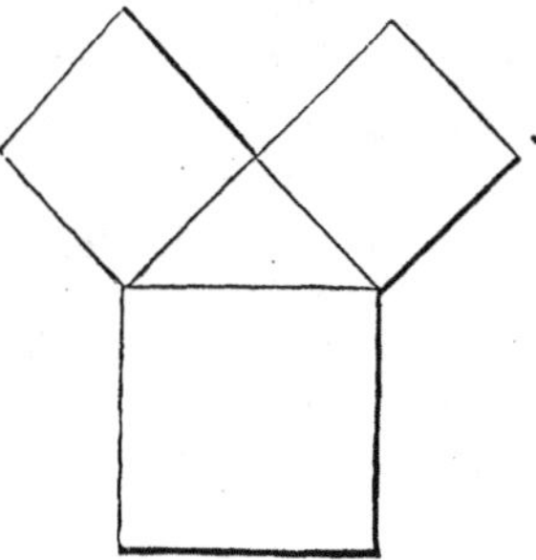

THE FORTY-SEVENTH PROBLEM OF EUCLID

Was an invention of our ancient friend and brother, Pythagoras, who, in his travels through Asia, Africa and Europe, was initiated into several orders of Priesthood, and raised to the sublime degree of a Master Mason. This wise Philosopher enriched his mind abundantly in a general knowledge of things, and more especially in Geometry and Masonry. On this subject he drew out many problems and theorems; and among the most distinguished he erected this, which in the joy of his heart, he called "Eureka," meaning, in the Grecian language, "I have found it;" and upon the discovery, is said to have sacrificed a hecatomb.

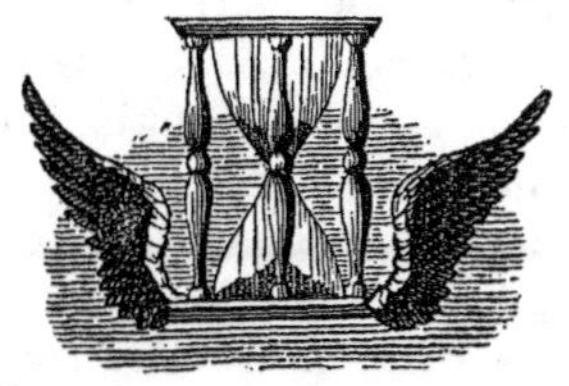

THE HOUR GLASS

Is an emblem of Human Life. Behold how swiftly the sands run, and how rapidly our lives are drawing to a close! We cannot, without astonishment, behold the little particles which are contained in this machine; how they pass away almost imperceptibly, and yet to our surprise, in the short space of an hour they are all exhausted. Thus wastes man. To-day, he puts forth the tender leaves of hope; to-morrow, blossoms and bears his blushing honors thick upon him. The next day comes a frost, which nips the shoot; and when he thinks his greatness is aspiring, he falls like autumn leaves, to enrich his mother earth.

THE SCYTHE

Is an emblem of Time, which cuts the brittle thread of life, and launches us into eternity. Behold what havoc the Scythe of Time makes among the human race! If by chance we should escape the numerous ills incident to childhood and youth, and with health and vigor arrive to the years of manhood, yet withal we must soon be cut down by the all-devouring Scythe of Time and gathered unto the land where our fathers have gone before us, "that bourne whence no traveler returns."

The explanation of the emblems is closed with the tenth or last class; which are

THE SETTING MALL, THE SPADE, THE COFFIN AND SPRIG OF ACACIA.

These emblems force upon us the solemn thought of Death, which without Revelation is dark and gloomy; but the Master Mason is suddenly revived by the ever green and ever living Sprig of Faith in the merits of the Lion of the Tribe of Judah, which strengthens him with confidence and composure to look forward to a glorious immortality beyond the grave.

* * * * * * * * * * *

Then let us imitate our Most Excellent Grand Master in his virtuous and amiable conduct; in his unfeigned piety to God; in his inflexible fidelity to his trust; that we may welcome the grim tyrant Death, and receive him as a kind messenger sent from our Supreme Grand Master, to translate us from this imperfect, to that all perfect, glorious and celestial Lodge above, where the Supreme Architect of the Universe in his glory presides.

CHARGE AT RAISING TO THE SUBLIME DEGREE OF MASTER MASON.

Brother A. B.

Your zeal for the Institution of Free Masonry, the progress you have made in the mystery, and your conformity to our regulations, have pointed you out as a proper object of our esteem and favor. You are now a Free and Accepted Mason, and as such, bound by duty, honor and gratitude, to be faithful to your trust, to support the dignity of your character on every occasion, and to enforce by precept and example, obedience to the tenets of our Order.

In the character of a Master Mason, you are authorized to correct the errors and irregularities of your less informed brethren, and to guard them against a breach of fidelity. To preserve the reputation of the Fraternity unsullied must be your constant care; and for this purpose it is your province to recommend to your inferiors obedience and submission; to your equals, courtesy and affability; to your superiors, kindness and condescension; universal benevolence you are always to inculcate; and by the regularity of your own behavior, afford the best example for the conduct of others less informed. The Ancient Landmarks of the Order, entrusted to your care, you are carefully to preserve, and never suffer them to be infringed, or countenance a deviation from the established usages and customs of the Fraternity.

Your virtue, honor and reputation are concerned in supporting with dignity the character you now bear. Let no motive, therefore, make you swerve from your duty, violate your vows, or betray your trust; but be true and faithful, and imitate the example of that celebrated Artist whom you this evening represent. Thus you will render yourself deserving of the honor which we have conferred, and merit the confidence we have reposed.

Grand and Subordinate Lodge Jewels.

Degree of Past Master.

This degree treats of the government of our Society, the disposition of its rulers, and illustrates their requisite qualifications. It includes the Ceremony of Opening and Closing Lodges in the several preceding degrees; it comprehends the Ceremonies and Forms of Constitution, Consecration, Installation, Laying the Corner Stones of Public Edifices, and also at Dedications and Funerals, by a variety of particulars explanatory of those ceremonies.

SECTION I.

This section contains the Form of a Petition for Letters of Dispensation or a Warrant of Constitution for a new Lodge, empowering them to work. The Ceremonies of Constitution and Consecration are considered with the form of a Grand Procession.

Any number of Master Masons desirous of forming a new Lodge, or reviving an old one, must present a petition (see page 137) therefor to the Most Wor. Grand Master.

This petition must be signed by at least seven regular Master Masons, and recommended by the Lodge nearest to the place where the new Lodge is to be held; it must then be forwarded to the Grand Secretary, whose duty it is to lay it before the Grand Lodge, or if received during the recess, before the Grand Master; and if approved, a Dispensation or Charter issues accordingly; if a Dispensation, the officers named continue their work without Installation until the ensuing Grand Annual Communication, when, if their work, &c., is approved, a Charter is issued for the Legal Constitution of said Lodge.

After a Charter is granted by the Grand Lodge, the Grand Master appoints a day and hour for Constituting and Consecrating the new Lodge, and for Installing the Master, Wardens and other officers. If the Grand Master cannot attend, he has the power to appoint three worthy Past Masters, with full powers to consecrate, constitute and install the petitioners.

CEREMONY OF CONSTITUTION AND CONSECRATION.

On the day and hour appointed, the Grand Master and his officers, or the Commission appointed by him,* meet in a convenient room near the Lodge to be constituted, and open in the third degree. After the officers of the new Lodge are examined by a committee appointed therefor by the Grand Master or Commission, they send a messenger to the Grand Master or Commission, with the following message:

MOST WORSHIPFUL:

The officers and brethren of ——— Lodge, who have now assembled at ———, have instructed me to inform you, that the Most Worshipful Grand Lodge was pleased to grant them a Charter, authorizing them to form and open a Lodge of Free and Accepted Masons in the ——— of ———. They are now desirous that their Lodge should be Consecrated and their officers Installed in due and ancient form; for which purpose they are now met, and await the pleasure of the Most Worshipful Grand Master.

When notice is given, the Grand Lodge walk in procession to the Hall of the New Lodge. When the Grand Master enters, the Grand Honors are given by the new Lodge, the officers of which resign their seats to the Grand Officers, and take their several stations on the left of each.

The necessary cautions are then given, and all except Present or Past Masters of Lodges are requested to retire until the Master of the New Lodge is inducted into the Oriental Chair of Solomon. He is then bound to the faithful performance of his trust, and invested with the characteristics of the Chair.

Upon due notice, the Grand Marshal reconducts the brethren into the Hall; and all take their places, except the members of the new Lodge, who form a procession on one side of the Hall. As they advance, the Grand Master addresses them: "BEHOLD YOUR MASTER!" They make the proper salutations as they pass.

* If the Ceremony is performed by a Commission, the word "Grand" is omitted on their record, wherever it occurs in this form.

A Grand Procession is then formed in the following order:

Marshall; | Marshall;

Tiler with a drawn Sword;
Two Stewards with white Rods;
Master Masons;
Junior Deacons;
Senior Deacons;
Secretaries;
Treasurers;
Past Wardens;
Junior Wardens;
Senior Wardens;
Past Masters;
Present Masters.

THE NEW LODGE.

Marshall; | Marshall;

Tiler with drawn Sword;
Two Stewards with white Rods;
Master Masons;
Junior and Senior Deacon;
Secretary and Treasurer;
Two brethren carrying the Flooring of the Lodge;
Junior and Senior Warden;
The Holy Writings,
(carried by the oldest member of the Lodge;)
The Worshipful Master;
Music.

THE GRAND LODGE.

Grand Tiler with drawn Sword;
Grand Stewards with white Rods;
A brother carrying a Golden Vessel of Corn;
Two brethren, each carrying a Silver Vessel—one of Wine, the other of Oil;
Grand Secretary;
Grand Treasurer;
A Burning Taper borne by a Past Master;
A Past Master bearing the Holy Writings, Square and Compasses, supported by two Stewards with white Rods;
Two Burning Tapers borne by two Past Masters;
The Tuscan and Composite Orders;

Marshall;

The Doric, Ionic and Corinthian Orders,
(each carried by a Master Mason;)
Past Grand Wardens;
Past Grand Masters;

Marshall;

The Globes borne by two Master Masons;
Chaplain and Orator;
R. W. Junior and Senior Grand Wardens;
R. W. Deputy Grand Master;
The Master of the oldest Lodge, carrying the Book of Constitutions;
The M. W. Grand Master;
The Grand Deacons on the right and left of the Grand Master, with black Rods;
Grand Sword Bearer, with drawn Sword;
Two Stewards with white Rods.

The Marshals conduct the Procession to the Church or house where the services are to be performed. When the front of the Procession arrives at the door, they halt and open to the right and left, and face inwards, while the Grand Master and others in succession pass through and enter the house, where a platform has been erected and provided with seats for the accommodation of the Grand Officers.

The Holy Bible, Square and Compasses, and Book of Constitutions, are placed upon a table in front of the Grand Master. The Flooring is then spread upon the platform, covered with white satin or linen, and encompassed by the Three Tapers and the Vessels of Corn, Wine and Oil.

SERVICE.

1. A piece of Music.

When earth's foundation first was laid,
By the Almighty Artist's hand,
'Twas then our perfect, our perfect laws were made,
Established by his strict command.
Chorus—Hail! mysterious, hail! glorious Masonry,
That makes us ever great and free.

As man throughout for shelter sought,
In vain from place to place did roam,
Until from heaven, from heaven he was taught
To plan, to build, to fix his home.

Hail! mysterious, &c.

Hence, illustrious rose our art,
And now in beauteous piles appear;
Which shall to endless, to endless time impart
How worthy and how great we are.

Hail! mysterious, &c.

2. A Prayer.
3. An Oration.
4. A piece of Music.

Nor we less fam'd for every tie,
By which the human thought is bound;
Love, truth and friendship, and friendship socially,
Join all our hearts and hands around.

Hail! mysterious, &c.

Our actions still by virtue blest,
And to our precepts ever true,
The world admiring, admiring shall request,
To learn, and our bright paths pursue.

Hail! mysterious, &c.

5. The Grand Marshal forms the officers and members of the new Lodge in front of the Grand Master, when the Deputy Grand Master addresses the Grand Master as follows:

MOST WORSHIPFUL:

A number of brethren duly instructed in the mysteries of Masonry, having assembled together at stated periods, by virtue of a Dispensation granted them for that purpose, do now desire to be constituted into a regular Lodge, agreeably to the ancient usages and customs of the Fraternity.

The Dispensation and records are presented to the Grand Master, who examines the records, and if found correct, proclaims:

The records appear to be correct and are approved. Upon due deliberation, the Grand Lodge has granted the brethren of this new Lodge a Charter, establishing and confirming them in the rights and privileges of a Regularly Constituted Lodge, which the Secretary will now read.

After the Charter is read, the Grand Master then says:

We shall now proceed, according to ancient usage, to Constitute these brethren into a regular Lodge.

Thereupon, the several officers of the new Lodge deliver up their jewels and badges to their Master, who presents them, with his own, to the Deputy Grand Master, and he to the Grand Master.

The Deputy Grand Master then presents the Master elect to the Grand Master, saying:

MOST WORSHIPFUL:

I present you Brother A. B., whom the members of the Lodge now to be constituted have chosen their Master.

The Grand Master asks them if they remain satisfied with their choice, when they bow in token of assent.

The Master elect then presents severally his Wardens and other officers. The Grand Master asks the brethren if they remain satisfied with each and all of them, when they bow as before.

The officers and members of the new Lodge are then formed in front of the Grand Master by the Grand Marshal, and the business of Consecration commences with a piece of solemn music.

6. Ceremony of Consecration.

The Grand Master, attended by the Grand Officers and the Grand Chaplain, form themselves in order round the Lodge, all devoutly kneeling.

7. A piece of solemn Music is performed while the Lodge is uncovered:

Great source of Light and Love,
To thee our songs we raise;
Oh! in Thy Temple, Lord, above,
Hear and accept our praise.

Shine on this festal day,
  Succeed its hoped design;
And may our Charity display
  A love resembling thine.

May this Fraternal Band
  Now CONSECRATED—*blest*,
In *Union* all distinguished stand,
  In purity be blest.

May all the Sons of Peace
  Their every grace improve;
'Till discord thro' the nations cease,
  AND ALL THE WORLD BE LOVE!

After which, the first clause of the Consecration Prayer is rehearsed as follows:

Great Architect of the Universe! Maker and Ruler of all Worlds! deign from Thy Celestial Temple, from realms of light and glory, to bless us in all the purposes of our present assembly! We humbly invoke Thee to give us at this, and all times, wisdom in all our doings, strength of mind in all our difficulties, and the beauty of harmony in all our communications! Permit us, O Thou Author of Light and Life, Great Source of Love and Happiness, to erect this Lodge, and now solemnly to consecrate it to the honor of Thy glory. Glory be to God on high.

As it was in the beginning, is now, and ever shall be, world without end. Amen!

The Deputy Grand Master takes the Golden Vessel of Corn, and the Senior and Junior Grand Wardens the Silver Vessels of Wine and Oil, and sprinkle the elements of consecration upon the Lodge. The Grand Chaplain then continues:

Grant, O Lord our God, that those who are now about to be invested with the government of this Lodge, may be endued with wisdom to instruct their brethren in all their duties. May brotherly love, relief and truth, always prevail among the members of this Lodge; and may this bond of union continue to strengthen the Lodges throughout the world! Bless all our brethren, wheresoever dispersed, and grant speedy relief to all who are either oppressed or distressed. We affectionately commend to Thee all the members of Thy whole family. May they increase in grace, in knowledge of Thee, and in the love of each other. Finally, may we finish all our work here below with Thy approbation; and then have our transition from this earthly abode to Thy Heavenly Temple above, there to enjoy light, glory and bliss ineffable and eternal. Glory be to God on high.

Response.—As it was in the beginning, is now, and ever shall be. So mote it be—Amen!

8. A piece of solemn Music is performed while the Lodge is covered:

Grant us, Great God, Thy powerful aid,
To guide us thro' this vale of tears;
For where Thy goodness is displayed,
Peace soothes the mind and pleasure cheers.

Inspire us with Thy Grace divine,
Thy sacred law our guide shall be:
To every good our hearts incline,
From every evil keep us free.

9. The Grand Chaplain then dedicates the Lodge in the following terms:

To the memory of the Holy Saints John we dedicate this Lodge. May every brother revere their character, and imitate their virtue. Glory be to God on high.

Response.—As it was in the beginning, is now, and ever shall be, world without end. So mote it be—Amen!

10. A piece of solemn music is performed while the brethren of the new Lodge advance in procession to salute the Grand Lodge, with their hands crossed upon their breasts, and bowing as they pass, they then take their places as they pass.

11. The Grand Master then rises, and constitutes the new Lodge in form following:

In the name of the Most Worshipful Grand Lodge of ———, I now constitute and form you, my beloved brethren, into a regular Lodge of Free and Accepted Masons. From henceforth I empower you to meet as a regular Lodge, constituted in conformity to the rites of our Order, and the charges of our Ancient and Honorable Fraternity, and may the Supreme Architect of the Universe direct and counsel you in all your doings.

Response.—So mote it be—Amen!

SECTION II.

CEREMONY OF INSTALLATION.

The Grand Master, or Presiding Officer, addresses the Master elect in the words following:

BROTHER:

Previous to your investiture, it is necessary that you should signify your assent to those ancient charges and regulations which point out the duty of the Master of a Lodge:

1. You agree to be a good man and true, and strictly to obey the moral law.
2. You agree to be a peaceable citizen, and cheerfully to conform to the laws of the country in which you reside.
3. You promise not to be concerned in conspiracies or plots against the government, but patiently to submit to the decisions of the Supreme Legislature.
4. You agree to pay a proper respect to the civil ma-

gistrates, to walk uprightly, work diligently, live creditably, and act honorably by all men.

5. You agree to hold in veneration the original rulers and patrons of the Order of Masonry, and their regular successors, supreme and subordinate, according to their stations; and to submit to the awards of your brethren, when convened, in every case consistent with the Constitutions of the Order.

6. You agree to avoid private piques and quarrels, and to guard against intemperance and excess.

7. You agree to be cautious in carriage and behavior, courteous to your brethren, and faithful to your Lodge.

8. You promise to respect genuine brethren, and to discountenance impostors, and all dissenters from the original plan of Masonry.

9. You agree to promote the general good of society, to cultivate the social virtues, and to propagate the knowledge of the Art.

10. You promise to pay homage to the Grand Master for the time being, and to his officers when duly installed; and strictly to conform to every edict of the Grand Lodge, or general assembly of Masons, that is not subversive of the principles and groundwork of Masonry.

11. You admit that it is not in the power of any man or body of men, to make innovations in the body of Masonry.

12. You promise a regular attendance on the Committees and Communications of the Grand Lodge, on receiving proper notice, and to pay attention to all the duties of Masonry on convenient occasions.

13. You admit that no new Lodge shall be formed without permission of the Grand Lodge, and that no countenance be given to an irregular Lodge, or to any

person clandestinely initiated therein, being contrary to the Ancient Charges of the Order.

14. You admit that no person can be regularly made a Mason in, or admitted a member of any regular Lodge, without previous notice and due enquiry into his character.

15. You agree that no visiter shall be received into your Lodge without due examination, and producing proper vouchers of his having been initiated into a regular Lodge.

These are the regulations of Free and Accepted Masons. Do you submit to, and promise to support them, as Masters have done in all ages before you?

Answer.—I do.

The presiding officer then addresses him:

BROTHER A. B.

In consequence of your cheerful conformity to the charges and regulations of the Order, you are now to be installed Master of this Lodge, in full confidence of your care, skill and capacity to govern the same.

The new Master is then regularly invested with the insignia of his office, and presented with the furniture and implements of his Lodge, all of which are carefully enumerated and duly commented on.

The Holy Writings, that great light in Masonry, will guide you to all truth; it will direct your paths to the temple of happiness, and point out the whole duty of man.

The Square teaches us to regulate our actions by rule and line, and harmonize our conduct by the principles of morality and virtue.

The Compasses teach us to limit our desires in every station; that rising to eminence by virtue and merit, we may live respected and die regretted.

The Rule directs that we should punctually observe our duty, press forward in the path of virtue, and, neither inclining to the right nor to the left, in all our actions have eternity in view.

The Line teaches the criterion of moral rectitude, to avoid dissimulation in conversation and action, and to direct our steps to the path which leads to a glorious immortality.

The Book of Constitutions you are to search at all times; cause it to be read in your Lodge, that none may pretend ignorance of the excellent precepts it enjoins.

You will also receive in charge the By-Laws of your Lodge, which you are to see carefully and punctually executed.

CHARGE UPON THE INSTALLATION OF A MASTER OF A LODGE.

WORSHIPFUL SIR:

Being appointed Master of this Lodge, you cannot be insensible of the obligations which devolve on you as their head; nor of your responsibility for the faithful discharge of the important duties annexed to your appointment.

The honor, reputation and usefulness of your Lodge will materially depend on the skill and assiduity with which you manage its concerns, while the happiness of its members will be materially promoted in proportion to the zeal and ability with which you propagate the general principles of our Institution.

For a pattern of imitation consider the great Luminary of Nature, which rising in the East, regularly diffuses light and lustre to all within its circle. In like manner, it is your province to spread and communicate light and instruction to the brethren of your Lodge. Forcibly impress upon them the dignity and high importance of Masonry, and seriously admonish them never to disgrace it. Charge them to practise out of the Lodge those duties which are inculcated in it; and by amiable, discreet and virtuous conduct, to convince mankind of the goodness of the Institution; so that when any one is said to be a member of it, the world may know that he is one to whom the burthened heart may pour out its sorrows; to whom distress may prefer its suit; whose hand is guided by justice, and his heart expanded by benevolence. In short, by a diligent observance of the By-Laws of your Lodge, the Constitutions of Masonry, and, above all, the Holy Scriptures, which are given as a rule and guide to your faith, you will be enabled to acquit yourself with honor and reputation, and lay up a crown of rejoicing which shall continue till time shall be no more.

The subordinate officers are then severally invested by the presiding officer, who delivers to each of them a short charge.

CHARGE TO THE SENIOR WARDEN.

BROTHER C. D.

You are appointed Senior Warden of this Lodge, and are now invested with the ensign of your office.

The Level demonstrates that we are descended from the same stock, partake of the same nature, and share the same hope; and though distinctions among men are necessary to preserve subordination, yet no eminence of station should make us forget that we are brethren; for he who is placed on the lowest spoke of fortune's wheel may be entitled to our regard, because a time will come, and the wisest knows not how soon, when all distinctions but those of merit and goodness shall cease, and death, the grand leveller of human greatness, reduce us to the same state.

Your regular and punctual attendance on our stated

meetings is essentially necessary. In the absence of the Master, you are to govern this Lodge; in his presence, you are to assist him in the government of it. I firmly rely on your knowledge of Masonry, and attachment to the Lodge, for the faithful discharge of the duties of this important trust. LOOK WELL TO THE WEST!

CHARGE TO THE JUNIOR WARDEN.

BROTHER E. F.

You are appointed Junior Warden of this Lodge, and are now invested with the badge of your office.

The Plumb admonishes us to walk uprightly in our several stations; to hold the Scales of Justice in equal poise; to observe the just medium between intemperance and pleasure; and to make our passions and prejudices coincide with the line of our duty.

To you is committed the superintendence of the Craft during the hours of refreshment; it is, therefore, indispensably necessary that you should not only be temperate and discreet in the indulgencies of your own inclinations, but carefully observe that none of the Craft be suffered to convert the means of refreshment into intemperance or excess.

Your regular and punctual attendance is particularly requested; and I have no doubt you will faithfully execute the duty which you owe to your present appointment. LOOK WELL TO THE SOUTH!

CHARGE TO THE TREASURER.

BROTHER G. H.

You are appointed Treasurer of this Lodge, and I invest you accordingly. It is your duty to receive all moneys from the hands of the Secretary, keep a fair and just account of the same, and pay them out by order of the Worshipful Master and the consent of the Lodge.

I trust your regard for the interests of the Fraternity will prompt you to the faithful discharge of the duties of your office.

CHARGE TO THE SECRETARY.

Brother I. K.

You are appointed Secretary of this Lodge, and now invested accordingly. It is your duty to observe all the proceedings of the Lodge; to keep a fair record of all things proper to be written; to receive all moneys due the Lodge, and pay them over to the Treasurer, and take his receipt for the same.

Your good inclination to Masonry and this Lodge, I hope, will induce you to discharge your office with fidelity; and by so doing you will merit and receive the esteem and applause of your brethren.

CHARGE TO THE SENIOR AND JUNIOR DEACONS.

Brothers L. M. and N. O.

You are appointed Deacons of this Lodge, and I now invest you with the badges of your office. To you is especially entrusted the reception and accommodation of visiting brethren. It is also your province to attend on the Master and Wardens, and to act as their proxies in all the active duties of the Lodge, particularly such as relate to the reception and conducting of candidates into the different degrees of Masonry, and in the immediate and responsible practice of our rites. Not doubting your vigilance and attention, I trust your faithful discharge of the duties of your offices will entitle you to the esteem of your brethren.

CHARGE TO THE STEWARDS.

Brothers P. Q. and R. S.

You are appointed Stewards of this Lodge, and I now present you the badges of your office. The duties of your office are to assist in the collection of dues and subscriptions; to keep an account of the Lodge expenses; to see that the tables are properly furnished at refreshment, and that every brother is suitably provided for; and generally to assist the Deacons and other officers in performing their duties.

Your regular and early attendance will afford the best proof of your zeal and attachment to the Lodge.

CHARGE TO THE TILER.

Brother T. U.

You are appointed Tiler of this Lodge, and I now invest you with the badge and implement of your office. As the Sword is placed in the hands of the Tiler, to enable him effectually to guard against the approach of cowans and eavesdroppers, and suffer none to pass and repass but such as are duly qualified, so it should morally serve as a constant admonition to us to set a guard at the entrance of our thoughts; to place a watch at the door of our lips, and to post a sentinel at the avenue of our actions, thereby excluding every unqualified and unworthy thought, word and deed; and preserving consciences void of offence towards God and towards man.

Your early and punctual attendance will afford the best proof of your zeal for the Institution.

The following charge is then given to the brethren generally:

Brethren:

Such is the nature of our Constitution, that as some must of necessity rule and teach, so others must of course learn to submit and obey. Humility in both is an essential duty. The officers who are appointed to govern your Lodge, and whom you have selected for that purpose, are sufficiently conversant with the rules of propriety and the laws of the Institution, to avoid exceeding the powers with which they are entrusted; and you are, as Masons, of too generous dispositions to envy their preferment. I therefore trust that you will have but one aim, to please each other, and unite in the grand design of being happy and communicating happiness.

Finally, my brethren, as this Association has been formed and perfected in so much unanimity and concord, in which we greatly rejoice, so may it long continue. May you long enjoy every satisfaction and delight which disinterested friendship can afford. May kindness and brotherly affection dlstinguish your conduct as men and as Masons. Within your peaceful walls may your children's children celebrate with joy and gratitude, the transactions of this auspicious solemnity. And may the Tenets of our Profession be transmitted through your Lodge, pure and unimpaired, from generation to generation.

The Marshal then proclaims the New Lodge in the following manner:

In the name of the Most Worshipful Grand Lodge of ———, I proclaim this New Lodge, by the name, title and designation of ——— Lodge, No. —, duly Constituted.

The Grand Chaplain then makes the concluding prayer, which ends the public ceremonies.

The Grand Procession is then formed in the same order as before, and returns to the Hall.

The Grand Master, Deputy Grand Master and Grand Wardens being seated, (or in their absence the officers appointed by the Grand Master to constitute and install the new Lodge,) the procession continues round the Hall, and upon passing the several Grand Officers, or their representatives, pays them homage by the usual congratulations and honors in the different degrees. During the procession, which passes three times round the Lodge, the following song is sung, which concludes the ceremony of Constitution and Installation:

1. Hail Masonry divine!
Glory of ages shine;
  Long may'st thou reign:
Where'er thy Lodges stand,
May they have great command;
  Thou Art Divine!

2. Great fabrics still arise,
And grace the azure skies;
  Great are thy schemes:
Thy noble Orders are
Matchless beyond compare;
No Art with thee can share,
  Thou Art Divine!

3. Hiram the Architect,
Did all the Craft direct
  How they should build;
Solomon, great Israel's King,
Did mighty blessings bring,
And left us room to sing,
  Hail Royal Art.
} *Chorus three times.*

The Lodge is then closed with the usual solemnities.

This is the usual ceremony observed by regular Masons at the Constitution of a new Lodge, which the Grand Master (if he attend) may abridge or extend at pleasure; but the material points are on no account to be omitted. The same ceremony and charges attend every succeeding Installation of Officers.

CEREMONY OF INSTALLING A GRAND MASTER, WHICH MUST ALWAYS BE PERFORMED BY A PAST GRAND MASTER.

The Grand Master elect is addressed as follows:

Most Worshipful:

It is my duty to install you into your high office, as Grand Master of Masons. Give me leave to invest you with this Badge of your office. This will silently admonish you always to do justice to the cause of Masonry; to consult, as the exalted rank you now hold demands of you, its real interests. It will instruct you to infuse into the many Lodges, of which you are now the head, the true spirit of our Order; to give due commendation to the worthy members of it, and to rebuke those who act contrary to its laws.

Take this Emblem of the Power with which you are invested. Always make use of it for the good of our benevolent Institution.

To you are committed those Sacred Writings, in which are to be found the sublime parts of our Ancient Mystery. In them are likewise most strongly inculcated the social and moral duties, without which no man can be a Mason. You will direct your Lodges to read, study and obey them.

Receive these Tools of Operative Masonry, which are to each of us the most expressive symbols. These will assist you, Most Worshipful, to reduce all matter into proper form; to bring to due subjection irregular passions, and to circumscribe them by harmony, order and duty.

And, lastly, I present to you the Book of Constitutions, in which are contained the Rules and Orders made for the good government of the Institution, and the Charges, which show its nature, its wisdom and its utility. With this Book, Most Worshipful, you will direct your Lodges to make themselves well acquainted—a work, eminently worthy the attention of men the most enlightened and judicious.

You are now, Most Worshipful, at the head of an Order which is calculated to unite men by true friendship, to extend benevolence, and to promote virtue—and give me leave to say, that the honor with which you are invested is not unworthy of a man of the highest rank, or most distinguished abilities. Permit me also to remind you, that your faithful attention to the duties of your office, and acceptable discharge of them, will render you of great benefit to one of the most liberal Institutions upon earth.

May you do honor to your exalted station, and long enjoy the highest respect and best wishes of all the Fraternity.

CHARGE TO THE DEPUTY GRAND MASTER.

Right Worshipful Brother:

The station to which you have been called by the suffrages of your brethren, is one of great dignity and much importance. In the absence of the Grand Master, you are to exercise his prerogatives in presiding over the Craft; in his presence you are to assist him with your counsel and co-operation. If his absence be permanent, being the result of death, resignation, or removal from the state, you are to enter upon and discharge with fidelity all the duties devolved on him by the laws, resolutions and edicts of this Grand Lodge, and the Constitution of Masonry. But while your powers and privileges are thus extensive, remember that they carry with them a heavy share of responsibility. The honor that has been conferred upon you, and the trust that has been reposed in you, demand a corresponding fidelity and attachment to the interests of those to whose kindness and confidence you are indebted for your official elevation. Let the Book of Constitutions be your constant study, that you may be the better enabled to preserve inviolate the laws and ancient landmarks of our Order, and that you may be ever ready to exercise the functions of that more exalted office to which you are so liable to be called. Receive this jewel of your office, and sit at our right hand to aid us with your counsel.

SECTION III.

This section contains the ceremony observed in laying the Foundation Corner Stones of Public Edifices.

This ceremony is usually conducted by the Grand Master and his officers, and such officers and members of subordinate Lodges as can conveniently attend. The Chief Magistrate and other civil officers of the place where the building is to be erected also generally attend on the occasion.

At the time appointed, the Grand Lodge, or Lodge appointed to preside, is convened in some suitable place approved by the presiding officer. A band of martial music is provided, and the brethren appear in the Insignia of the Order.

The Lodge is then opened with the usual formalities, and the rules for regulating the procession are audibly read by the Secretary; the Lodge is then adjourned, after which the procession sets out in due form in the following order:

PROCESSION AT LAYING FOUNDATION CORNER STONES.

Tiler with drawn Sword;
Music;
Two Stewards with white Rods;
Master Masons;
Treasurers;
Secretaries;
Junior Deacons;
Senior Deacons;
Junior Wardens;
Senior Wardens;
Past Masters;
Present Masters.

Marshall; Marshall;

Tiler of the Presiding Lodge, with drawn Sword;
Stewards with white Rods;
A Past Master with a Golden Vessel containing Corn;
Three Masters with Square, Level and Plumb;
Two Past Masters with Silver Vessels, one containing Oil and the other Wine;
Secretary and Treasurer;
Five Master Masons carrying the Five Orders;

Marshall; | Marshall;

One large Light borne by a Past Master;
The Holy Bible, Square and Compasses, borne by a Master of a Lodge, supported by one Steward on the right and left;
Two large Lights borne by two Past Masters;
Deputy Grand Master, (if present;)
Chaplain;
Clergy and Orator, if Masons;
Senior and Junior Warden;
Master of the oldest Lodge, carrying the Book of Constitutions on a Velvet Cushion;
Grand Master or Presiding Master;
Deacons on each side of the Master, seven feet apart;
Two Stewards with white Rods.
Sword Bearer with Drawn Sword.

A Triumphal Arch is usually erected at the place where the ceremony is to be performed. The Procession passes through the Arch, and the brethren repair to their stands, the Presiding Master and his officers take their place on a temporary platform covered with carpet. The brethren are brought to order and silence. An ode to Masonry is sung:

To Heaven's high Architect all praise,
  All gratitude be given,
Who deigned the human soul to raise
  By secrets sprung from Heaven.

CHORUS—Then sound the Great JEHOVAH'S praise,
To Him the glorious structure raise.
Now swells the Choir in solemn tone,
  And hovering Angels join;
Religion looks delighted down
  When votaries press the shrine.

(CHORUS.)

Blest be the place! thither repair
  The true and pious train:
Devotion wakes her anthem there,
  And Heaven accepts the strain.

(CHORUS.)

After which the necessary preparations are made for laying the stone, on which is engraved the year and date of Masonry, the names of the Grand Officers, Chief Magistrates, &c., &c.

The stone is raised up by means of an engine erected for that purpose, and the Chaplain repeats a short prayer.

The Treasurer then, by the Master's command, places under the stone the various sorts of coin and medals of the present age. Solemn music is introduced, and the stone is let down into its place.

Let Masonry from pole to pole
 Her sacred laws expand,
Far as the mighty waters roll,
 To wash remotest land;
That virtue has not left mankind,
 Her social maxims prove,
For stamp'd upon the Mason's mind,
 Is UNITY AND LOVE.

Ascending to her native sky,
 Let Masonry increase;
A glorious Pillar raised on high,
 INTEGRITY its base.
Peace adds to Olive boughs, entwined,
 An EMBLEMATIC DOVE,
As stamp'd upon the Mason's mind,
 Is UNITY AND LOVE.

The Principal Architect of the building then comes forward and presents the working tools to the Master, who applies the Square, Level and Plumb to the stone in their proper positions, and pronounces it to be well formed, true and trusty.

The Gold and Silver Vessels are next brought, and successively presented to the Master, who, according to ancient ceremony, pours the Corn, Wine and Oil on the stone, saying:

May the all-bounteous Author of Nature bless the inhabitants of this place with all the necessaries, conveniences and comforts of life; assist in the erection and completion of this building; protect the workmen against every accident, and long preserve this structure from decay; and grant to us all a supply of the Corn of nourishment, the Wine of Refreshment, and the Oil of joy.

Response.—So mote it be—Amen!

He then strikes the stone three times with the Mallet, and the public grand honors are given, after which the Master delivers over to the Architect the various implements of architecture, entrusting him with the superintendence and direction of the work; he then, with his officers, reascends the platform, and an Oration suitable to the occasion is delivered.

A voluntary collection is made for the workmen, and the sum collected is placed upon the stone by the Treasurer.

A suitable Song in honor of Masonry is sung, which concludes the ceremony.

Let there be Light, the Almighty spoke,
Refulgent streams from chaos broke,
To illume the rising earth!
Well pleas'd the Great Jehovah stood;
The power supreme pronounc'd it good,
And gave the Planets birth.
In choral numbers Masons join
To bless and praise the Light Divine.

Parent of light accept our praise,
Who shed'st on us thy brightest rays,
The light that fills the mind.
By choice selected, lo, we stand,
By friendship join'd a social band,
That love, that aid mankind!
In choral, &c.

The widow's tear, the orphan's cry
All wants, our ready hands supply,
As far as power is given.
The naked clothe, the prisoner free,
These are thy works, sweet Charity!
Reveal'd to us from heaven.
In choral, &c.

After which the procession returns to the place whence it set out, and the Lodge is closed in due form.

SECTION IV.

This section contains the ceremony observed at the Dedication of Free Masons' Halls.

On the day appointed, the Grand Master, or Presiding Officer, accompanied by the officers and members of the presiding Lodge, meet in a convenient room near the place where the ceremony is to be performed, and open in due and ample form.

The Master of the Lodge to which the Hall to be dedicated belongs, being present, addresses the Grand Master or Presiding Officer as follows:

WORSHIPFUL SIR AND BROTHER:

The brethren of ——— Lodge, No. —, being animated with a desire of promoting the honor and interest of the Craft, have, at great pains and expense, erected a Masonic Hall, for their convenience and accommodation. They are desirous that the same should be examined by the M. W. Grand Lodge, and if it should meet their approbation, that it should be solemnly dedicated to Masonic purposes agreeably to ancient form.

The Grand Master, or Presiding Officer, then directs the Secretary to read the Order of Procession, (as at page 206,) which is delivered over to the Marshal; and a general charge respecting propriety of behavior is given.

A procession is then formed, accordingly, in the order laid down, and moves forward to the Hall which is to be dedicated, and upon the arrival of the front of the procession at the door, they halt, open to the right and left and face inward, while the Grand Master, or Presiding Officer, and others in succession pass through and enter. The music continues while the procession marches three times round the Hall.

Offspring of Heav'n, mankind's best friend,
Bright Charity, inspire the lay;
On these terrestrial shores descend,
And quit the realms of cloudless day:
CHORUS.—To thee our constant vows are paid,
Thy praise we hymn, Angelic Maid.

The house a dismal ruin lies,
Where mirth late tun'd her lyre of joy;
And tears of anguish fill your eyes,
Poor orphan girl and houseless boy:—

CHORUS.—But thou, sweet maid, with pity's glow,
Inspir'st each heart to soothe their wo.

Come then, all-bounteous as thou art,
And hide thee from our sight no more;
Touch every soul, expand each heart,
That breathes on freedom's chosen shore:

CHORUS.—Columbia's sons with pity's glow
Inspire to feel for human wo.

The Lodge or Flooring is then placed in the centre, and the Grand Master, or Presiding Officer having taken the Chair, under a Canopy of State, the Grand Officers and the Masters and Wardens of the Lodges repair to the places assigned them, and previously prepared for their reception. The Three Lights, and the Gold and Silver Pitchers with the Corn, Wine and Oil, are placed round the Lodge, at the head of which stands the Altar with the Holy Bible open, and the Square and Compasses laid thereon, with the Charter, Book of Constitutions and By-Laws. An Anthem is then sung

Let Masons ever live in love;
Let harmony their blessings prove;
And be the sacred Lodge the place,
Where freedom smiles in every face.
Live Free Masons, Free Masons live and love,
And show your types are from above.

Behold the world all in amaze,
Each curious eye with transport gaze;
They look, they like, they wish to be,
What none can gain, except he's free.
Live Free Masons, &c.

Let Masons then, with watchful eye,
Regard the works of Charity;
Let Union, Love and Friendship meet,
And show that Wisdom's ways are sweet.
Live Free Masons, &c.

And an Exordium on Masonry is given; after which the Architect addresses the Grand Master as follows:

MOST WORSHIPFUL:

Having been entrusted with the superintendence and management of the workmen employed in the construction of this Edifice, and having according to the best of my ability accomplished the task assigned me, I now return my thanks for the honor of this appointment, and beg leave to surrender up the implements which were committed to my care, when the foundation of this fabric was laid; humbly hoping, that the exertions which have been made on this occasion will be crowned with your approbation, and that of the Most Worshipful Grand Lodge.

To which the Grand Master or presiding officer, makes the following reply:

BROTHER ARCHITECT:

The skill and fidelity displayed in the execution of the trust reposed in you at the commencement of this undertaking, have secured the entire approbation of the Grand Lodge, and they sincerely pray that this edifice may continue a lasting monument of the taste, spirit and liberality of its founders.

An Ode in honor of Masonry is sung, accompanied with instrumental music.

By Mason's art the aspiring dome,
On stately columns shall arise,
All climates are their native home,
Their Godlike actions reach the skies.
Heroes and Kings revere their name,
While Poets sing their lasting fame.

Great, noble, gen'rous, good and brave;
All virtues they must justly claim;
Their deeds shall live beyond tne grave,
And those unborn their praise proclaim.
Time shall their glorious acts enroll,
While LOVE and FRIENDSHIP charm the soul.

The Deputy Grand Master then rises and says:

MOST WORSHIPFUL:

The Hall in which we are now assembled, and the plan upon which it has been constructed, having met with your approbation, it is the desire of the Fraternity that it should now be dedicated, according to ancient form and usage.

A procession is then formed in the following order, viz:

Grand Tiler;
Grand Sword Bearer;
A Past Master with a Light;
A Past Master with a Bible, Square and Compasses on a Velvet Cushion;
Two Past Masters, each with a Light;
Grand Secretary and Treasurer with Emblems;
Grand Junior Warden with Pitcher of Corn;
Grand Senior Warden with Pitcher of Wine;
Deputy Grand Master with Pitcher of Oil;
Grand Master;
Two Stewards with Rods.

All the other brethren keep their places and assist in performing an Ode, which continues during the procession, excepting only at the intervals of dedication.

GENIUS OF MASONRY! descend,
And with thee bring thy *spotless* train;
Constant our sacred rites attend,
While we adore thy peaceful reign.

The Lodge being uncovered, the first time passing round it, the

Junior Grand Warden presents the Pitcher of Corn to the Grand Master, who pours it out upon the Lodge, at the same time pronouncing:

In the name of the Great Jehovah, to whom be all honor and glory, I do solemnly Dedicate this House to MASONRY.

The Grand Honors are given.

Bring with thee VIRTUE! brightest maid;
Bring Love, bring Truth, bring Friendship here;
While social mirth shall lend her aid,
To smooth the wrinkled brow of care.

The second procession is then made round the Lodge, and the Grand Senior Warden presents the Pitcher of Wine to the Grand Master, who sprinkles it upon the Lodge, at the same time saying:

In the name of the Holy Saints John, I do solemnly Dedicate this Hall to VIRTUE.

The Grand Honors are twice given.

Bring CHARITY! with goodness crowned,
Encircled in thy heavenly robe!
Diffuse thy blessings all around,
To every corner of the GLOBE!

The third procession is then made round the Lodge, and the Deputy Grand Master presents the Pitcher of Oil to the Grand Master, who sprinkles it upon the Lodge, saying:

In the name of the whole Fraternity, I do solemnly Dedicate this Lodge to UNIVERSAL BENEVOLENCE.

The Grand Honors are thrice given.

A solemn Invocation is made to Heaven by the Chaplain, and an appropriate Anthem sung:

To Heaven's high Architect all praise,
All praise, all gratitude be given,
Who deigned the human soul to raise,
By mystic secrets sprung from Heaven.

CHORUS.—Sound aloud the Great Jehovah's praise,
To him the dome, the temple raise.

After which the Lodge is covered, and the Grand Master retires to his Chair. An Oration is then delivered, and the ceremonies conclude with music.

Lo CHARITY! with VIRTUE blest,
With open hand, and tender heart
Which wounded is at man distrest,
And bleeds at every human smart!

Ye HAPPY FEW! who hence extend
In peaceful lines from East to West;
With fervent zeal the Lodge defend,
And lock its secrets in your breast.

Since ye are met upon the Square!
Bid LOVE AND FRIENDSHIP jointly reign;
Be PEACE AND HARMONY your care,
They form an *Adamantine Chain!*

The Grand Lodge is then closed in due and ample form.

[NOTE.—Dedications. Consecrations and Constitutions of Subordinate Lodges would seem to be the appropriate and exclusive duty of the Grand Lodges, and therefore it will be seen by reference to old Authors upon these subjects that they everywhere direct Grand Lodge Processions, and recognize the presence of the Grand Officers, without reference to their practicability or convenience.

In those states or Masonic Jurisdictions of small extent, and where the Grand Lodge may conveniently be summoned and attend, it would be desirable to keep up this usage; but in large states or Grand Masonic Jurisdictions, where this would necessarily be attended with great inconvenience and expense, no possible injury can result to the Craft, if the brethren wishing such services performed be required to address the Grand Master through the Grand Secretary, requesting him to issue a Letter of Dispensation to some regular and warranted Lodge in their vicinity, to perform the several duties required.

Such Lodge, however, should not as is sometimes done, style themselves a Grand Lodge, and their officers Grand Officers; but should keep their record of the ceremony as performed by a subordinate Lodge in the usual manner.]

SECTION V.

This section contains the ceremony observed at Funerals according to ancient customs, together with the service used on such occasions.

No Mason can be interred with the formalities of the Order unless he has been raised to the sublime degree of a Master Mason, and as no Fellow Craft or Entered Apprentice is entitled to funeral obsequies, neither are they permitted to attend Masonic processions on such occasions.

All the brethren who walk in procession should observe as much as possible an uniformity in their dress; decent mourning round the left arm, a suit of black, with white aprons and gloves, are most suitable.

THE FUNERAL SERVICE.

The brethren being assembled at the Lodge Room, (or some other convenient place,) the Presiding Officer opens the Lodge in the Third Degree, with the usual forms, and having stated the purpose of the meeting, and given the brethren strict charge upon their deportment during the procession, the service begins as follows:

Master. What man is he that liveth and shall not see death? Shall he deliver his soul from the hand of the grave?

Response. Man walketh in a vain shadow, he heapeth up riches and cannot tell who shall gather them.

Master. When he dieth, he shall carry nothing away; his glory shall not descend after him.

Response. Naked he came into the world and naked he must return.

Master. The Lord gave and the Lord hath taken away, blessed be the name of the Lord.

The Master, then taking the Roll in his hand, says:

Let us live and die like the righteous, that our last end may be like his.

Response. God is our God forever and ever; he will be our guide unto death.

The Master then records the name, age and day of death of the deceased upon the Roll, and says:

Almighty Father! in Thy hands we leave with humble submission the soul of our deceased brother.

The brethren answer three times—giving the Grand Honors each time:

The will of God is accomplished! So mote it be—Amen!

The Master then deposits the Roll in the Archives, and the following prayer is repeated:

Most glorious God! author of all good and giver of all mercy, pour down Thy blessing upon us, and strengthen our solemn engagements with the ties of sincere affection. May the present instance of mortality remind us of our approaching fate, and draw our attention towards Thee, the only refuge in time of need! That when the awful moment shall arrive, that we are about to quit this transitory scene, the enlivening prospects of Thy mercy may dispel the gloom of death; and after our departure hence in peace, and in Thy favor, may we be received into Thine everlasting kingdom, to enjoy, in union with the souls of our departed friends, the just rewards of a pious and virtuous life. Amen!

A procession is then formed, which moves to the house of the deceased, and from thence to the place of interment, in the following order:

ORDER OF PROCESSION.

Tiler with a drawn Sword;
Stewards with white Rods;
Musicians, (if Masons,) otherwise they precede the Tiler;
Master Masons;
Past Masters;
Senior and Junior Deacons;
Secretary and Treasurer;
Senior and Junior Wardens;
The Holy Bible on a cushion covered with black crape, and carried by the oldest member of the Lodge;
The Master;
Clergy;
Chaplain of Lodge;

The body with the 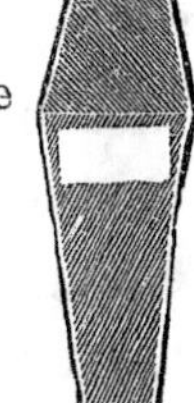 Insignia thereon;

Pall Bearers; Pall Bearers;

Relatives and Mourners;
Two Stewards with white Rods.

When the Procession arrives near the place of interment, the whole halt, and opening to the right and left, six feet apart, face inwards and uncover their heads, while the Body is borne by the Pall Bearers through the Procession, who then move on in inverse order, and having arrived at the grave, the members of the Lodge form a circle round the grave, the Clergyman and Officers of the Lodge take their stations at the head of the grave, and the mourners at the foot. The service is then resumed, the Coffin placed over the grave, and the following exhortation is given:

MY BRETHREN:

Here we view a striking instance of the uncertainty of life and the vanity of all human pursuits. The last offices paid to the dead are only useful as lessons to the living; from them we are to derive instruction, and to consider every solemnity of this kind as a summons to prepare for our dissolution.

Notwithstanding the various mementoes of mortality with which we daily meet; notwithstanding Death has established his empire over all the works of nature; yet, through some unaccountable infatuation, we forget that we are born to die, we go on from one design to another, add hope to hope, and lay out plans for the employment of many years, till we are suddenly alarmed with the approach of Death, when we least expect him, and at an hour which we probably conclude to be the meridian of our existence.

What are all the externals of majesty, the pride of wealth, or charms of beauty, when Nature has paid her just debt? Fix your eyes on the last scene, and view life stripped of her ornaments, and exposed in her natural meanness; you will then be convinced of the futility of these empty delusions. In the grave all fallacies are detected, all ranks are levelled, and all distinctions are done away.

While we drop the sympathetic tear over the grave of our deceased friend, let charity incline us to throw a veil over his foibles, whatever they may have been, and not withhold from his memory the praise that his virtues may have claimed; suffer the apologies of human nature to plead in his behalf. Perfection on earth has never been attained—the wisest as well as the best of men have erred.

Let the present example excite our most serious thoughts and strengthen our resolutions of amendment. As life is uncertain and all earthly pursuits are vain, let us no longer postpone the all-important concern of preparing for eternity, but embrace the happy moment, while time and opportunity offer, to provide against the great change, when all the pleasures of this world shall cease to delight, and the reflections of a virtuous and holy life, yield the only comfort and consolation. Thus our expectations will not be frustrated, nor we hurried unprepared into the presence of an all-wise and powerful Judge, to whom the secrets of all hearts are known.

Let us, while in this state of existence, support with propriety the character of our profession, advert to the nature of our solemn ties, and pursue with assiduity the sacred tenets of our Order. Then, with becoming reverence, let us seek the favor of the Eternal God, whose goodness and power know no bounds, and prosecute our journey, without dread or apprehension, to that far distant country from whose bourne no traveller returns. By the light of the Divine countenance we shall then pass without trembling through those gloomy mansions where all things are forgotten; and at that great and tremendous day, when arraigned at the Bar of Divine and Unbiassed Justice, judgment shall be pronounced in our favor; we shall receive the reward of our labor and virtue, and acquire the possession of an immortal inheritance, where joy flows in one continued stream, and no mound can check its course.

The following Invocations are then made by the Master:

Master. May we be true and faithful, and may we live in love and die in peace.

Response. So mote it be.

Master. May we profess what is good, and always act agreeably to our profession.

Response. So mote it be.

Master. May the Lord bless us and prosper us, and may all our good intentions be crowned with success.

Response. So mote it be.

Master. Glory be to God in the highest; on earth peace and good will towards men.

Response. So mote it be now, from henceforth and forever more—Amen!

The Apron is taken from the coffin and handed to the Master; the coffin is deposited in the grave, and the Master, taking the Apron in his hand, says:

This Lamb Skin, or White Leather Apron, is an emblem of Innocence, and the time-honored badge of a Free and Accepted Mason—more ancient than the Roman Eagle or Golden Fleece; more honorable than the Star and Garter, when worthily worn. This emblem I now deposit in the grave of our deceased brother. By this we are reminded that through the universal dominion of death our brother has finished his earthly labor, and that his account now rests with his God. The Arm of Friendship cannot oppose the King of Terrors, nor the charms of Innocence elude his grasp.

The Master then takes from his pocket a white Glove, and holding it up to public view, says:

This Glove is an emblem of Innocence and a token of Friendship, and though death in the present instance has severed and destroyed our social connexion with the deceased, let us remember that it has not impaired or weakened our obligations to the living.

The Glove is then deposited in the grave, and the Master presenting a Sprig of Evergreen, says:

The Evergreen is an emblem of Masonic faith in the immortality of the soul; or that better part of man, which neither cross, accident, pain, sickness, nor death itself can destroy, but shall continue to bloom with an eternal verdure through an ever beginning to a never ending eternity; and though the body of our deceased brother, now clothed in the habiliments of the dead and deposited in the silent grave, will soon mingle with the common mass of senseless matter, yet his spirit has ascended to God who gave it. And we hope and trust hath ere this passed the portals of the Grand Temple of Jehovah, and before the Grand Tribunal of unbiased Justice in the presence of myriads of intelligent beings, received the heavenly plaudit of "well done, good and faithful servant, enter thou into life eternal."

The brethren then standing round the grave, severally drop into it the Sprig of Evergreen. After which the public Grand Honors are given. The Master then continues the ceremony in the following words:

From time immemorial it has been the custom among Free and Accepted Masons, at the request of a brother, to accompany his corpse to the place of interment, and there to deposit his remains with the usual formalities.

In conformity to this usage, and at the request of our deceased brother, whose memory we revere, and whose loss we now deplore, we have assembled in the character of Masons to offer up to his memory before the world, the last tribute of our affections, thereby demonstrating the sincerity of our past esteem, and our steady attachment to the principles of the Order.

The Great Creator having been pleased out of his mercy to remove our brother from the cares and troubles of this transitory existence, to a state of eternal duration, and thereby to weaken the chain by which we are united man to man, may we who survive him anticipate our approaching fate, and be more strongly united in the ties of union and friendship; that during the short space allotted to our present existence, we may wisely and usefully employ our time, and in the reciprocal intercourse of kind and friendly acts, mutually promote the welfare and happiness of each other.

The Master then taking the Spade in his hand, strews earth three times on the grave, and says:

Unto the grave we resign the body of our deceased friend and brother, earth to earth, dust to dust, and ashes to ashes; there to remain until the General Resurrection, in favorable expectation that his immortal soul will then partake of joys which have been prepared for the righteous from the beginning of the world; and we pray Almighty God of His infinite goodness, at the dread tribunal of unbiassed justice, to extend His saving mercy to him and all of us, and to crown our felicity with everlasting bliss in the expanded realms of unbounded eternity; and this we beg for the honor of His holy name, to whom be glory now and forever.

Response. So mote it be—Amen!

The whole ceremony is then concluded by the following Prayer from the Chaplain:

Almighty and Eternal God, in whom we live and move and have our being, and before whom all men must appear in the judgment day to give an account of their deeds in life, we who are daily exposed to the flying shafts of Death, and now surround the grave of our deceased brother, most earnestly beseech Thee to grant us Thy divine assistance, Oh! merciful God, to redeem our misspent time; and in the discharge of the important duties Thou hast assigned us in the erection of our moral edifice, may we have Wisdom from on high to direct us, Strength commensurate with our task to support us, and the Beauty of holiness to adorn and render all our performances acceptable in Thy sight; and when our work is done, and our bodies mingle with the mother earth, may our souls, disengaged from their cumbrous dust, flourish and bloom in eternal day, and enjoy that rest made perfect, which Thou hast prepared for all good and faithful servants, in that Spiritual House—that Holy Temple not made with hands, eternal in the Heavens. Amen!

Response. So mote it be—Amen!

The Procession then returns to the place from whence it set out, where the necessary duties are complied with and the Lodge closed in due and ancient form.

METHODICAL DIGEST

OF

THE LAWS

OF

THE GRAND LODGE OF VIRGINIA.

20

Methodical Digest.

CHAPTER I.

OF THE QUALIFICATIONS REQUIRED FOR ADMISSION INTO THE SOCIETY OF ANCIENT MASONS.

Before entering on the duties of Free Masons, whether in their individual or social capacity, it is proper to give a summary view of those qualities which recommend candidates for initiation into the mysteries of our Ancient Fraternity:

1st. It is indispensably necessary that every applicant expecting to gain admission into the Masonic Society should exercise a firm belief in the Eternal God, paying him that worship which is due to the Great Architect and Governor of the Universe.

2d. And while on one hand he shuns the darkness of Atheism, he will with equal solicitude avoid the gloomy errors of bigotry and superstition, making a free and independent use of his understanding, the most invaluable attribute of intelligent beings.

3d. At the same time that he embraces with a firm hold these fundamental principles of universal or natural religion, it will be no objection that he subjoin such other principles of faith, or forms of worship and adoration, as his own mind may deliberately approve.

4th. Whoever would be a Free Mason, is further to know, that in that character, his civil and social obligations will in no degree be relaxed, but acquire additional force. He is to be a lover of quiet, peaceable and obedient to the civil powers, so far as they infringe not the inalienable rights of reason and of religion, and to consider the welfare of his country an object of his peculiar care.

5th. In regard to himself, a candidate for Masonry should know and practise all the private virtues, avoiding every species of intemperance and excess, which unfit him for the enjoyment of rational pleasure, and degrade him in the estimation of society. He ought to pursue the duties of his profession with diligence and assiduity, devoting his hours of leisure to improvement in those branches of knowledge, by which he may be rendered useful in the various relations of life. And for the more successful attainment of these valuable objects, he should cultivate with unwearied diligence the virtues of patience, self-denial, forbearance, and all others which afford a control over the human passions, and enable him to discharge all his duties, whether to his family or to the world, with affection, dignity and prudence.

6th. He should have a disposition, and possess the ability of preserving with inviolable fidelity, all secrets which may be confided to him. On this point a candidate ought to examine his own character with scrupulous precision; since no defect would more expose him to ridicule and contempt, or more completely exclude him from the happy results of Masonic information, than a disposition to unfold what ought to be a sacred deposit in the bosoms of faithful Craftsmen.

7th. In addition to these religious and moral qualifications, it is moreover necessary that every candidate for Masonry should be a free born man, of the age of twenty-one years or upwards, of good reputation; of sufficient natural and intellectual endowments; with an estate, office, trade, occupation, or some other obvious source of honest subsistence; from which he may also be enabled to spare something for works of charity, and for maintaining the ancient dignity and utility of the Masonic Institution. He must also be free from such corporeal deformity as would render him incapable of complying strictly with every requirement of the Ritual of the Degrees; or prevent him from procuring a livelihood, in case he should be necessitated so to do.

CHAPTER II.

OF A LODGE AND ITS MEETINGS.

1st. A Lodge is a place in which Masons meet to work. An assembly or organized body of Masons is also called a Lodge—just as the word Church is expressive both of the congregation of worshipers, and of the building wherein they assemble to worship.

2d. A Lodge must consist of one Master, a Senior and a Junior Warden, a Treasurer, a Secretary, a Senior and a Junior Deacon, a Steward and Tiler, and as many members as the Master and a majority of the members shall from time to time think proper.

3d. Thus constituted, a Lodge ought to assemble for work at least once in every calendar month, and must hold all their Sessions in the Third Degree of Masonry, except for the purpose of Lecturing and Working in the First and Second Degrees.

4th. For the preservation of secresy, and to guard the Lodge from interruption or surprise, while engaged in serious and solemn labors, a well skilled Master Mason shall be appointed and paid for Tiling the Lodge door during its convocation.

5th. Every Lodge shall practice the Ancient York Ritual, and shall keep a book, containing its By-Laws, the names of its members, and a list of all the Lodges under this Grand Lodge, with their usual times and places of meeting, and such other necessary parts of their transactions, as may with propriety be committed to writing.

6th. It is inexpedient and improper for any Masonic Lodge to be incorporated by law.

CHAPTER III.

OF INITIATION, ADVANCEMENT, ADMISSION TO MEMBERSHIP, AND VISITING.

1st. Every person desirous of being made a Free Mason in any Lodge, shall be proposed by a member thereof, who shall give an account of the candidate's name, age, quality, profession, place of residence, description of his person, and all requisite qualifications mentioned in the first chapter. And it is generally required that such proposal be seconded by one or more members possessing some knowledge of the candidate. It shall also be made during Lodge hours, at a Stated Communication of the Lodge, and at least one month before initiation, except by Dispensation from the Grand Master, in order that the brethren may have sufficient time and opportunity to make a strict enquiry into his circumstances, principles, character and connections, and shall in no case be referred to a committee; and the ballot *must* be unanimous for the admission of all candidates.

2d. The brother who proposes a candidate, shall at the same time deposit such a sum of money for him as the By-Laws of the Lodge may require; which is forfeited to the Lodge if the candidate should not attend according to his proposal; but is to be returned to him if he should not be approved and accepted; and in case he is received, he is to pay, in addition to his deposit, such further sum as is prescribed by the By-Laws of the Lodge; and the fee for each degree must be paid up in full before the degree shall be conferred.

3d. No candidate for initiation who shall be rejected, in any Lodge under the jurisdiction of this Grand Lodge, shall be eligible to a second recommendation in that or any other such Lodge, until the expiration of twelve months.

4th. It shall be the duty of every Master of a Lodge rejecting a candidate, to cause his Secretary to notify the same immediately to the Grand Secretary.

5th. No Lodge shall make more than five new brethren at one time, unless by Dispensation from the Grand Master, or his Deputy in his absence; nor shall they initiate, pass and raise a brother for a less sum than twenty dollars, (where a fee is required,) for the three degrees; or ten dollars for the First, five for the Second, and five for the Third; nor confer any portion of either degree, except the Explanatory Lectures, on more than one candidate at a time.

6th. In all cases of advancement from one degree to another, it shall be necessary for the brother wishing to be advanced, to undergo an examination in open Lodge, in the degree from which he proposes to be advanced; after which his eligibility to such advancement, predicated upon his Masonic proficiency, shall be decided by ballot, and the suffrages of the majority present shall determine on the subject; but it is necessary for the ballot to be taken and to be *clear* in the degree to which the brother prays to be advanced, as a test of his moral fitness, before he can be received into the proposed degree.

7th. No Lodge shall confer a degree on any brother who is not of their household; for every Lodge ought to be competent to its own business, and without doubt, most capable of judging of the qualifications of its own members; nor shall any Lodge under this Grand Jurisdiction, initiate, pass, or raise any person, who is a resident of any state or territory in which there is a Grand Lodge, nor initiate a candidate living within the proper Masonic Jurisdiction of another Lodge: *that is*, whose residence is nearest such other Lodge, without its consent: provided, that where two or more Lodges are situated in the same city or town, their jurisdiction shall be concurrent.

8th. All applications of brethren for membership in any Subordinate Lodge, must be made one month before a decision can be given; and the balloting thereon shall be confined to Master Masons.

9th. When on application for membership a rejection takes place, it is not indispensably necessary that the name of the rejected brother should be inserted in the return to the Grand Lodge; nor is he precluded from applying to the same or any other Lodge at any subsequent meeting; and no Lodge shall make public through any *public print*, any rejection, suspension or expulsion.

10th. No member can be imposed on any Lodge without its consent, by any power whatever.

11th. If any Lodge shall admit to membership a brother who may be in arrears to another Lodge, the Lodge thus admitting him becomes responsible for the arrearages due to the other Lodge.

12th. Any brother may be a member of as many Lodges as choose to admit him, and must always be a member of some Lodge, unless excused by vote of the

Lodge nearest his residence; and every brother so excused, is required to pay annually the sum of one dollar to the Lodge nearest his residence, for the benefit of the Charity Fund of said Lodge, and which sum the Master thereof is empowered to receive and collect.

13th. No brother shall be admitted to visit any Subordinate Lodge a second time, unless he is a member of some warranted Lodge in Virginia, or a sojourner from some other grand jurisdiction, carrying with him proper certificates; unless for satisfactory reasons such Lodge may by vote dispense with the provisions of this regulation: nor shall he be entitled to join in any Masonic procession, or be entitled to Masonic burial, or to any pecuniary aid from a Lodge, unless he has been excused from membership by a vote of his Lodge.

14th. Each Subardinate Lodge must in general be the best judge of the moral fitness of all applications for visiting.

CHAPTER IV.

OF ATTENDANCE AND DEPORTMENT IN LODGE.

1st. Every brother must always appear in his Lodge properly clothed, and in clean and decent apparel.

2d. He must attend all meetings, whether stated or emergent, when duly summoned, unless he can offer such plea of necessity for his absence, as the By-Laws and General Regulations admit; and to all these Laws and Regulations, render a willing and cheerful obedience.

3d. While the Lodge is engaged in its usual labors, Masons must hold no private conversations or committees, without leave from the Master; nor introduce any remarks irrelevant to the business before them. They must not interrupt the Master or Wardens, or any brother addressing the Presiding Officer, nor act ludicrously while the Lodge is engaged in what is serious and solemn; but every brother shall show due respect to the Master and Wardens and other brethren.

4th. No discussions relating to *nations*, *religion*, or *politics*, must ever be introduced within the walls of a Lodge; Masons as such, professing the *universal religion*, recognizing those political maxims only in which all men agree, and considering all nations as members of the same human family.

5th. The working hours of the Subordinate Lodges shall be from seven o'clock in the evening until ten, between the 25th of March and the 25th of September; and from six till nine, between the 25th of September and the 25th of March, when their meetings are held at night; but when held in the day time, the three first hours of each session shall be considered technically the working hours.

CHAPTER V.

OF UNMASONIC CONDUCT AND ITS CONSEQUENCES.

SECTION I.

Of the Powers and Mode of proceeding thereon, in Subordinate Lodges.

1st. Every Lodge under the jurisdiction of this Grand Lodge shall have full power and authority to enquire into, and punish unmasonic conduct in any of its members, except Masters of Lodges and regular Past Masters: provided they do not interfere in disputes between brethren of a pecuniary nature, and in these only by request, or consent of all parties interested.

2d. In hearing all complaints and punishing delinquents, according to the laws of the Craft, they are to adhere most religiously to the old Hebrew regulation, viz: "If a complaint be made against a brother, and he be found guilty, he shall stand to the determination of the Lodge; but if the accuser or complainant cannot support his charge, and it should appear to the Lodge to be groundless, being the result of hatred, malice or some unwarrantable passion, he shall incur such penalty as the accused would have done, had he been duly convicted."

3d. Every Lodge possesses an inherent power of suspending or expelling members, for a non-compliance with its Rules and By-Laws; and of enacting and enforcing its regulations, with respect to monthly, quarterly, and annual fees.

4th. Should any brother resident in Virginia, who may not belong to any Lodge under the jurisdiction of this Grand Lodge, deport himself so immorally as to merit the reprobation of his brethren, the Subordinate Lodge nearest to the place of his residence, shall have power to take cognizance of such reprehensible conduct, in the same manner as if the said brother were a member of that Lodge.

5th. Every brother who may be charged with unmasonic conduct, shall in due time be furnished with a copy of the charges to be exhibited against him, if they be of a nature that will admit of being written; and if they be not, the said charges shall be made known to him by a committee, to be appointed for that purpose.

6th. Should any brother whose conduct has been regularly impeached, fail to attend the summons of the Lodge, or of the committee appointed to examine into his said conduct, such brother, so failing, shall stand suspended from all the benefits of Masonry, until he do come forward, and answer to the charges alleged against him; and should such brother fail to appear and answer said charges for one month after such suspension, the Lodge shall be authorized to proceed to examine into the merits of the charges, and pronounce such judgment as they shall deem proper in the premises.

7th. If any member of a Lodge under the jurisdiction of this Grand Lodge, shall visit or work in any Lodge of Masons commonly called Clandestine Masons; or any Lodge of Masons not working agreeably to the ancient usages of York Masons, he shall be reprimanded by the Lodge to which he belongs; and if he should afterwards be guilty of a similar offence, he shall be expelled from the Lodge, and excluded from the benefits of Masonry.

8th. In all cases of suspension, the person suspended, is thereby absolutely precluded from all the benefits and privileges of Masonry, throughout the Masonic world during the term of said suspension; and which suspension should in every case be for an indefinite period: provided always, that the Lodge imposing a suspension, shall have the power of reinstatement.

9th. In all cases of expulsion, the person expelled is thereby absolutely precluded from all the benefits and privileges of Masonry throughout the Masonic world *forever*.

10th. Balloting in the Subordinate Lodges, in all cases, shall be confined to Master Masons, and consequently must be taken in a Master Mason's Lodge.

11th. All suspensions and expulsions in any Subordinate Lodge, shall immediately be communicated to the Grand Secretary; and if a suspension is for a non-payment of dues, the cause, as well as the amount due, shall be mentioned in the report of the suspension.

12th. No Master of a Lodge, or regular Past Master,

can, without his own consent previously obtained, be called to an account, or tried for misconduct before any other body than the Grand Lodge, or a committee to be appointed by the Grand Lodge, or the Grand Master.

13th. No Master, Warden, or other Subordinate Officer of any Subordinate Lodge, against whom any specific charges of unmasonic conduct are preferred, is competent to discharge the duties of his office until a final decision shall be made on said charges; nor can any brother elected to office while charges are preferred against him, be installed, until such charges are disposed of.

14th. When any Masonic accusations shall be brought against a brother in any Lodge, Subordinate or other, the same shall not be withdrawn for private adjustment, except by unanimous consent of the Lodge.

15th. Where a member of a Lodge is liable, under the By-Laws of the Lodge, to suspension for nonpayment of dues, and no notice can be served upon him after an order of the Lodge directing him to be summoned to show cause why he should not be suspended for nonpayment of dues, and the lapse of three months, the Lodge is hereby authorized and empowered to suspend such brother without any further notice.

16th. When a member of a Subordinate Lodge removes from the geographical jurisdiction of said Lodge, and fails to make a remittance sufficient to liquidate his dues to the Lodge with which he is affiliated, for the space of twelve months, the Lodge may suspend such member for non-payment of dues without notice.

17th. Whenever a charge is preferred against a brother for unmasonic conduct, the Subordinate Lodge having jurisdiction in the case, shall issue a summons for the brother charged to appear and answer; and if the officer directed to execute the summons, make return that the brother charged "has absconded, and is believed to be beyond the jurisdiction of Virginia," the Subordinate Lodge having the case before it, having first appointed some brother to defend the absentee, may proceed to trial as though the brother were present, and inflict such punishment by suspension or expulsion as by them may be deemed just: provided, no trial shall be had under three months from the date of the charges.

SECTION II.

Of carrying Appeals from the decisions of Subordinate Lodges.

1st. In all cases where a brother may consider himself aggrieved by the decision of a Subordinate Lodge, he has the right of appeal to the District Deputy Grand Master of the District in which such Lodge may be holden.

2d. When any brother appeals from a decision of his Lodge, he shall lodge a copy thereof with the D. D. G. Master, who shall summon the parties and their witnesses to appear before a committee, to be by him appointed, for a rehearing and decision of the case.

3d. Each District Deputy Grand Master shall have jurisdiction of all appeals within his district, in the following manner: on notice by him duly received of any appeal, he shall forthwith summon five or more officers, or skilful Master Masons, to meet at such time and place as may be most convenient to hear and determine the whole subject matter of the appeal, and to make report of their proceedings to him, the said District Deputy Grand Master, reserving to either party the right of final appeal to the Grand Lodge upon the record.

4th. Immediately after the receipt of the report and proceedings of said Committee, it shall be the duty of such D. D. G. Master to furnish the Master of the Lodge with a copy of the decision, and forward to the Grand Secretary a copy of all proceedings held under the commission: provided that evidence not proper to be written may be communicated verbally.

5th. In all cases where a brother or Lodge may consider themselves aggrieved by the decision of said committee, they have an undoubted right of final appeal therefrom to the Grand Lodge; and

6th. Whereas in cases of appeal to the Grand Lodge from any vote, ballot, or resolution of said committee, it is necessary to have a copy of the whole of the written proceedings in such case present at the consideration of such appeal; therefore it shall be the duty of the Master of every Lodge, in all cases of appeal, forthwith to cause a copy of such proceedings to be forwarded to the Grand Secretary. But no copy of such proceedings shall be granted to any brother whatever.

7th. When any brother or Lodge appeals from a decision of said committee, they shall lodge a copy thereof with the Grand Secretary, who shall summon the parties to appear with the record at the next ensuing Grand Communication, in order to a rehearing and final determination of the controversy.

8th. In all cases of trial of brethren charged with unmasonic conduct, *all* the testimony relating to the matters in question, and which may be proper to be committed to writing, *shall* be taken in writing before the Lodge or before a committee appointed by the Lodge for that purpose, after due notice to the opposite party, and shall constitute a portion of the record of the case; and in all cases of appeal, a certified copy thereof, together with other parts of the record, shall be forwarded to the Grand Secretary; and *no oral* testimony shall be received by the Grand Lodge or Committee on Grievances and Appeals, unless such testimony be of a character improper to be written.

9th. When any Lodge or Lodges requires that a commission be sent to their vicinity, for the purpose of investigating any difficulty which may exist in or between such Lodges, or between the members of any Lodge, that the Lodge or Lodges making such request, shall do so in writing, and shall pay to the Grand Treasurer the expenses attending the visit of such commission.

SECTION III.

Of Reinstatements.

No reinstatement of a suspended or expelled Mason shall hereafter be made by any Lodge under the jurisdiction of this Grand Lodge, unless the following regulations be strictly complied with:

1st. Any suspended or expelled Mason who may desire to be reinstated to the benefits and privileges of Free Masonry, shall make application by petition in writing to the Lodge which suspended or expelled him, praying for such reinstatement, and setting forth the reasons which prompt him to ask this favor; which petition shall be presented to the Worshipful Master, who shall cause the same to be audibly read by the Secretary at the first stated Communication after its reception; when it shall be ordered to lie over for one month (or until the next stated Communication, if the Lodge holds not more than one stated Communication in a month.) The Worshipful Master shall then order due notice to be given to all the members of the Lodge, of the application, and have them notified to attend.

2d. The Lodge being thus duly notified and assembled, shall then proceed to consider the application; when the question of granting or refusing the request shall be determined by vote or ballot, as the Lodge may see fit.

3d. In all votes or ballots on the question of re-instating a suspended or expelled Mason, every member present shall be required to vote, unless for good cause he may be excused by unanimous consent of the Lodge.

4th. If, upon taking a vote or ballot on the petition of a suspended Mason for re-instatement, a *less* number than *two-thirds* of the members present vote for the re-instatement, the petition shall be declared *rejected;* and in case of the petition of an expelled Mason, the vote for re-instatement must be *unanimous.*

5th. The action of a Lodge on the question of restoring or reinstating a suspended or expelled Mason, may be the subject of appeal by any member who may think proper to do so. And in case of an appeal, the re-instatement shall not take effect until the appeal is decided by the proper tribunal.

6th. Any Mason who has been, or may hereafter be suspended for *nonpayment* of dues, may be reinstated at any stated Communication of the Lodge which suspended him, upon paying the amount of his dues; and, with the consent of a majority of the members present, may be restored to membership.

7th. The re-instatement of an expelled or suspended Mason, does not restore such brother to membership in the Lodge which suspended or expelled him, but only to the general rights and privileges of Masonry; and to be restored to membership, he must, after reinstatement, petition as any other nonaffiliated Mason, except in cases of suspension for nonpayment of dues as above provided for.

8th. The Lodge which suspends or expels a Mason, is the only Lodge which can reinstate him. But if that Lodge has become extinct (or otherwise incapable of working), and there is no Working Lodge in the former jurisdiction of that extinct Lodge, the petition shall be presented to the D. D. G. Master of the District in which the Lodge was located, who shall refer the petition to a commission of five skilful Past Masters or Officers of Lodges, who, after due notice to all the former members of the extinct Lodge who can be found within its jurisdiction, shall proceed to hear and determine the application. This commission shall keep a full record of their proceedings, which they shall transmit to the Grand Secretary, who shall lay the same before the Grand Lodge; and if no objection be then urged, it shall be confirmed.

9th. In a case of a Working Lodge being in existence in the former jurisdiction of an extinct Lodge, the D. D. G. Master may, at his option, refer the petition to that Lodge, when the same proceedings shall be held as provided for when the petition is presented to the Lodge inflicting the suspension or expulsion, and their decision need not be submitted to the Grand Lodge for confirmation, unless by appeal.

CHAPTER VI.

OF THE ELECTION, POWERS AND DUTIES OF THE OFFICERS OF SUBORDINATE LODGES.

SECTION I.

Of the Election of the Officers in general.

1st. The election of officers in the Subordinate Lodges shall be annually on the twenty-fourth of June. Nevertheless, when particular circumstances may render it expedient for any Lodge, the election of its officers may be on the evening of the stated meeting immediately preceding the anniversary.

2d. Whenever a vacancy shall happen, either by the death, removal, or resignation of any officer of a Subordinate Lodge, such vacancy shall be filled either at the next stated meeting, or at a meeting specially called by the Master or presiding Warden, for that purpose.

3d. In all cases of election of officers, the suffrages of a majority of all the members present, who are entitled to vote, shall be necessary to constitute a proper election.

4th. In the election of officers, every free member, namely, every member who has paid all arrearages, or has been excused from payment according to law, has one vote.

5th. In selecting candidates for the different offices, great care is to be taken that none be nominated from any other considerations than real merit, and pre-eminent ability to discharge the duties attached to them.

SECTION II.

Of the Master of a Lodge.

1st. No brother can be Master of a Lodge till he has regularly served in the office of Warden, unless in extraordinary cases, or where a new Lodge is about to be formed, and no Past Warden is to be found among the members. In such cases, a well informed Master Mason may be constituted Master of the new Lodge, or of any old Lodge similarly situated; but previous to entering on the functions of his office, he must receive the degree of Past Master.

2d. In the election of the Master, the present Wardens where they have regularly served, shall always be among the number of candidates for the Chair.

3d. After the nominations are all made, the candidates

shall withdraw, while every free member gives his vote in favor of him whom he deems most worthy.

4th. When the ballot is closed, the acting Master shall direct that the candidates return to the Lodge room and take their seats. He shall then carefully examine the poll, through a committee appointed therefor, and declare the brother having the majority of votes duly elected.

5th. The Master of every Lodge thus duly elected and installed, has it in special charge to see that the By-Laws of his Lodge, as well as the General Regulations from the Grand Lodge, be duly observed; that his Wardens discharge their duties with fidelity, and be examples of diligence and propriety to the Craft; that true and exact minutes and records of all the proceedings be kept by the Secretary; that the Treasurer keep and render accurate and just accounts, at the stated times required by the By-Laws and Orders of the Lodge; and in general, that all the goods and moneys belonging to the Lodge be correctly managed and dispensed, as if they were his own private property, according to the vote and direction of the majority.

6th. The Master has the power of appointing some brother, (who is generally the Secretary,) to keep the book of By-Laws, and other laws given by proper authority; containing likewise the names of all the members of the Lodge, and the list of Lodges in Virginia, with their usual times and places of meeting.

7th. The Master has also the power of preventing the removal of his Lodge from one house to another, unless sanctioned by the course of proceeding pointed out in Chapter XIV.

8th. The Master of every Subordinate Lodge shall have power and authority to assemble his Lodge, upon the application of any of the brethren, and upon any emergency which in his judgment may require their meeting.

9th. The Masters of all Subordinate Lodges, where they have abilities and members, are permitted to perform the ceremonies of Installation, Dedication, Consecration, Funerals, Laying Corner Stones of Public Edifices, &c., and are required to report their proceedings to the first Grand Annual Communication thereafter.

10th. It is likewise the duty of every Master of a Lodge to attend all meetings of the brethren in Grand Communication, as a representative of his Lodge.

11th. The Master of every Lodge is required either to have the proceedings of each Grand Annual Communication read in open Lodge, or referred to a special committee, with instructions to report to the Lodge any matter that demands their specific attention, at the first regular meeting after the receipt of said proceedings.

12th. It is the duty of the Master, immediately upon the death of a regular member of his Lodge, *in good standing*, to have a record made of said death upon the Lodge Book, and report the same to the Grand Secretary, who shall thereupon transmit to the Master of said Lodge a Grand Lodge Diploma, filled up with the name of the deceased brother, free of expense, for the benefit and use of the widow and orphans, or either.

13th. When sitting in Grand Communication, the Master and Wardens, or such of them who may attend, have full power and authority to represent their Lodge, and to transact all business therein, as fully as if all their members were there present. Nevertheless, the representatives of every Lodge are subject to such instructions as may be given them by their respective Lodges, for their conduct in Grand Communication.

SECTION III.

Of the Wardens of a Lodge.

1st. None but Master Masons can be Wardens of a Lodge; and must receive the degree of Past Master before entering upon the duties of that office.

2d. From among these the Master elect shall nominate one for the office of Senior Warden, and the present Master and brethren shall nominate one in opposition; and in balloting for this and all the remaining officers, the Lodge shall proceed in the same manner as in choosing a Master.

3d. The Senior Warden succeeds to all the duties of the Master when he is absent. And if the Master resigns, or becomes otherwise disqualified, the Senior Warden takes his place till it is supplied by election. And although it was formerly held that in all such cases, the Master's authority ought to revert to the last Past Master who is present, yet it is now the settled rule that the authority devolves upon the Senior Warden, and in his absence upon the Junior Warden, even although a former Master be present. And if the presiding Warden should call on any Past Master who may be in Lodge to take the Chair, on the presumption of his superior skill in conducting the business of the Lodge; nevertheless, such Past Master still derives his authority from the Warden, and cannot act till that officer congregates the Lodge.

4th. The business of the Wardens is generally to assist the Master in conducting the labors of the Lodge, to perform that duty in his absence, and to attend as representatives of their Lodge in Grand Communication.

SECTION IV.

Of the Treasurer of a Lodge.

1st. The Treasurer is to receive all moneys paid in for the use of the Lodge, and to pay all orders drawn on him by its authority. He is to keep regular entries both of his receipts and disbursements, and to have his books and vouchers always ready for examination, at such stated times as the By-Laws require, or when specially called on by order of the Master and brethren.

2d. The Treasurer is likewise to have the charge and custody of the jewels and furniture of the Lodge, unless when the Master and majority may judge it more convenient to assign that duty to some other responsible brother; or when the officers may take the charge immediately on themselves.

SECTION V.

Of the Secretary of a Lodge.

1st. The Secretary shall keep regular minutes of all the proceedings of a Lodge that may properly be committed to writing, which shall be afterwards faithfully entered in the record books, with such previous corrections as the brethren may approve.

2d. He shall keep an accurate list of all the members of the Lodge, with the times of admission of new members, and make a return thereof to the Grand Secretary, just before each Grand Annual Communication, which shall be signed by the Master and attested by the Secretary with the seal of each Lodge, in order that the Grand Secretary, and consequently the members of the Grand Lodge may be at all times enabled to know the number and names of members in every Lodge under their jurisdiction, with the handwriting of the different officers; and to pay all due respect to the brethren recommended, or certified by them from time to time.

SECTION VI.

Of the Deacons of a Lodge.

It is the duty of the Senior and Junior Deacons to attend on the Master and Wardens, and to act as their proxies in the active duties of the Lodge—such as the reception of candidates into the different degrees of Masonry, the introduction and accommodation of visitors, and in the immediate practice of our rites.

SECTION VII.

Of the Stewards of a Lodge.

It is the duty of the Stewards to assist in the collection of dues and subscriptions, to keep an account of the Lodge expenses, to see that the tables are properly furnished at refreshment, and that every brother is suitably provided for; and generally to assist the Deacons and other officers in performing their respective duties.

SECTION VIII.

Of the Tiler of a Lodge.

1st. The Tiler should be a Master Mason of knowledge and experience; and generally a brother is to be preferred to whom the fees of the office may be necessary and serviceable.

2d. His principal duty is to take care that no person (even a member) shall be admitted while the Lodge is in session, without the knowledge and consent of the presiding officer; neither shall he admit any visitor (that is not a member of a warranted Lodge) a second time, sojourners producing certificates excepted.

3d. If he is a member of a Lodge, he is entitled to all the privileges which any other member is entitled to.

CHAPTER VII.

OF THE GRAND LODGE OF VIRGINIA.

SECTION I.

Of whom the Grand Lodge is composed.

1st. The Grand Lodge of Virginia is composed of the Masters and Wardens of all the regular Lodges therein, or of such representatives as may occasionally be appointed in the room of Masters or Wardens unable to attend.

2d. Of the Grand Master, Deputy Grand Master, Grand Wardens, Treasurer, Secretary and Deacons.

3d. Of the District Deputy Grand Masters.

4th. Of the regular Past Masters of the different Lodges.

5th. Of the Past Grand Masters, Past Deputy Grand Masters, and Past Grand Wardens.

6th. When any Master or Warden of a Subordinate Lodge, from such urgent business as may reasonably plead his excuse, cannot attend the Grand Lodge, his Lodge may appoint any one of their members, or other brother Mason, to supply his place in Grand Communication: provided that no brother shall represent a Subordinate Lodge in the Grand Lodge, unless he be a resident of the Masonic District wherein such Lodge is situated, or the Master or Warden of the Lodge which he may represent; and no brother shall represent more than three Lodges.

7th. Any Lodge under the jurisdiction of the Grand

Lodge of Virginia, and *not within this Commonwealth*, may be represented by any eminent brother or brethren, not a member or members of such Lodge, who shall be entitled to one vote for each Lodge he may so represent: provided that no brother shall represent more than three Lodges.

8th. Every brother thus deputed to represent a Lodge, shall be furnished with a certificate of his appointment, under the seal of the Lodge appointing him, and the attestation of the Secretary thereof; without which, he cannot take his seat in the Grand Lodge.

9th. No brother residing in the State of Virginia can be a member of this Grand Lodge, unless he is actually a contributing member of some chartered Lodge under its jurisdiction.

10th. To constitute a quorum of this Grand Lodge so as to proceed to business, there must be present the representatives of at least five regular Lodges.

11th. If the Grand Master is absent from any meeting of the Grand Lodge, the Deputy Grand Master shall supply his place; if the Deputy Grand Master be likewise absent, the Senior Grand Warden shall preside, and in his absence the Junior Grand Warden; and if neither of the Presiding Grand Officers is present, the Master of the oldest Subordinate Lodge who may be present, shall act as Grand Master *pro tem.* In all cases, the presiding member may nominate his deputy, and call on any eminent brethren to fill the temporary vacancies of the Grand Lodge.

12th. The Grand Master when he finds he must necessarily be absent, shall nevertheless have the power at all times of giving a special commission under his hand and seal of office, authorizing any eminent brother, a member of the Grand Lodge, to officiate in his place; provided the Deputy Grand Master should not attend.

13th. In case of the death of a Grand Master, or any other Grand Officer, the same order of succession shall take place as is above set forth, till the next succeeding election.

SECTION II.

Of the Meetings and Powers of the Grand Lodge.

1st. The Grand Lodge thus formed, shall meet at the Masons' Hall in the city of Richmond, by six o'clock in the evening of the second Monday in every December; and may close from day to day until its business is finished: and the Grand Treasurer and Grand Secretary shall attend at four o'clock P. M. of the first day of each Grand Annual Communication to receive dues and returns.

2d. The Grand Lodge shall have power and authority at all times to make local ordinances and new regulations, as well as to amend old ones, for their own particular benefit, and the good of Masonry in general: provided always, that the ancient landmarks be carefully preserved.

3d. The Grand Lodge at the Annual Communication, shall seriously consider, discuss and transact all matters that concern the prosperity of the Fraternity in general, or private Lodges and individual brethren in particular. Here, therefore, are all differences to be deliberately considered and decided that cannot be accommodated privately, nor by particular Lodges.

4th. The members of the Grand Lodge, and of all warranted Lodges within their jurisdiction, so far as they have abilities and numbers, have an undoubted right to exercise all degrees of the ancient Craft, and consequently the Royal Arch; but no Masons of any denomination can hold any Lodge without a warrant for the place where held. Nevertheless, Royal Arch

Masons must not at Processions, nor in any other place, except in the Royal Arch Lodge, be distinguished by any garment or badge, different from what belongs to them as officers or members of the Grand or their own private Lodges.

SECTION III.

Of the Manner of Voting in the Grand Lodge.

1st. All questions before the Grand Lodge shall be determined by a majority of votes, to be regulated on the following principles, viz:

2d. The Representatives of each Subordinate Lodge shall collectively have one vote.

3d. The Grand Master, or Presiding Officer, one vote, except in cases of an equal division, when he shall have two votes: provided they are not cases of election.

4th. The Deputy Grand Master one vote.

5th. The Grand Wardens, Treasurer, Secretary and Deacons, collectively, one vote.

6th. The District Deputy Grand Masters, collectively, one vote: provided they are not representatives of a Subordinate Lodge, or officers of the Grand Lodge.

7th. The Past Grand Masters and Deputy Grand Masters collectively, one vote.

8th. The Past Masters and Past Grand Wardens collectively, one vote, who are not representatives of any Subordinate Lodge, or Officers of the Grand Lodge.

9th. For the sake of convenience in voting, the Grand Master, or Presiding Officer, shall direct every collective body to sit together, that when a question is before the Lodge, they may consult among themselves how the vote shall be given; and when the question is put, one member of each collective body shall vote for the whole, and that duty shall be performed by the senior Mason.

SECTION IV.

Of admitting Visitors into the Grand Lodge.

1st. Any Master Mason having business before the Grand Lodge, or whose attendance becomes necessary to give evidence or information, or who is of respectable standing, may be admitted to visit the Grand Lodge; but such brother shall not be allowed to vote, nor shall he speak to any question without leave, or when requested to give his opinion: provided, that no brother whatever can be admitted into the Grand Lodge, unless he is a member of some regular Lodge.

2d. Every brother admitted to visit the Grand Lodge, shall pay to the Grand Treasurer one dollar on every admission, for the benefit of the Grand Charity Fund, unless he is attending on business with the Grand Lodge, or his circumstances will not admit of the payment thereof.

3d. Visitors are permitted to take their seats before the opening of the Grand Lodge.

4th. Upon the invitation of any member of the Grand Lodge, a Master Mason being a member of some Lodge, may be admitted to visit without paying a fee: provided no member of the Grand Lodge shall be permitted to invite more than one brother.

CHAPTER VIII.

RULES TO BE OBSERVED IN CONDUCTING BUSINESS BEFORE THE GRAND LODGE.

1st. At the third stroke of the Grand Master's Gavel, there shall be a general silence, and whoever breaks it without permission from the Chair, shall be publicly reprimanded.

2d. Under the same penalty, every brother shall keep his seat and observe silence whenever the Grand Master, Deputy, or Grand Warden, shall think proper to call to order.

3d. No member of the Grand Lodge shall ever appear therein without the jewels he ought to wear in his own private Lodge, unless for some good reason to be allowed in the Grand Lodge.

4th. Every member shall take his seat according to the number of his Lodge, and avoid moving about during Communication, except the Grand Deacons, as having more immediately the care of the Grand Lodge, and such other officers whose official duties may call them to different parts of the Lodge room.

5th. No brother shall speak more than twice on the same subject, unless to explain, or when called upon by the Chair to speak.

6th. Every brother who speaks shall rise and in a respectful manner address the Chair; and while speaking no member shall presume to interrupt him, under the aforesaid penalty. But if the speaker is wandering from the point under consideration, and the Grand Master should call him to order, he shall sit down, and after being set right, may again proceed if he chooses.

7th. If any member shall be twice called to order during the same evening, for a violation of these rules, and is guilty of a third offence of the same nature, the Chair shall peremptorily order him to quit the Lodge room for the night.

8th. Whoever shall be so rude as to hiss or laugh at any brother, or at what he may have advanced, shall be forthwith solemnly excluded the Communication, and rendered incapable of membership till he shall have made satisfactory concessions.

9th. For the purpose of admitting witnesses, it is deemed most proper to try all controversies in a committee, and therefore the Presiding Officer shall direct a committee of the whole Grand Lodge to meet in the Hall, on the second day of Communication, for the aforesaid purpose; and this committee shall examine and determine on every kind of business that may be referred to them, and report their proceedings to the Grand Lodge the same evening, for their ratification.

10th. No resolution having for its object the introduction of a new regulation in the Constitution of the Grand Lodge, or the alteration of an existing one, shall be acted upon, unless it be handed up in writing to the Chair on the first or second night of the Grand Annual Communication, and audibly read by the Grand Secretary; after which it must be referred to the Grand Committee for consideration; and after being reported on by the committee, it shall be finally determined.

11th. No motion or resolution once disposed of by the Grand Lodge, shall be reconsidered during that Communication, unless the motion to reconsider be entered up during the evening on which such motion or resolution shall have been made.

12th. The Grand Master shall lay before the Grand Lodge, minutes of all his proceedings during the recess, particularly those relating to questions of jurisprudence; which shall be read previously to the election of Grand Officers.

CHAPTER IX.

OF RETURNS, CONTRIBUTIONS AND FEES.

1st. The several Lodges on record shall transmit to each Grand Annual Communication, a list of all the officers and members of each Lodge, distinguishing their various grades, with such other matters relating to the Craft, as may be deemed proper to communicate; as also a list setting forth as accurately as may be, the names of all Masons residing in their vicinity who are not members of any Lodge, and consequently not contributing to the Masonic Society; and the said lists shall be recorded by the Grand Secretary, in a book specially appropriated for that purpose.

2d. Every Subordinate Lodge shall pay annually, as a contribution to this Grand Lodge, the sum of fifty cents for each member of such Subordinate Lodge, according to the returns made: provided that no Lodge shall pay less than ten dollars.

3d. And when any Subordinate Lodge shall fail to send its contribution, and to make a return of its members, such Lodge shall be chargeable on the books of the Grand Treasurer with the sum of ten dollars; and when a return shall be made without the contribution, the Grand Secretary shall furnish the Grand Treasurer with the amount of contribution due from such Lodge.

4th. It shall be the duty of the Grand Secretary to send out a list of such contributions as may be paid to the Grand Lodge, after every Annual Communication.

5th. If any Subordinate Lodge shall fail of attending the annual meetings of the Grand Lodge, or in the discharge of contributions to the Grand Charity Fund, for three years successively, as reported by the Grand Secretary, such Lodge so failing, shall thereby be *suspended;*

and all its workings thereafter be considered null and void, until it shall be regularly reinstated; and if not reinstated at the next succeeding Grand Annual Communication, they shall become *extinct* and be so declared. The numbers of such extinct Lodges shall be used in subsequent Charters, beginning with the oldest, unless otherwise requested by the petitioners for such Charter.

6th. For every Charter granted by the Grand Lodge, the members of the Lodge thereby constituted, shall pay to the Grand Lodge the sum of thirty-three and one-third dollars, and to the Grand Secretary a fee of six dollars and sixty-seven cents.

7th. But the Lodges constituted anterior to the Grand Communication in October, 1791, may have new Charters, without the fee of thirty-three and one-third dollars to the Grand Lodge.

8th. For every Dispensation to form a new Lodge, the applicants shall pay to the Grand Secretary a fee of five dollars.

9th. For every Grand Diploma, the brother receiving it shall pay to the Grand Treasurer, for the benefit of the Charity Fund, the sum of three dollars; and two dollars to the Grand Secretary as his fee: provided, that all Ministers of the Gospel who are Master Masons and members of Lodges, upon their producing the requisite certificate of good standing, shall be entitled to a Diploma free of charge.

10th. Every person admitted to any degree of Masonry in this Grand Lodge, shall pay for the benefit of the Grand Charity, sixteen dollars and sixty-seven cents.

CHAPTER X.

OF THE GRAND CHARITY FUND.

SECTION I.

Its Origin, Increase and Investment, and of Insurance Quotas.

1st. A permanent fund shall be established by the Grand Lodge of Virginia, in manner and form following, and shall not be touched but for the purposes therein expressed.

2d. All the cash that shall remain in the Grand Treasurer's hands, after discharging the expenses of each Grand Annual Communication, all Charter and Dispensation Fees, and all fees arising from affixing the seal of the Grand Lodge, shall be appropriated to the said fund.

3d. There shall be a subscription paper opened in every Lodge, and presented to the brethren on each St. John's day, for the purpose of receiving their voluntary donations, in aid of the aforesaid fund.

4th. All the moneys which shall thus accrue to the Grand Charity Fund shall be laid out in some public stock, by and in the name of a committee of five members, to be appointed by the Grand Master annually for that purpose, of whom the Grand Treasurer shall always be one; and that they, or a majority of them, be authorized to make such investments in such public stock as the said committee shall deem most advantageous; and that all certificates of such stock be deposited with the Grand Secretary immediately after purchase; and the said committee, or a majority of them, are hereby authorized and required, immediately after the close of each Grand Annual Communication, also to invest in some public stock all such sums of money as may have been received and unaccounted for by the Grand Treasurer in his last settlement with the Grand Lodge; and that the said committee be, and they are hereby required to make report of their proceedings to every Grand Annual Communication.

5th. The interest alone arising out of the said stock, shall be applied to the purpose of educating Master Masons' orphans, and relieving their distressed widows; and the principal shall remain untouched.

6th. As soon as the net proceeds of the said fund shall amount to one hundred dollars, the Grand Lodge may then, and not till then, at their Grand Annual Communication, dispose of the said annual proceeds, in such way as to them in their wisdom and discretion may seem best, in educating the orphan children, and relieving the widows of Master Masons; and that all the Lodges may have an equal opportunity of making their wishes known as to the appropriation of said fund, every proposition for disposing of the proceeds thereof, shall be made and decided on, either on the first or second night of each Grand Annual Communication.

7th. The annual taxes on the Masons' Hall in the city of Richmond, owned by the Lodges Nos. 10 and 19, shall be paid out of the funds of the Grand Lodge.

SECTION II.

Of the Beneficiaries and Mode of Distribution.

1st. The surplus proceeds of the Grand Charity Fund, after defraying the expenses of each Grand Annual Communication, shall be annually distributed to the Masonic Districts, as follows:

2d. Each District shall be entitled to one or more Beneficiaries, and the number of the Working Lodges in each District shall be separately drawn for biennially, in open Grand Lodge, on the first night of its session.

3d. As many Lodges shall be drawn for as the Grand Lodge may determine the interest of the fund will usefully serve the ensuing year.

4th. Not more than TWENTY dollars shall be allowed any Subordinate Lodge for its Beneficiary for one year.

5th. Each Subordinate Lodge so chosen by allotment, shall select its own Beneficiary.

6th. No Beneficiary, so chosen shall continue for a longer term than two years.

7th. It shall be the duty of the Master of the Subordinate Lodge to enter at school the aforesaid Beneficiary to some good teacher, on the best terms he may, and to have the same taught spelling, reading, writing and arithmetic; and it shall be the duty of the Master and Wardens especially, to see to and superintend the education of the Beneficiary aforesaid.

8th. Should there be any Masonic District in which there is no Working Lodge, then the District Deputy Grand Master of such District shall attend to all the duties hereby imposed on the Subordinate Lodges, and execute all the requirements of the Masters, Wardens and Treasurers of the same.

9th. Whenever, from the thriving condition of any Subordinate Lodge, by addition to the sum allowed it by the Grand Lodge, for any Beneficiary, it shall be able to send one or more children of poor worthy Masons to school under like care and management, it is earnestly recommended to her to do so.

10th. The Grand Secretary shall make and keep an exact record of all the Lodges who may first become recipients of said Charity, and they shall not be included in subsequent allotments, until all the Working Lodges under the jurisdiction of this Grand Lodge, have in like manner received the aid of said fund.

11th. The Grand Secretary shall also keep a correct

list of the Beneficiaries aforesaid, and report the same annually to the Grand Lodge.

12th. The Grand Treasurer shall also keep a separate and correct account in his books with the Treasurer of each Subordinate Lodge, who shall be a recipient of any part of this charity; and no second payment shall be made to the Treasurer of any Lodge, until he shall have returned to the Grand Treasurer, evidence showing that all previous payments have been applied to the objects for which they are hereby appropriated.

13th. No Subordinate Lodge which shall be chosen as a beneficiary, shall be entitled to and receive its quota, unless the same be called for within the ensuing Masonic year from and after the time it shall have been so chosen by ballot; and on failure thereof, it shall forfeit its quota back to the Grand Charity Fund, and the Grand Treasurer shall make the proper entries thereof, and shall account for the same in like manner as for any other money falling due, and coming to his hands as Grand Treasurer.

CHAPTER XI.

OF ISSUING CHARTERS, DISPENSATIONS AND DIPLOMAS.

1st. No set of Masons shall ever take upon themselves to work together, or form a new Lodge, without a Warrant or Dispensation, issued according to the Laws of the Grand Lodge.

2d. Charters for forming new Lodges can only be granted by the brethren assembled in Grand Annual Communication.

3d. Before application can be made to the Grand Lodge by brethren already members of a Lodge, for a

Charter to form a new one, the applicants shall pay up all dues to their Lodge, and notify them in writing that they intend applying for a Charter to a establish a new Lodge.

4th. Whenever application is made to the Grand Lodge, by a sufficient number of brethren, for a Charter to form a new Lodge, the Grand Lodge shall carefully ascertain whether their skill as Masons, and their good conduct as men, will justify a compliance with their petition. And only after perfect satisfaction on these points, shall the Grand Lodge issue a Charter.

5th. When a Lodge becomes too numerous for working with convenience, and application shall be made by some of the members for leave to separate and form a new Lodge, the cause of their separation must be certified by their Lodge to the Grand Communication, together with a recommendation of the brethren most proper to be appointed officers of the new Lodge, before a Charter shall issue.

6th. The Grand Master, or in his absence out of the state, the Deputy Grand Master, may grant a Dispensation for forming a new Lodge, to continue in force until the next Grand Communication: provided the petitioners are furnished with the same recommendations as are necessary for obtaining Charters: and further, provided said Lodge shall work according to a code of By-Laws to be furnished by the Grand Secretary. But it shall be discretionary with the succeeding Grand Annual Communication, whether a Charter shall be granted or not, and if granted, the Dispensations shall continue in full force and effect until such Charter shall be received and the new Lodge installed.

7th. And the Grand Lodge of Virginia will hold no communication with any Lodge in this state, which shall in future be constituted by the authority of any other Grand Lodge.

8th. No Charter or Dispensation to Constitute a Lodge, shall be granted to any number of Masons residing in any other state where a Grand Lodge adopting this principle is held, unless such Grand Lodge shall furnish the petitioners with a written acquiescence, properly authenticated.

9th. The Lodges within the jurisdiction of this Grand Lodge in October, 1791, may have new Charters, so numbered as to preserve their priority of rank, agreeably to the dates of their original Charters.

10th. Every Charter issued from this Grand Lodge shall be signed by the Grand Master, or in case of his death or absence out of the state, by the Deputy Grand Master and Wardens, sealed with the seal of the Grand Lodge, and attested by the Grand Secretary, directed to three reputable brethren, authorizing them to call in other brethren to their assistance, and to enter Apprentices, pass Fellow Crafts, and raise Master Masons, and perform all other work agreeably to ancient customs and usages.

11th. Every Dispensation granted for forming a new Lodge shall have the Seal of the Grand Lodge, and the attestation of the Grand Secretary, and be entered by him in the book of proceedings.

12th. Whenever a Charter shall issue from this Grand Lodge to form a new Lodge, it shall be accompanied by a Dispensation, signed by the Presiding Officer, with the Seal of the Grand Lodge, and attested by the Grand Secretary, directed to some Past Master, with power to appoint his Wardens, and to install the Officers of the new Lodge, and set them to work, agreeably to ancient customs and usages; but the Master of the new Lodge shall previously receive his Degree in the presence of three Past Masters at least. And all these things must be done before the new Lodge can be entitled to representation in Grand Lodge.

13th. Every newly constituted Lodge shall be furnished with three copies of the Text-Book, at the expense of the Grand Lodge.

14th. Every brother previously obtaining a certificate from the Lodge of which he is a member, setting forth his regular behavior, and that he has regularly discharged all Lodge dues, shall be entitled on application to receive a Grand Lodge certificate or diploma, impressed on parchment, and signed by the proper Officers, (the Grand Master or Deputy, and Grand Secretary,) and having also the signature of the member himself, opposite the seal: provided said application is made within thirty days after the date of such certificate, and when the Grand Secretary has no good reason to believe he has been guilty of any criminal offence since said date.

15th. Every member of a Lodge under a Dispensation, shall be considered a member under a subsequent Charter.

CHAPTER XII.

OF THE MANNER OF CONSTITUTING A LODGE.

1st. A sufficient number of brethren being convened in conformity to Dispensation, as set forth in the 12th paragraph of the foregoing chapter, together with the brethren of the intended new Lodge, the Constituting Lodge shall be opened in the Third Degree of Masonry.

2d. The brethren designated as Master and Wardens of the new Lodge being yet promiscuously among their

Fellows, the Acting Master shall ask his Senior Warden if he has examined them, and found them well skilled in the mysteries of Masonry, &c. The Warden answering in the affirmative, shall, by the Master's order, take the Senior Candidate from among his Fellows, and present him to the Master saying, "Right Worshipful Master, the brethren here assembled desire to be formed into a regular Lodge, and I present my worthy brother A. B., to be installed their Master, whom I know to be of good morals and great skill, true and trusty, and a lover of the whole Fraternity, wheresoever dispersed over the face of the Earth."

3d. Then the Master placing the Candidate on his left hand, and having asked and obtained the unanimous consent of the brethren, shall say, (after some other ceremonies and expressions that cannot be written,) *I constitute and form these good brethren into a new regular Lodge, and appoint you brother A. B. the Master* thereof, not doubting of your capacity and care, to preserve the cement of the Lodge, &c.

4th. Whereupon the Senior Warden, or some other brother for him, shall rehearse the charge of a Master, and the Master shall ask the Candidate saying, "Do you submit to these charges as Masters have done in all ages?" And the new Master signifying his cordial submission thereto, the Master shall by certain significant ceremonies and ancient usages, install him, and present him with his Warrant, the Book of Constitutions, the Lodge Book, and the Instruments of his office, one after another; and after each of them, the Master, his Warden, or some brother for him, shall rehearse the short and expressive charge, suitable to the thing presented.

5th. Next the members of this new Lodge bowing to the Acting Master, shall return him thanks according to the custom of Masons, and shall immediately do homage to their own Master, and as faithful Craftsmen signify their promise of obedience to him, with usual congratulations.

6th. The Wardens and such other brethren as are not members of this new Lodge, shall now congratulate the new Master, and he shall return becoming acknowledgments, first to the Acting Master and other officers, and then to the rest in order.

7th. The Acting Master then instructs the new Master to enter immediately on the exercise of his official functions; and the new Master calling forth his Senior Warden, presents him to the Acting Master for his approbation, and to the new Lodge for their consent; whereupon the Senior or Junior Acting Warden, or some other brother for him, rehearses the charges of a Warden, &c., and he signifying his cordial submission thereto, the new Master shall present him with the several Instruments of his office in succession, and install him in due and ancient form.

8th. In like manner, the Master of the new Lodge shall call forth his Junior Warden, and present him to be duly installed. And the members thereof shall signify their obedience to their Wardens, by the usual congratulations.

9th. The acting Master then gives all the brethren joy of the Master, Wardens, &c., and recommends harmony, &c., hoping their only contention will be a laudable emulation in cultivating Masonic and social virtues.

10th. Then the Secretary, by the Acting Master's order, in the name of the Grand Lodge, proclaims this new Lodge duly constituted No. —, &c.; upon which all the members of the new Lodge, (after the customs of Masons,) return their cordial thanks for the honor of this Constitution, and the Lodge is closed.

11th. The Master thus acting under Dispensation,

makes return to the Grand Secretary of his proceedings therein.

12th. No Warden of a Subordinate Lodge shall enter upon the duties of his office until he shall have taken the Degree of Past Master, which degree the officers being Past Masters have the undoubted right to confer.

CHAPTER XIII.

OF PROCEEDINGS IN RETURNING CHARTERS.

1st. Whenever a question shall be agitated in a Subordinate Lodge, having in view the return of its Charter to the Grand Lodge, the said Subordinate Lodge shall be convened by summonses, issued at least one month before the first discussion of the question of returning the Charter shall be had; and the Tiler or person appointed to summon the brethren, shall make due return of the persons summoned.

2d. When in conformity to the aforesaid summonses, the Lodge shall be convened, the concurrence of a majority of at least two-thirds of the members present shall be necessary, before the proposal for returning the Charter shall be entered of record. If such majority be found, this proposition shall lie over until the next regular meeting of the Lodge; and summonses and return thereof shall be made as before. At the said next regular meeting of the Lodge, the subject shall again be discussed; and if two-thirds of the attending members shall be in favor of giving up the Charter, the reasons on which such resolution is founded, shall be entered of record.

3d. Immediately after the passage of such resolution, a schedule shall be made out and entered of record, of all the books, papers, jewels, furniture, funds, &c., belonging to the Lodge, and also a list of all the creditors of, and debtors to the Lodge.

4th. When these measures shall have been taken, the said Lodge shall cause to be laid before the Grand Lodge, at the next succeeding Annual Communication, an accurate copy of the whole of their proceedings, with the reasons, schedule, and list aforesaid, when the Grand Lodge will on thus possessing the whole subject, take such order on the case of such private Lodge, as shall appear to be right and proper.

5th. When the determination of any Lodge to return its Charter, shall be confirmed by the Grand Lodge, or when a Lodge shall be declared dormant or extinct, the books, papers, funds, furniture, and everything else belonging to such Lodge, should come under the control, direction and safe-keeping of the Grand Lodge, as the paternal representative of the Craft throughout its jurisdiction.

CHAPTER XIV.

OF PROCEEDINGS IN REMOVING LODGES.

1st. No motion can be made for the removal of a Lodge, in the absence of the Master. But if a motion be made while he is present, for moving the Lodge to some other more convenient place, within the district assigned by the Charter; and the said motion be seconded and thirded, the Master shall order summonses to every individual member of the Lodge, specifying the business, and appointing a time, not less than ten days distant, for discussing and determining thereon. And if on the ultimate vote, the Master is not of the majority, the Lodge shall not be removed, unless two-thirds of the members present vote for such removal.

2d. But if the Master refuse to direct such summonses to be issued, then either of the Wardens may authorize the same; and if the Master neglects to attend on the day therein appointed, the Lodge may, under the direction of the Warden, proceed to a decision.

3d. If the Lodge thus regularly decide on a removal, the Master or Warden shall send notice to the Grand Secretary, that such removal may be recorded in the books of the Grand Lodge.

CHAPTER XV.

OF THE GRAND COMMITTEES AND GRAND LECTURER.

SECTION I.

Of the Committee on Work.

On the first evening of every Grand Annual Communication, a Committee of five members shall be appointed by the Grand Master, to be called the "Working Committee;" whose duty shall be, to attend on the second and third days of each Annual Communication, or oftener if required by the Grand Lodge, to exemplify to any brother or brethren wishing it, the three degrees of Masonry.

Of the Steward's Committee.

1st. A Steward's Lodge or Committee, consisting of five Master Masons, shall be appointed annually, for the purpose of regulating the Steward's Department, whose duty shall commence at the close of the Grand Annual Communication at which they are appointed, and continue until the close of the next succeeding Grand Annual Communication.

2d. In performing the duties thus assigned them, they shall authorize no expenditures beyond the aggregate amount of fifty dollars, during any Grand Communication.

Of the Committee of Correspondence.

A Committee of Correspondence, consisting of five members, shall be appointed annually by the Grand Master during the sitting of the Grand Lodge, whose duty it shall be during the recess of each Grand Annual Communication, to peruse, and when in the opinion of said Committee it may be necessary, to answer any communication which may from time to time be addressed to this Grand Lodge by other Grand Lodges; and the said Committee is hereby required to make report of their proceedings at every Grand Annual Communication succeeding its said appointment.

Of the Committee of Investment.

1st. A Committee of Investment of the Funds of the Grand Lodge in aid of the Grand Charity Fund, consisting of seven members, of which the Grand Treasurer shall always be one, shall be appointed annually by the Grand Master during the sitting of the Grand Lodge, whose duty it shall be to invest the same in some public stock immediately after the rising of each Grand Annual Communication.

2d. It shall be the duty of said Committee to audit and examine semi-annually the Grand Treasurer's and Grand Secretary's books and accounts, and annually to report the same to each Grand Lodge; to them also shall be referred all accounts, and all applications for appropriations not otherwise disposed of, to be reported upon with such recommendation with regard to them as they shall think right.

Of the Other Committees.

1st. A Committee on Dispensations and Charters, to consist of three.

2d. A Committee on Grievances and Appeals, to consist of seven, whose duties shall commence at the close of the Grand Annual Communication at which they are appointed, and continue until the close of the next succeeding Grand Annual Communication, and that they have power to sit during recess.

3d. A Committee on Masonic Jurisprudence, to consist of three.

4th. A Committee on the Proceedings of the Grand Officers during recess; to consist of three, to whom shall be referred the minutes of the Grand Secretary during recess, and whose duty it shall be to report to the Grand Lodge the subjects therein contained which require their action.

SECTION II.

OF GRAND LECTURER.

1st. Immediately after the election of officers, annually, the Grand Master shall nominate and appoint a Grand Lecturer, whose duty it shall be to visit and instruct the Lodges and members thereof when requested so to do.

2d. In his instructions he shall conform to the Ancient York Ritual, as taught by the Grand Working Committee, and revised and adopted by the Grand Lodge in 1855, and to the Laws of the same, as contained in the Virginia Text-Book.

3d. He shall be *ex officio* Chairman of the Grand Working Committee. He may also appoint one or more deputies, for whose competency and energy he shall be responsible.

4th. The Grand Lecturer and his deputy shall receive as compensation for their services, the sum of five dollars per day while engaged in lecturing or travelling to and from said Lodges or members; and such expenses to be paid by the Lodges or parties to whom such services are rendered.

5th. On any such visit of instruction, if he shall discover any immoral or masonic irregularity among the members of said Lodges, or in the Lodges themselves, he shall report the same to the District Deputy Grand Master of the District.

6th. He shall annually on the first night of each Grand Annual Communication, make a report in writing of his acts and doings during the year.

CHAPTER XVI.

OF DISTRICTS, AND DISTRICT DEPUTY GRAND MASTERS.

1st. All the Subordinate Lodges under this jurisdiction, shall be laid off in the following Districts, and any Lodge which may be revived, or any new Lodge which may be established, shall be assigned its position and number by the Grand Lodge accordingly:

District No. 1.

Norfolk City	Norfolk Lodge	No.	1
"	Atlantic Lodge	"	2
Elizabeth City	St. Tammany Lodge	"	5
Isle of Wight	Mount Olivet Lodge	"	25
Princess Anne.			

Nansemond	Suffolk Lodge	No.	30
"	Chuckatuck Lodge	"	77
Northampton	Northampton Lodge	"	90
Nansemond	Somerton Lodge	"	99
Norfolk County	Portsmouth Naval Lodge	"	100
Nansemond	Harmony Lodge	"	149
Southampton	Franklin Lodge	"	151
Norfolk County	Mount Vernon Lodge	"	166
Nansemond	McAlister Lodge	"	185
Accomack.			

District No. 2.

James City	Williamsburg Lodge	No.	6
Gloucester	Botetourt Lodge	"	7
Matthews.			
Warwick.			
York.			

District No. 3.

Charles City.
New Kent.
King & Queen.
King William.
Middlesex.
Essex.

District No. 4.

Westmoreland	Montross Lodge	No.	76
Lancaster	Lancaster Union Lodge	"	88
Northumberland	Benevolentia Lodge	"	105
Richmond.			

District No. 5.

Dinwiddie	Blandford Lodge	No.	3
"	Petersburg Lodge	"	15
"	Corinthian Lodge	"	29
Sussex	Astræ Lodge	"	85
Prince George	Prince George Lodge	"	115
Greenesville	Widow's Son Lodge	"	150
Sussex	Relief Lodge	"	169

District No. 6.

Isle of Wight	Smithfield Union Lodge	No.	18

Southampton	Berlin Lodge	No. 42
Surry	Jefferson Lodge	" 65
Southampton	Acacia Lodge	" 84
Isle of Wight	Mayfield Lodge	" 134
"	Temperance Lodge	" 164
Surry	Cabin Point Lodge	" 177

District No. 7.

Brunswick	Brunswick Lodge	No. 52
Lunenburg	Warren Lodge	" 59
Lunenburg	Flat Rock Lodge	" 83
Brunswick	Starke Lodge	" 90
Mecklenburg	Washington Union Lodge	" 118
"	Meherrin Lodge	" 119
Lunenburg	Blue Stone Lodge	" 123
"	Fitzwhylsonn Lodge	" 152

Nottoway.

District No. 8.

Henrico	Richmond Lodge	No. 10
"	Metropolitan Lodge	" 11
Chesterfield	Manchester Lodge	" 14
Henrico	Richmond Randolph Lodge	" 19
"	St. John's Lodge	" 36
"	Dove Lodge	" 51
"	Loge Française	" 53
Chesterfield	Black Heath Lodge	" 89
Henrico	Henrico Union Lodge	" 130
Chesterfield	Chesterfield Lodge	" 161
Hanover	Ashland Lodge	" 168
Henrico	Capitol Lodge	" 184

Goochland.

District No. 9.

Powhatan	Powhatan Lodge	No. 68
Cumberland	De Witt Clinton Lodge	" 141
Buckingham	Buckingham Union Lodge	" 143
Cumberland	Cumberland Doric Lodge	" 146

Amelia.

District No. 10.

Amherst	Warren Lodge	No. 33
"	Clinton Lodge	" 73

Nelson	Friendship Lodge	No. 74
"	New Glasgow Union Lodge	" 87
"	Fleetwood Harmony Lodge	" 92
"	Friendship Lodge	" 163

District No. 11.

Campbell	Marshall Lodge	No. 39
"	Prudence Lodge	" 44
"	Mackey Lodge	" 69
Bedford	Boonsborough Lodge	" 70
"	Liberty Lodge	" 95
Campbell	Staunton River Lodge	" 155
"	Leesville Lodge	" 181
"	Hill City Lodge	" 183

District No. 12.

Rappahannock	Blue Ridge Lodge	No. 7
Culpeper	Fairfax Lodge	" 43
Greene	Piedmont Lodge	" 50
Rappahannock	Washington Lodge	" 78
"	Front Royal Lodge	" 102
Madison	Linn Banks Lodge	" 126
Fauquier	Mt. Carmel Lodge	" 133
"	Patmos Lodge	" 189

District No. 13.

Caroline	Kilwinning Cross Lodge	No. 2
Spotsylvania	Fredericksburg Lodge	" 4
"	Fredericksburg American Lodge	" 63
King George.		
Stafford.		

District No. 14.

Pittsylvania	Chestnut Grove Lodge	No. 17
"	Pittsylvania Lodge	" 24
Franklin	Rocky Mount Lodge	" 75
Pittsylvania	Vincent Witcher	" 87
Henry	Washington Lodge	" 127
Patrick	Patrick Henry Lodge	" 140
Halifax	Dan River Lodge	" 153

District No. 15.

County	Lodge	No.
Alexandria	Alexandria Washington Lodge	No. 22
Fairfax	Henry Lodge	" 40
Alexandria	Lafayette Lodge	" 67
Loudoun	Salem Lodge	" 81
"	Olive Branch Lodge	" 114
Alexandria	Andrew Jackson Lodge	" 120
Prince William.		

District No. 16.

County	Lodge	No.
Albemarle	George Lodge	No. 32
Fluvanna	Bowlesville Lodge	" 34
Albemarle	Scottsville Lodge	" 45
Fluvanna	Palmyra Lodge	" 55
Louisa	Day Lodge	" 58
Albemarle	Widow's Son Lodge	" 60
"	Blue Ridge Lodge	" 71
Louisa	Green Spring Lodge	" 79
Orange	Independent Orange Lodge	" 138

District No. 17.

County	Lodge	No.
Berkeley	Excelsior Lodge	No. 54
Jefferson	Malta Lodge	" 80
Berkeley	Mount Nebo Lodge	" 91
Jefferson	Charity Lodge	" 111
"	Triluminar Lodge	" 117
"	Avon Lodge	" 124
Berkeley	Equality Lodge	" 136

District No. 18.

County	Lodge	No.
Frederick	Hiram Lodge	No. 21
Clarke	George Washington Lodge	" 57
"	Greenway Court Lodge	" 94
Frederick	Dallas Lodge	" 132
Hampshire	Clinton Lodge	" 139
Clarke	Chandler Lodge	" 148
"	Prospect Hill Lodge	" 157
Frederick	Mount Olivet Lodge	" 175

District No. 19.

Rockingham	Rockingham Union Lodge	No.	27
Shenandoah	Central Lodge	"	38
"	Hunter Lodge	"	135
Page	Lafayette Lodge	"	137
Shenandoah	Cassia Lodge	"	142
Hardy	Moorfield Lodge	"	192
Pendleton.			

District No. 20.

Augusta	Staunton Lodge	No.	13
"	Worthington Smith Lodge	"	46
Rockbridge	Natural Bridge Lodge	"	64
"	Mountain City Lodge	"	67
Augusta	New Hope Lodge	"	103
Bath.			
Highland.			

District No. 21.

Roanoke	Taylor Lodge	No.	23
Alleghany	Friendship Lodge	"	66
Botetourt	James Evans Lodge	"	72
Craig	Door to Virtue Lodge	"	109
Alleghany	Covington Lodge	"	171
Roanoke	Lakeland Lodge	"	190

District No. 22.

Wythe	Wytheville Fraternal Lodge	No.	82
Montgomery	McDaniel Lodge	"	86
Grayson	Independence Lodge	"	129
Floyd	Leitch Lodge	"	131
Montgomery	Hunter's Lodge	"	156
Pulaski	Henry Clay Lodge	"	165
Carroll	Fulton Lodge	"	193

District No. 23.

Smythe	Marion Lodge	No.	31
Scott	Catlett Lodge	"	35
Lee	Preston Lodge	"	47

Washington ....Abingdon Lodge..................No. 48
Tazewell.............Tazewell Lodge.................. " 62
Washington ....Shelby Lodge.................... " 162
Russell..............Hope Lodge...................... " 173
Scott................Rye Cove........................ " 187
Lee..................Martin's Station................ " 188

District No. 24.

Monroe...............Monroe Lodge....................No. 12
Greenbrier...........Greenbrier Lodge................ " 49
" ....Frankfort Lodge................. " 97
Giles................Giles Lodge..................... " 106
Mercer...............Princeton Lodge................. " 116
Nicholas.............Wakoma Lodge.................... " 179

District No. 25.

Cabell...............Minerva Lodge...................No. 56
Fayette..............Fayetteville Lodge.............. " 74
Kanawha..............Kanawha Lodge................... " 104
Cabell...............Western Star Lodge.............. " 110
Kanawha..............Salina Lodge.................... " 145
Putnam...............Kanawha Valley Lodge............ " 178
Wayne................Wayne Lodge..................... " 182
Mason.
Boone.
Logan.
Wyoming.

District No. 26.

Lewis................Franklin Lodge..................No. 20
" ....Western Lodge................... " 26
Braxton.
Gilmer.
Upshur.

District No. 27.

Marion...............Fairmount Lodge.................No. 9
Barbour..............Bigelow Lodge................... " 28
Monongalia...........Morgantown Union Lodge.......... " 93
Harrison.............Herman Lodge.................... " 98
Marion...............Mannington Lodge................ " 158

Preston	Preston Lodge	No. 167
Taylor	Fetterman Lodge	" 170
Doddridge.		
Randolph.		

District No. 28.

Marshall	Marshall Union Lodge	No. 37
Ohio	Ohio Lodge	" 101
Wetzell	Wetzell Lodge	" 104
Brooke	Wellsburg Lodge	" 108
Ohio	Wheeling Lodge	" 128
Hancock	New Cumberland	" 174
Brooke	Bethany	" 176
Marshall	Cameron	" 180
Tyler.		

District No. 29.

Prince Edward	Farmville Lodge	No. 41
Appomattox	Monroe Lodge	" 107
Charlotte	Laurel Lodge	" 112
"	St. John's Lodge	" 144
"	Keysville Lodge	" 154
Appomattox	South Side Lodge	" 191

District No. 30.

Halifax	Roanoke Lodge	No. 8
"	Brooklyn Lodge	" 16
Pittsylvania	Polk Lodge	" 61
Halifax	Halifax Hiram Lodge	" 96
Pittsylvania	Roman Eagle Lodge	" 122

District No. 31.

Wood	Mt. Olivet Lodge	No. 113
Jackson	Ashton Lodge	" 121
"	Ripley Lodge	" 160
Pleasants.		
Wirt.		
Ritchie.		

2d. Every Subordinate Lodge, at the stated meeting in the months of September, October, or November, shall recommend some brother of respectability and skill, who is a Master of a Lodge, or regular Past Master, and a resident in the Masonic district in which the Lodge so recommending is situated, as District Deputy Grand Master for the said District, for the year then next ensuing; and said Lodge shall return the name of the person so recommended, with the annual return, to each Grand Annual Communication.

3d. Every brother so recommended and nominated as a District Deputy Grand Master, shall be satisfactorily vouched for as a Past Master of a Lodge, and well skilled in the first, second and third degrees of Masonry, as the work is now prescribed by this Grand Lodge.

4th. The Most Worshipful Grand Master, with the advice of the Deputy Grand Master, the Grand Senior Warden, Grand Junior Warden and Grand Lecturer, shall be vested with the power to appoint, annually, on the third night of each Grand Annual Communication, a District Deputy Grand Master for each district, who shall exercise all the functions and enjoy all the privileges prescribed thereby.

5th. Every District Deputy Grand Master so appointed, shall be furnished with a warrant of his appointment, signed by the Grand Master or his Deputy, and attested by the Grand Secretary, with the seal of the Grand Lodge affixed; upon receipt whereof, in all cases where they decline to act, they are required forthwith to return the warrant of appointment; whereupon the Grand Master is authorized and requested to make a new appointment, to continue in force until the next Grand Annual Communication.

6th. Immediately after every appointment of District Deputy Grand Masters as aforesaid, the Grand Secretary shall forward to each of the Subordinate Lodges a list of the names of the persons appointed, with the

Lodges composing the Districts placed under their superintendence respectively.

7th. The Duties of the District Deputy Grand Masters shall be as follows; and each of them by virtue of his appointment, shall possess full power and authority to carry these duties into full effect:

8th. Each District Deputy Grand Master shall have jurisdiction of all appeals within his District, in the following manner, to wit: on notice by him duly received of any appeal, he shall forthwith summon five or more officers or skilful Master Masons, to meet at such time and place as may be most convenient, to hear and determine the whole subject matter of the appeal, and to make report of their proceedings to him, the said District Deputy Grand Master—reserving to either party the right of final appeal to the Grand Lodge, upon the record.

9th. Each District Deputy Grand Master shall visit every Lodge in his District, at least once during the term of his appointment; and of such intended visit, he shall give the Master or Secretary of the Lodge notice.

10th. At every such visit, the District Deputy Grand Master is to preside in the Lodge, after it is opened, and he is introduced. He is to examine the records of the Lodge, and see if they are regularly kept, to inform himself of the number of members, and whether they are generally punctual in their attendance; to inquire whether the Lodge be in a flourishing or a declining state; to point out any errors he may observe in their conduct or manner of working, and to use every effort to enforce a compliance with the Work of the Grand Lodge; to instruct them in every particular wherein he may conceive them to require information; to recommend attention to the moral and benevolent principles of our Institution; caution in the admission of candidates, and a punctual representation of their Lodge, at every meeting of the Grand Lodge.

11th. When any District Deputy Grand Master shall discover, either in his own District, or in any other part of the jurisdiction of this Grand Lodge, any Masonic error or evil, whether it appertain to an individual or to a Lodge, he shall immediately endeavor by Masonic means to arrest its progress; and if he shall judge it expedient, he is forthwith to forward to the Grand Master or Grand Secretary, full information of the whole subject.

12th. The several District Deputy Grand Masters are authorized and required to receive the whole property belonging to any dormant or extinct Lodge; and except in cases where a different disposition has been made, or may hereafter be made, in relation to any part or the whole thereof, to forward to the Grand Secretary the several Charters, Jewels, Seals, Books, Papers, Floor Cloths, &c., and to sell the other Furniture and personal property of such extinct or dormant Lodge, and account for the proceeds thereof to the Grand Lodge.

13th. Previously to every annual meeting of the Grand Lodge, every District Deputy Grand Master shall, so far as is proper to be done, make out in writing a candid and faithful report of the state of each Lodge in his district, and forward it to the Grand Secretary, to be laid before the Grand Lodge; and such report shall be read to the Grand Committee on the second day of the session; and on failure to send said report, shall be ineligible to reappointment.

14th. In all cases where it may occur that there are no Working Lodges in any given district, the District Deputy Grand Master shall be empowered and required to carry out the provisions of the Grand Lodge in relation to beneficiaries of the Grand Charity Fund.

15th. In the Grand Lodge, the District Deputy Grand Masters, who are not officers or representatives thereof, shall sit as a distinct body; and in all questions shall have one vote collectively.

16th. It is recommended to all the Subordinate Lodges under this jurisdiction, to pay all the necessary expenses of their District Deputy Grand Masters, while in the discharge of their official duties.

CHAPTER XVII.

OF THE ELECTION AND DUTIES OF THE OFFICERS OF THE GRAND LODGE.

SECTION I.

Of the Election of the Grand Officers generally.

1st. The election of *all* the officers of the Grand Lodge shall take place by ballot, on the second evening of every Grand Annual Communication, and shall have the priority of all other business of that evening, the minutes of the Grand Master's proceedings during the recess, having been previously read.

2d. In all cases of election of officers, the suffrages of a majority of all the members present who are entitled to vote, shall be necessary to constitute a proper election.

3d. There shall be at least two candidates in nomination in the election of every officer.

4th. All these elections shall be for one year, and until another election shall be made; nevertheless, the Grand Master, the Deputy Grand Master and Grand Wardens, may be elected for two years successively, and the other

Grand Officers as often as may be the pleasure of the Lodge.

5th. Every member of this Grand Lodge shall with the preceding limitations, be eligible to any office therein, and may be elected whether he be present or absent.

6th. Election to an office in the Grand Lodge shall be no cause of disqualification from holding an office in a Subordinate Lodge.

SECTION II.

Of the Grand Master.

1st. The Presiding Officer shall request the Grand Lodge to nominate some skilful brother or brethren for the office of Grand Master. Should there be only one member in nomination, it shall be the indispensable duty of the Most Worshipful to nominate one other in opposition, with this exception, that if the present Grand Master is again eligible, and willing to serve another year, he shall instruct his Deputy to nominate the candidate in opposition.

2d. The Grand Master, if eligible, shall be at all times in the nomination.

3d. The members shall then prepare their ballots for one of the brethren in nomination, to be collected by one of the Grand Deacons, when the Grand Master shall instruct two of the members to examine the ballots, and report to him in writing the number of votes in favor of each candidate, and he shall immediately cause the brother having the greatest number of votes, to be thrice proclaimed aloud by the Grand Secretary, GRAND MASTER OF MASONS.

4th. The Presiding Officer shall then cause the Grand Master elect to be conducted to the Chair, and after introducing him to the members as a skilful and faithful brother, shall proceed to invest him with the badges of his office, and install him in due form; upon which all the members shall salute him according to the ancient customs of Masons.

SECTION III.

Of the Deputy Grand Master, Grand Wardens, &c.

1st. The Grand Master elect shall next nominate some skilful brother for the office of Deputy Grand Master, and the Grand Lodge shall nominate one or more in opposition, and the member having the greatest number of votes shall be declared duly elected, and shall in like manner be introduced, installed, and saluted by the brethren.

2d. In like manner shall the Grand Lodge proceed in the election of the Grand Wardens, and all the remaining officers.

SECTION IV.

Of the Grand Secretary and his Deputy.

1st. The office of Grand Secretary is of very great importance in the Grand Lodge, from the variety and multiplicity of business committed to his care, and from the learning, abilities and attention necessary for the proper management of it.

2d. All the proceedings of the Grand Lodge are to be drawn into form and recorded by him.

3d. All petitions, applications and appeals, are to pass through his hands; and no Charter or other instrument of writing is authentic without his attestation, and affixing the Grand Seal.

4th. As soon as possible after each Grand Annual Communication, he is to transmit to each Lodge four copies of the proceedings of the Grand Lodge, a list of contributions paid to the Grand Treasurer, and accurate lists of the Officers, Past Masters and Members of every Lodge in Communication.

5th. The general correspondence with Lodges, and with brethren throughout the world, is to be conducted by him, agreeably to the voice of the Grand Lodge, and the instructions of the Grand Master or his Deputy. And it is particularly his duty, once a year, to write Circular Letters to all the Grand Lodges in North America, and such as are known to be established in Europe.

6th. He shall have bound in volumes of uniform and convenient size, each year's proceedings of our sister Grand Lodges from year to year as they accumulate, to be placed in and form part of the Grand Lodge Library; and shall have printed with each year's proceedings of this Grand Lodge, such standing Laws, Resolutions and Edicts as may be passed after the publication of this Text-Book, in form of an appendix.

7th. The Grand Secretary, by virtue of his office, shall be a member of the Grand Lodge, and have a right to vote along with the Grand Wardens in all cases except in choosing Grand Officers.

8th. He shall also have the right of appointing his own Deputy or Assistant, who must be a Master Mason; but such Deputy shall not by virtue of that appointment, be a member of the Grand Lodge.

9th. He shall furnish each Lodge working under a Dispensation, with a code of By-Laws, under which they are required to work.

SECTION V.

Of the Grand Treasurer and his Assistant.

1st. To the Grand Treasurer is committed the care of all moneys raised for the General Charity and other uses of the Grand Lodge, an account of which he is regularly to enter in a book, with the respective purposes for which the several sums are intended. He is likewise to disburse the same on legal orders, and to keep an accurate account of his disbursements, and as compensation for his services shall be allowed five per centum commission on all moneys which may come into his hands as Grand Treasurer.

2d. The Grand Treasurer, or his Assistant, shall always be present in Grand Lodge, and ready when required, to attend the Grand Master and other officers, with his books for inspection, as well as any Grand Committee that may be appointed, for examining and adjusting his accounts.

3d. The Grand Treasurer shall receive in payment of annual contributions, all sums that may be offered by the Subordinate Lodges, if in notes of chartered banks; and should any loss be thereby sustained, he shall charge the same to the Grand Lodge.

4th. He shall regularly render his accounts, up to the close of each Annual Communication, and shall furnish the Grand Secretary annually, a list of Delinquent Lodges, including the preceding Grand Annual Communication, which shall be published with the proceedings; he shall also open and keep an account against the Grand Secretary, in which he shall charge him with all fees for Charters, Revivals, Diplomas, &c.

5th. The Grand Treasurer shall *ex officio* be a member of the Grand Lodge, and of the Committee of Investment of the surplus funds, and vote with the Grand Wardens.

6th. He shall have a right to appoint an assistant, who must be a Master Mason; but such assistant shall not thereby be a member of the Grand Lodge.

SECTION VI.

Of the Grand Deacons.

1st. The Grand Deacons are *ex officio* members of the Grand Lodge.

2d. Their duty is principally to assist the Grand Master and Senior Grand Warden, in conducting the business of the Grand Lodge.

SECTION VII.

Of the Grand Tiler and Grand Pursuivant.

1st. The Grand Tiler and Grand Pursuivant must be intelligent Master Masons. But neither of them is by virtue of his office, a member of the Grand Lodge.

2d. The Grand Tiler's duty is to attend at the outside of the Hall door, and to take care that none but members or visitors duly authorized, shall enter; and not even members or visitors while the Lodge is in session, without first reporting them through the Grand Pursuivant, and receiving the Grand Master's permission.

3d. The Grand Tiler is also to summon the members on any special emergency, by order of the Grand Master or his Deputy, signified to him under the signature of the Grand Secretary or his Clerk.

4th. The business of the Grand Pursuivant is to attend withinside the door of the Grand Lodge, and to report from the Grand Tiler the names of all brethren applying for admission. He is also to carry messages while the Grand Lodge is open, and to perform sundry other services, only known in the Grand Lodge.

SECTION VIII.

Of the Grand Stewards.

1st. Previously to each Grand Annual Communication, the Grand Stewards shall wait on at least two members of the Steward's Committee, and obtain their sanction to a specific Bill of Fare, which shall in no respect be exceeded by the Grand Stewards; nor shall the Committee authorize the expenditure of more than fifty dollars, during any Communication; and the refreshments shall be limited to eatables only.

2d. The Grand Stewards shall at no time admit any brother into either of the rooms appropriated for their department, except the members of the Grand Lodge, and those who shall be regularly admitted to visit.

CHAPTER XVIII.

THE MASONIC TEMPLE ASSOCIATION.

A committee of nine members of the Order shall be appointed to petition the Legislature of Virginia, or other proper authority, for an act incorporating a joint stock company, under the style and title of The Masonic Temple Association, for the purposes of purchasing a site in the City of Richmond, and erecting thereon a suitable building adapted to the use of the Grand Lodge and other Masonic Bodies in Virginia, both supreme and subordinate, as set forth in the preamble—the capital stock of said company to be not less than twenty-five thousand dollars, nor more than one hundred thousand dollars. The affairs of said company to be managed by a Board of Trustees, consisting of nine. The members of the committee, which shall be raised under this chapter, shall constitute the first Board of Trustees, to remain in office, with full powers, until the next annual meeting of the Grand Lodge, at which time another election shall be had, and annually thereafter. The trustees shall have power to open, under their own superintendence, or that of any other person or persons whom they may appoint, books for subscription to the capital stock of the company, at such times and places as they may think proper; and as soon as the minimum amount of stock is subscribed, they shall then organize by the appointment of one of their own body as President, and shall have power to appoint a Treasurer, Secretary, and such other officers and agents as they may deem necessary, and to fix their salaries. No member of the Board of Trustees shall be eligible to any office within the gift of the Board other than that of President. The Board of Trustees to have power to pass such rules and regulations for the government of the company as may be necessary, not contrary to the laws of this State. They shall have power to determine the location, to purchase the ground for, and to adopt the plan and arrangement of the building; to contract for and superintend the erection of the same; to collect the subscription of stock, in such requisitions as may be necessary for the payment of the purchase of the ground, and the completion of the building. When completed, the Board of Trustees shall have power, through their officers and agents, to take charge of the building, to rent out the various parts, determine the rate, collect the income arising therefrom, to alter and repair the buildings, to declare and pay out any revenues out of the nett profits which they may deem proper, and shall have power to do and perform all things necessary and proper for the best interest of the corporation generally; except that they shall not have power to sell and convey the property after the building shall be erected, without the consent of the Grand Lodge of Virginia. The Board of Trustees shall report annually to the Grand Lodge a full and fair account of their acts and doings for the year ending the 30th September next preceding each annual meeting, which report shall be spread upon the minutes of the Grand Lodge, and be published with the proceedings thereof.

As soon as books are opened for subscriptions to the capital stock of the company for building the Masonic Temple, the Committee on Investments are authorized to subscribe, through their Chairman, for so much of the capital stock of said company as they may think advisible, and to pay for the same as called for out of the Charity Fund, or any other Funds of the Grand Lodge; and the said Committee is also authorized to sell, for that purpose, any stocks or other securities held by the Grand Lodge.

The Committee on Finance and Investment of this Grand Lodge are instructed to subscribe to the capital stock of the Masonic Temple Association, the sum of twenty thousand dollars, to be paid for out of any moneys or stocks under their control, or which may be hereafter under their control—payment of said subscription to be made at such time and in such manner as may be required by the Trustees of the Masonic Temple Association.

The Grand Master shall, annually appoint three Proxies to represent the Grand Lodge at any meeting of the Stockholders of the Masonic Temple Association of Virginia.

CODE OF BY-LAWS

FOR THE

GOVERNMENT OF A LODGE.

ARTICLE I.

OF THE MEETINGS OF THE LODGE.

The Stated Meetings of —— Lodge, No. ——, shall be held on the evening of ——, in each month: on the Festival of St. John the Baptist, and St. John the Evangelist; and on the eve of St. John the Baptist, for the installation of officers.

ARTICLE II.

OF THE ELECTION OF OFFICERS.

Sec. 1. The officers of the Lodge shall be chosen by ballot, at the Stated Meeting preceding the Feast of St. John the Baptist, in every year, and shall be installed on the eve of that Festival.

Sec. 2. Before the election of officers takes place, the list of delinquents shall be called over; and no member who may be in arrears to the Lodge, to the amount of —— dollars, shall be entitled to hold an office, ballot or vote in any case whatever.

Sec. 3. No brother holding an office in any other Subordinate Lodge, (the Steward and Tiler excepted,) shall be eligible to any office in this Lodge.

ARTICLE III.

OF SOME PARTICULAR DUTIES.

Sec. 1. It shall be the duty of the Master at every meeting, when time will admit of it, to give the brethren the benefit of a lecture in one of the degrees.

Sec. 2. The Treasurer shall keep a regular account of all receipts and disbursements, and also a list of all the members, with an account of their respective arrearages annexed, which he shall call over at each Stated Meeting, in order that they may be collected.

Sec. 3. The Treasurer shall collect the introductory fee for each degree, and shall acknowledge himself satisfied in this respect, before any degree shall be conferred.

Sec. 4. The Secretary, on application, shall furnish any member of this Lodge with a Diploma, for which he shall be entitled to one dollar: provided the said member produces to him the Treasurer's receipt for all dues.

Sec. 5 The Steward shall provide such refreshments as the Master or Presiding Warden shall direct: provided that the expenses of the Lodge for any one meeting, all things included, (except the Tiler's fee and occasional charges for music,) shall not exceed —— dollars; and provided, that this law shall not interfere with the right of individuals, at Called Meetings, to provide such refreshments as they may judge necessary.

Sec. 6. The Livery of the Lodge shall be blue, and it shall be the duty of the Tiler to see that every brother is properly clothed before he enters the Lodge.

Sec. 7. Any brother who may wish to speak on any subject, shall rise and address the Worshipful Master in due form, and no brother shall be allowed to speak more than twice on any subject, without leave.

Sec. 8. No brother shall absent himself from the Lodge after having taken his seat, without leave from the Worshipful Master.

Sec. 9. No initiation shall take place on the evening of annual election, unless the candidate be about to travel.

Sec. 10. Any member wishing to obtain a Grand Lodge Diploma, shall make application to the Lodge in person or by proxy; and if he has paid all Lodge dues, and be recommended to the Grand Secretary, he shall obtain a certificate signed by the Master and attested by the Secretary, with the Seal of the Lodge attached thereto, setting forth his good Masonic character.

ARTICLE IV.

OF RECOMMENDATIONS AND BALLOTINGS.

Sec. 1. No brother shall be recommended as a candidate for membership to this Lodge, unless he has resided in the City of ———, or County of ———, at least six months, unless he is a person whose character is well known to the generality of the members.

Sec. 2. Every candidate for Initiation must possess the requisites specified in the Book of Constitutions; must have resided in the State of Virginia for two years, and in the City of ——, or County of ——, twelve months; and must be recommended by petition in writing, signed by himself, and seconded by two or more members of the Lodge, at a Stated Meeting, and shall stand recommended one month, (except in cases of emergency,) after which time he shall be balloted for.

Sec. 3. Every member who recommends a candidate for Initiation, shall deposit —— dollars in the hands of the Treasurer, the said —— dollars to be returned if the candidate be rejected; if he be received and initiated, it shall be considered as part of his Initiation Fee; but if he be received and do not apply to be initiated within —— months, it shall be forfeited to the Special Charity Fund.

Sec. 4. Every member who recommends a candidate for membership, shall deposit —— dollars in the hands of the Treasurer at the time, the said —— dollars to be returned if he be rejected; but if he be received, it shall constitute the fee for membership.

Sec. 5. The mode of recommending and balloting for brethren who may wish to become members of this Lodge, shall, in every respect, (except the petition and fee) be the same as in recommending candidates for Initiation.

Sec. 6. Every candidate for Membership or Initiation, after having been regularly recommended, shall be balloted for and disposed of by the Lodge.

Sec. 7. In balloting for a candidate for Initiation, one dissentient shall reject him, and, when rejected, he shall not be again eligible for twelve months.

Sec. 8. Each person Initiated, Passed, and Raised in this Lodge, shall be permitted to declare himself a member hereof without the fee for membership.

ARTICLE V.

OF FEES AND EXPENSES.

Sec. 1. Every member, except the Chaplain, Secretary, Treasurer, Steward and Tiler, shall pay into the hands of the Treasurer —— dollars per annum, in monthly payments.

Sec 2. The Fee for Initiation shall be —— dollars; for Passing —— dollars; and for Raising —— dollars.

Sec. 3. The expenses attending any extraordinary or called meeting, shall be defrayed by the person or persons for whose convenience or benefit the meeting may be called.

Sec. 4. The Tiler, as a compensation for his services, shall receive —— dollars for every meeting, and the Steward —— dollars.

Sec. 5. The fee for membership shall be —— dollars, and shall constitute a contribution to the Charity Fund of that amount.

Sec. 6. Should any member absent himself from the Lodge for twelve months successively, or be in arrears to the Lodge to the amount of —— dollars, he shall be summoned to appear at the next regular Lodge, to show cause why he should not be suspended therefor, during the pleasure of the Lodge.

ARTICLE VI.

OF COMMITTEES.

Sec. 1. In the appointment of all committees, the Master shall have the right to nominate two members, after which the Lodge may nominate as many others as they may think proper.

Sec. 2. A Standing Committee shall be appointed after every Annual Election, to examine the Treasurer's accounts, who shall report the situation thereof at the Stated Meeting in June.

Sec. 3. The Master and Wardens, or any two of them, shall be a Committee of Charity, for the relief of transient brethren in distress, and shall report their proceedings at the Stated Meeting in May.

ARTICLE VII.

OF THE SPECIAL CHARITY FUND.

Sec. 1. A fund shall be established by this Lodge, to be called "*The Special Charity Fund,*" and set apart and held sacred to the purposes hereinafter mentioned.

Sec. 2. To establish and support the said fund, the admission fee of —— dollars, paid by every brother who may become a member of this Lodge, and —— dollars out of every fee received for making, passing and raising, shall be placed to the credit of said fund.

Sec. 3. At every meeting of the Lodge, whether stated or occasional, the Special Charity Fund Box shall be sent round, in order to collect whatever may be voluntarily contributed to said fund. The amount so collected shall be entered on the minutes, and passed by the Treasurer to the credit of said fund.

Sec. 4. The proceeds of this fund shall be appropriated exclusively to the relief of such distressed Master Masons, their widows and orphans, as are or have been residents of the city of ——— or county of ———, and whose claims to our relief are personally and positively known to be real and grievous, and not to have resulted from habits of intemperance or idleness.

Sec. 5. Not more than —— dollars shall be voted out of this fund to any one applicant, at any one session of the Lodge.

Sec. 6. It shall be the duty of the Treasurer of the Lodge so to keep the accounts of this fund, that he may be enabled, at any moment, to inform the Lodge of the actual state of it.

ARTICLE VIII.

OF VISITORS.

Every brother of good standing and of regular habits, is at liberty to visit this Lodge once, free of expense, but on the second visit, (unless he be a contributing member of a Lodge,) he is to pay the Treasurer, for the use of the Lodge, —— cents, which it shall be the duty of the Treasurer to collect, except when such visitor may be invited by a member of this Lodge.

ARTICLE IX.

OF WITHDRAWALS.

Any member may withdraw himself from the Lodge on producing the Treasurer's receipt for all dues, and giving notice to the Lodge, either personally or by proxy, but no member shall be considered as having regularly withdrawn himself, until he has complied with this article.

ARTICLE X.

OF THE BY-LAWS.

Sec. 1. Whoever may wish to introduce a new law or alter an existing one, shall, at a Stated Meeting, hand up the said law or alteration, in writing; if it be then seconded, it shall be audibly read by the Secretary, and lie over until the next Stated Meeting, and then submitted to the determination of the brethren present.

Sec. 2. Whoever may wish to introduce a general revision of these By-Laws, shall, at a Stated Meeting, hand up a written notice thereof, which shall, if the majority agree thereto, lie over until the next Stated Meeting, and then be determined on by the brethren present.

Sec. 3. Every member shall be furnished with a printed copy of these By-Laws at the expense of the Lodge.

Sec. 4. These laws shall go into operation from the passage thereof, and all laws heretofore passed, are hereby repealed.

A HISTORY

OF THE

M. W. Grand Lodge of Virginia:

ITS

Origin, Progress and Mode of Development,

BY WORSHIPFUL JOHN DOVE, M. D.

Delivered at the Request of RICHMOND RANDOLPH LODGE, No. 19,
before the Brethren of Lodges Nos. 10, 14, 19, 36, 51
and 53, on the 26th of October, 1853.

History of the Grand Lodge of Virginia.

BY WORSHIPFUL JOHN DOVE, M. D.

BRETHREN OF LODGES NOS. 10, 14, 19, 36, 51 AND 53:

At the request of Richmond Randolph Lodge, No. 19, of which I am now, and have been for thirty-six years, a member, I have undertaken the pleasurable but difficult task of imparting to my young Brothers a history of the Most Worshipful Grand Lodge of Virginia; its origin, progress, and mode of development. It will at once be seen by all, that this is rendered extremely difficult: first, from the character of our records, which requires that nothing shall be written which is not essentially necessary to the simple narration of the facts under consideration; and, second, that this requirement is often confided to timid minds, who in their anxiety to keep within the prescribed rule, render their records frequently obscure by a too laconic style.

Thus with access to all the records of our Grand Lodge, of which I have been an active member since 1816, and Grand Secretary since 1835, I am able only to furnish you a very imperfect account of its origin. I could have wished this subject had been therefore allotted to abler hands, and many such could have been found, or at any rate, to one whose engagements would have permitted him to devote more time to such an interesting subject; but feeble as I know my capacity is for such a task, I will venture upon it, if with no higher motive than the hope of inducing others more capable to improve upon the meagre number and importance of the facts I have been able to collect.

A History of this, or of any other Grand Lodge, is of two kinds; one, very easy of accomplishment, confined to the fact that on such a day, in such a year, a Convention of Lodges met by their representatives, brothers A., B. and C., and resolved to form a Grand Lodge; that they adopted such and such Laws, and established a Ritual of Work, and adjourned in brotherly Love and Harmony;

that from this Grand Lodge have emanated many Charters, name and number so and so, and that brother such a one was Grand Master and Master. To perform my task in this manner would be easy enough indeed; but would you gain anything by the information to enlighten your minds masonically, or make you wiser and better men? If not, it becomes then my duty as a Mason to abandon the task in this form, and to tax your patience and crave your indulgence while in my humble manner I attempt a history of the second kind, which, comprising all the facts above alluded to, refers to, if it does not account for, cotemporary developments, social, moral and political, which seem to the distant reader in succeeding ages, if not a necessary consequence of those facts, so intimately connected with them as to be part and parcel of the same operating agency.

In preparing this Autobiography of our dear and common parent, I could not pay your respectful request the poor compliment to suppose your intelligence would be satisfied with less than a faithful delineation of her Laws, Usages and Ritual, as far as they are permitted to be written, as well as a truthful account of the authentic sources from whence they derive their origin.

The time has past when what was termed a "bright Mason" is satisfied, and stops his education at a knowledge of the mere details, however minute, of what we technically call the "work." The philosopher in Masonry of the present day must be informed, and capable of teaching, what that "work" means; whence derived; what its object; and to what good and useful end it tends. Whence, says he, at the very commencement of his studies, this first word "Worshipful" Lodge, if its teachings are not holy? For nothing earthly can be "worshipful" which does not teach and practise those Cardinal Virtues, or rather Essential Principles, of Brotherly Love which train the heart and mind to a grateful adoration of their Great Creator, and make the professors of them wiser and better men.

Southey, the reputed author of that most eccentric of all eccentric books, called the "Doctor," in a chapter devoted to a criticism on Prolixity of Style, relates the following anecdote in, what he supposes, pungent language: "A certain lawyer, pleading a case in the United States Supreme Court at Washington, found that a witness essential to the success of his cause was absent in Kentucky, and that it was, therefore, necessary for him to consume the time, and occupy the attention of the court, until the arrival of the witness. He, accordingly, set himself industriously to the task, and so thoroughly analyzed every part of the law of the case, and presented the most minute points of his defence for several successive days, that the presiding Chief Justice, (John Marshall,) the biographer of Washington, and most patient of listeners, at last modestly interrupted him, saying, 'Mr. ———: There are some things with which the court ought to be presumed to be acquainted.'" Southey meant this as a satire on Marshall's Life of Washington, in five octavo volumes. Five octavo volumes, of five hundred pages each, to write the biography of one man! and embracing a period of only sixty-seven years!!

Short sighted man—how little could he have scanned and appreciated the overwhelming influence which the interesting incidents in the eventful life of that most illustrious of men, have exercised on all the political and social relations of man in every part of the civilized globe! By their instrumentality, governments which had been the admiration of historians for ages, were to be upturned; customs, forms and usages, which had received the sanction of time and experience, were to be revolutionized; and, amid the mighty upheavings of these untried experiments, a great and powerful nation was to come into existence, the embodiment of those principles, which were to teach crowned heads and privileged classes, that among this free and enlightened people, the great, the god-like potency of a government based upon the equal rights of man, would be exercised under the blessings of heaven, until its influence should be felt in the remotest corners of the earth, and its example appealed to by the oppressed in every clime; and finally, its protection sought and claimed as the asylum of all God's children, who duly appreciate the inestimable blessings which must in all future time result from such a government, based upon the equal and inalienable rights of man, and which is so beautifully typified by the symbolic teachings of our Masonic Level.

This hasty and imperfect sketch will serve at least to give some idea of the almost inappreciable difficulties which our Most Worshipful Brother John Marshall must have encountered in giving to the world a truthful biography of our Illustrious Brother George Washington. In like manner, I feel myself overwhelmed with the task of giving you, my Brothers, a truthful history of the Grand Lodge of Virginia, and the necessary and inseparable part she and her subordinates acted in the eventful political drama which closed the last century.

The pulpit, the press, the rostrum, have all teemed with eloquent arguments, to prove the interposition and continued influence of an Almighty Providence in carrying this nation through the mighty and unequal struggle she made, and gloriously achieved, when, "like the stripling of Israel, with scarce a weapon to attack, and without a shield for defence, she met and undismayed engaged the gigantic greatness of the British lion."

The quiet but unobtrusive part which the Genius of Masonry acted in that mighty moral struggle for supremacy of merit, is only to be inferred from the visible associations of the principal actors in those eventful times—operating as she does uniformly, in all ages and in every clime, by the suasive but not less potential means of her moral teachings, and confining those teachings to her retired meetings, she has never sought, claimed, or received any honor from the mass of mankind for the inestimable blessings which have resulted from her associations with those whose hearts have shown themselves imbued with those attributes which she requires from all her votaries. Those attributes are Friendship, Morality and Brotherly Love, as typified in our beautiful Masonic emblem, the Compasses.

How admirably the mighty influence of these attributes was illustrated in the lives and actions of the prominent sons of Masonry, who figured in the concerns of men during the last century, by their virtuous adaptation of the tenets of Masonry to the social and political wants of society, let the plaudits of an admiring world testify, by their oft-repeated hosannas to the heroism, valor, skill, and devoted patriotism of our generals, all of whom were Masons, in warring successfully against fearful odds, in defence of the inestimable privileges claimed by the wisdom, firmness and decision of that patriotic band, who drew and signed that priceless document, the Declaration of American Independence, forty-four of whom, out of fifty-six, were Masons. If this was accident or chance, it is most wonderful indeed! But to my task, more specifically.

From the year 2992, when the Genius of Masonry laid the first corner stone of a Grand Lodge, in the presence of, and under the protection and aid of our Heavenly Grand Master, the Almighty God of Nature, and commenced the erection of Solomon's Temple, we have the authority of writers, sacred and profane, to date the first organized association of Masons, for work as well as worship. Up to this time the Druidical mode of worship in the open air prevailed; men assembled in woods or groves, and each, for himself, addressed the Deity, according to his own idea of form or ritual, in public; and each bearing his idol before which he knelt, as representing some one of his mighty attributes. Now, for the first time, were the children of God to be assembled in church form, to offer their devotions to his holy name, as including all his attributes, as well as his eternity of existence, the Great I AM. The solemnization of its completion and dedication, in the presence of the assembled Craft, A. M. 3000, filled the world with wonder and admiration; and within its sacred courts, nothing was to be seen or heard but Harmony and Brotherly Love.

It pleased Almighty Providence, to fulfil some wise end, that this organization should be short of duration, for by the middle of the next century, the enemies of Masonry were let loose upon her, her beautiful earthly Temple razed to its foundation by fire and plunder, and her votaries made prisoners of war, and translated to a foreign and barbarous country; and though in the year 3470 it pleased the same All-merciful Providence to release the surviving remnant from captivity, and permit them to return and rebuild their Masonic Temple for his worship, we have few, and very faint intimations of the organization of a Grand Lodge, unless indeed the Tabernacle of Zerubabel may be so called; nor do we again hear of one until the year 5717, embracing a period of 2247 years. It is true, and history bears evidence, that in different countries and localities the Craft were occasionally assembled and elected a Grand Master, but he only assumed the title, and exercised the functions of Grand Master of the Craft for practical or operative, as well as speculative, purposes. Prominent, though promiscuous assemblages of this kind, seem to mark great and important events in the moral world, with such remarkable coincidence and promptness as to leave little doubt on the minds of the most skeptical of the direct interposition of an Almighty Providence in appointing their time of meeting.

St. Albans, the first Christian martyr, assembled the Craft in the year 300 A. C., and as their Grand Master gave them as his legacy some wise and wholesome instruction for their future conduct, and, Solon like, obligated them to certain written laws for their government and protection. This Worthy Brother Albanus, or St. Alban, as called after his martyrdom for the cause of Christianity, to which he had been converted by the preaching of Amphibalus at Caerleon, was a man wisely skilled in Geometry and Architecture, and therefore employed by King Carausius to surround the town of Verulam, in Britain, with a stone wall, and in it to build him a magnificent palace.

Our old constitutions affirm, and the following record proves, the position and influence of this brother thus: "St. Albans also loved Masons well, and cherished them much, and he made their pay right good, viz: two shillings per week, and three pence to their cheer; whereas, before that time, thro' all the land, a Mason had but a penny a day and his meat.

"He also obtained of the king a Charter for the Free Masons, for to hold a General Council, and give it the name of Assembly, and was thereat himself as Grand Master, and helped to make Masons, and gave them good Charges and Regulations."

This assemblage of the Craft at that momentous period in the world's history, could not have been without its influence under Divine Providence, in disseminating and establishing the wise and wholesome Code of Laws which had just been but a little while promulgated by the blessed Saviour of mankind as the will of his Heavenly Father, for the preservation and government of the human family; but which was being sternly, wickedly, and in some instances ferociously resisted by the barbarian ignorance which pervaded the world.

The agency which the Genius of Masonry was enabled to exercise through her intellectual teachings in the moral code, upon these unnatural, but powerful efforts of error and prejudice to destroy truth and religion, reason is not left to inference; for at this and all subsequent periods her sons are found nobly battling, even to the sacrifice of life, in the great, the god-like struggle for the promotion and establishment of virtue, as taught in that Holy Code.

Again the Craft are silent until the year 926 A. C., when Athelstane, the grandson of Alfred the Great, at the close of that memorable period, the Saxon Heptarchy, became the first anointed king of England, and feeling a deep and glowing interest in the Code of Laws above referred to, undertook, for the accomplishment of this holy purpose, to translate the Holy Bible, Hebrew and Greek, intc the Saxon language. And having accomplished this Herculean task, he sought thereby to diffuse the rays of knowledge and wisdom from this, our Great Masonic Light, to every corner of the dark and benighted world.

While he was being engaged in this Divine and giant labor, he caused his brother Edwin to assemble the Craft at York, and the record reads: "That the said king's brother, Prince Edwin, being taught Masonry, and taking upon him the charges of a Master Mason, for the love he had to the said Craft, and the honorable principles whereon it is founded, purchased a free charter of his father, for the Masons to have a Correction among themselves, as it was anciently expressed, or a Freedom, and Power to regulate themselves, to amend what might happen amiss within the Craft, and to hold a yearly Communication, and General Assembly.

"That accordingly Prince Edwin summoned all the Masons in the Realm to meet him in a Congregation at York, in June, Anno Domini 926, who came and composed a General or Grand Lodge of which he was Grand Master.

"And having brought with them all the old records and writings of the Craft extant, some in Greek, some in Latin, some in French and other languages, from the contents thereof that Assembly formed the Constitution and charges of an English Lodge, and made a law to preserve and observe the same in all time coming, and ordained good pay for the Working Masons."

This translation of our Divine Great Light, now illuminated the altar of every Lodge, when assembled for work, and the propagation of its great and holy truths and axioms were rapidly and widely disseminated through the British realm and her dependencies, and the name and title of Ancient York Mason was hailed in every country, as the advocate of Virtue, and patron, protector and defender of her holy tenets, Brotherly Love, Relief and Truth.

Peaceably, silently, harmoniously, the Genius of Masonry again pursues her high and holy calling amidst the busy scenes of real life in hamlet, town and country, until the year 1663, when, as if forewarned by an Almighty Providence, Charles II, who had been made a Mason during his exile, and yielding to the temptations of dissipation and sensuality, had neglected the high requirements of the Order; upon his restoration, immediately called the Craft together; who assembled under Henry Jermyn, Earl of St. Albans, G. M., Sir John Denham, D. G. M., Sir Christopher Wren and Mr. John Webb, Wardens, who passed some wise and wholesome regulations for the promotion and good of the Craft.

To show the deep and abiding interest which these skillful and zealous brothers felt and exercised for the promotion of Masonry, we will here quote from their record these six regulations, passed two hundred years ago:—

1. "That no person, of what degree soever, be accepted a Free Mason, unless in a regular Lodge, whereof one to be a Master, or Warden of that Division in which such Lodge is kept, and another to be a Craftsman in Masonry.

2. "That no person be hereafter accepted, but such as are able of body, honest in parentage, of good reputation, and an observer of the laws of the land.

3. "That no person, who shall be accepted a Free Mason, shall be admitted into any Lodge, until he has brought a certificate of the time and place of his acceptation, from the Master of the limit where he was made, and the Lodge kept; and the Master shall enrol the same in parchment, and shall give an account of such acceptation at every General Assembly.

4. "That every person, who is now a Free Mason, shall bring to the Master a note of the time of his acceptation, to the end that it may be enrolled in such priority of place as the brother deserves; and that the whole company and fellows may the better know each other.

5. "That for the future the said fraternity of Free Masons shall be regulated and governed by one Grand Master, and as many Wardens as the said society shall think fit to appoint at every General Assembly.

6. "That no person shall be accepted, unless he be twenty-one years old, or upwards."

From this period Masonry seems to have pursued the even tenor of her way, under this independent form of discipline, holding Lodges in different localities in England, for operative purposes, in the then Gothic style of architecure, until the memorable union of the Crowns in 1603. At this time the last of the Royal Tudors expired, and the first of the Royal Stewarts became king of all Britain, in the person of James I. At the same period the great Inigo Jones, the protege of William Herbert, Earl of Pembroke, returned from his travels into Italy, whither he had gone at the expense of that distinguished patron of the arts, to perfect himself in painting and drawing. He, however, laid aside the easel, and took up the Square, Level and Plumb, became the Vitruvius of Britain, the rival of Andrea Palladio, and of all the Italian reformers. The record goes on to say, "James I, Stewart, now the first king of all Britain, a Royal Brother Mason, and Royal Grand Master by prerogative, wishing for proper heads and hands for establishing the Augustan style here, was glad to find such a subject as Inigo Jones; he accordingly ordered the building a new palace at Whitehall. For this purpose he approved of the election of Brother Jones by the Craft, as Grand Master of England, to preside over the Lodges" until 1607; when, as the record further says,

"The king, with Grand Master Jones, and his Grand Wardens, Sir William Herbert, Earl of Pembroke, and Nicholas Stone, Master Masons to his Majesty, attended by many brothers in due form, and many eminent persons, walked to Whitehall gate, and leveled the footstone of the new banqueting house, with three great knocks, loud huzzas, sound of trumpets, and a purse of broad pieces of gold laid upon the stone, for the Masons to drink to the King and the Craft." It was the ceiling of this splendid room which afterwards received the fine pencil of the accomplished Peter Paul Rubens.

The best Craftsmen, from all parts, resorted to Grand Master Jones, who always allowed good wages, and seasonable time for instruction in the Lodges, which he constituted with excellent by-laws, and made them like the schools or academies of designs in Italy. He also held the Quarterly Communications of the Grand Lodge of Masters and Wardens, and the Annual General Assembly and Feast on St. John's Day. Under him and his expert and skilful Wardens, William Herbert and Nicholas Stone, the Augustan style of architecture was revived and flourished; men of great eminence, wealth and talents crowded the Lodges; he encouraged and received into them, Painters, Sculptors, Statuaries, Plasterers, &c.. from all parts; but no foreign architects, lest the true Augustan style should be rendered impure. It was this Nicholas Stone who had and kept up an authentic and precious copy of the laws and usages of Masonry, from the celebrated meeting at York, but which, as we shall see in our narrative, was burnt with many others equally valuable, at a subsequent period, by some too timid and over zealous Masons.

Scarcely had these eminent, wise and skilful brothers effected the publicity of these regulations, and put their Masonic household in order, when the devastating fire of 1666 laid the city of London in ashes. Sir C. Wren was then made D. G. Master, and to him and his associates in Masonry, as such, was confided the difficult task of remodeling the old, and rebuilding the new city, with all its public buildings, churches, &c. With what dexterity, neatness, order and dispatch, they performed this arduous task, it would take volumes to recount; volumes have been written in commendation of their operations. And their venerable and illustrious Grand Master, Sir Christopher Wren, lived to witness the realization of his judicious plans for rebuilding the city, and the erection of that stupendous sample of architecture, St. Paul's church.

The fame of Grand Master Wren and his Masonic associates now became world-wide; and kings, princes and noblemen sought admission into the Fraternity as "Free and Accepted Masons;" the benign influences of the Genius of Masonry in ameliorating the unbridled passions of men, were now seen and felt in every condition of society in which it had been brought to bear; and their superior skill in Geometry and Architecture rendered them desirable objects of patronage to the wealthy and powerful in all nations.

During all the period I have passed over, Lodges of Masons as such were only occasional or particular, for the purpose of receiving or initiating the profane man into the secrets of Masonry, and were held by any one or more Master Masons, at any place, or time, and without Charter or Warrant from any superior authority for so doing.

This, in the chronology of our History, brings us to the year 5717, before referred to, when the only four old Lodges then existing in England, met in London, and formed the first legally constituted Grand Lodge which had ever been held subjected to, and under the provisions of a Written Constitution; and at this time, and for all time to come, required all Lodges to be held by virtue of a Charter or Warrant from some legally constituted Grand Lodge.

Preston, writing in London in 1795, says:

"1. The old Lodge of St. Paul, now named the Lodge of Antiquity No. 1, formerly held at the Goose and Gridiron, in St. Paul's churchyard, is still extant, and regularly meets at the Free Masons Tavern, in Great Queen street, Lincoln's Inn Fields, on the 4th Wednesday of every month. This Lodge is in a very flourishing state, and possesses many valuable records and other eminent relics.

"2. The old Lodge No. 2, formerly held at the Crown, in Parker's Lane, in Drury Lane, has been extinct for fifty years, from the death of its members.

"3. The old Lodge No. 3, formerly held at the Apple Tavern, in Charles street, Covent Garden, has been dissolved for many years, on account of some schism among its members.

"4. The old Lodge No. 4, formerly held at the Rummer and Grapes, in Channel Row, Westminster, was removed to the Horn Tavern, in New Palace Yard, and finding it declining, merged itself into the Somerset House Lodge, and became a new and flourishing Lodge under the Constitution of the Grand Lodge."

They also requested Dr. Thos. Desaguliers and Rev. James Anderson to search all the old records, and to draw up for their approval, a literal copy of the old charges and regulations, and to submit them in the form of a Constitution for revision and adoption.

This duty Brother Anderson performed, and submitted it to the Grand Lodge, in 1721, at which time his report was received and referred to a committee of fourteen old and experienced Masons, for their revisal and criticism. The report of this committee was made to the Grand Lodge in 1722, and unanimously confirmed, and ordered to be printed under the care and supervision of Brother Anderson.

We have now arrived at the origin of the M. Wor. Grand Lodge of Virginia, or more properly speaking in narrative style, at one of those ever memorable epochs in the annals of time, the interesting incidents of which are seen and felt, for good or for evil, by the actors in them, and propagated through their successors, until by the unerring tests of the lights and experience of time, future generations shall realize to which they belong. And here I beg you to bear with me while I invite you to look back, and hastily speculate on the governments which have existed, and controlled the destiny of Masons and Masonry up to this time.

All forms of government, in every country, had acknowledged a privileged class, who being anointed, *jure divino*, gave laws for the government of the people, who were considered and treated as the subjects, or in some degree, the property of their governors. These laws were often the result of whim, caprice or passion, and were enforced without any regard whatever to the wishes, feelings or wants of the governed. A government and laws predicated upon the consent of the governed, or in other words, the equal rights of man to a voice in the laws creating a government for himself, had never entered into the minds of existing powers.

But in the meantime a continent had been discovered, separated from these powers by two thousand miles of water, roamed over, but not possessed, by the nomadic Red Man of the forest, without law, government or restraint of any kind. This continent was now fast growing in population and wealth, by emigrants from the old world, for the most part conscientious dissenters from her laws, governments and restraints of religion. At this distance, too, the plea of immemorial usage lost its influence, amid the chrystal springs and virgin soil which furnished them bread and water.

Here it pleased Divine Providence to put it into the heart of man to make the experiment of man's governing himself, or in other words, he should so carry out the holy injunction of "doing unto others as under like circumstances he would be done by," and thus enact only such laws as, while governing others, should exercise the same wholesome control over himself.

The executive officers of these laws being selected for their capacity, firmness and skill, by the united suffrages of the governed, and thereby requiring their implicit obedience; and the strict accountability of these officers at certain and stated periods of re-election, develop at once the internal polity of a well regulated Lodge of Masons.

The wise predicate indispensably necessary to this happiest system of government and laws is, that none but Master Masons are suffragans; and why so? because every Initiate is required to prove himself a man of virtuous principles, and as he progresses from one degree to another, to be subject to a critical examination of his acquirements, until finally he proves himself well educated in the law and ritual of his profession.

Is it at all wonderful, then, that an intimate acquaintance with the high behests of Masonry should at once actuate the patriot and philanthropist to bring them to bear upon the social and political relations of his fellow man, in this great and untried experiment of self-government? We think not. And accordingly we find them applying for a Charter to hold a Lodge in the village of Norfolk, in Virginia, on the 22d day of December, 1733.

The first Lodge of Ancient York Masons, then, chartered for Virginia, was in 1733, by the name, title and designation of the Royal Exchange Lodge, No. 172, and held its meetings in the above borough on the first Thursday of every month: prophetic period, indeed! The infant Washington was now on the banks of the noble Potomac unconsciously nursing with his mother's milk, and growing in physical form and symmetry; and from her richly stored mind receiving the primordial germs of that heroism and devotion to the cause of Virtue and Patriotism, which, in their maturity, were to inspire inextinguishable confidence in the cause of civil liberty; and personally to lead the handful of combatants for the equal rights of man, against the pampered hordes of privileged classes, to a successful and glorious victory on the plains of Yorktown.

The second Lodge was chartered by the Grand Lodge of Scotland for Port Royal, Caroline county, Va., by the mother-name of Kilwinning Cross, in 1755.

The third was chartered by the same for Petersburg, Va., by the name of Blandford Lodge, No. 83, in 1757.

The fourth was chartered by the R. W. G. Lodge of Massachusetts for Fredericksburg, Va., on 21st July, 1758, having some years before obtained a Dispensation under which they worked until they were duly constituted by Charter on this day.

The fifth was chartered by the Grand Lodge of England for Hampton, in Virginia, on 6th November, 1773, by the name of St. Tamany; and on the same day, by the same, No. 6 was chartered for Williamsburg, Va., by the name of Williamsburg.

The seventh was chartered by the same for Gloucester on 6th November, 1773, by the name of Botetourt.

The eighth was chartered by the Grand Lodge of Scotland for Cabin Point, April 5, 1775, by the name of Cabin Point Royal Arch.

Beside these, I find on the Registry of the Grand Lodge of Scotland, that St. John's Lodge, No. 111, was constituted at Norfolk, Virginia, in 1741. I also find there was a Lodge at Falmouth, Virginia, and a Lodge chartered for Yorktown, in Virginia, August 1, 1755, No. 204.

It will be seen that these Charters embrace a period of time from 1733 to 1775, or 42 years of the existence of the Grand Lodge of England. During this interval, schisms and intestine troubles convulsed this Grand Lodge; and as they exercised a manifest influence on the Lodges in Virginia in law, ritual and work, it is necessary we should pause here in our history, and review the most prominent of them.

The Grand Lodge of "Ancient York Masons," assembled at York by Edwin, A. D. 926, in the North of England, acting under charges and regulations of immemorial origin and constitution, continued its existence but feebly; occasionally meeting, and receiving the reports of the names of Masons made in "Occasional" Lodges, as those were called which merely assembled without Charters, for that purpose alone; and also to register and supervise the doings of "Particular" Lodges, as those were called which held regular monthly meetings and practised the Ancient York Ritual. Of these last, four only were left in the South of England at the beginning of the 18th century, as before stated, and feeling the necessity of a more efficient organization, met at London in 1717 and formed a Grand Lodge for England of Free and Accepted Masons, giving to the Grand Lodge of York the more imposing title of Grand Lodge for all England.

At this Grand Lodge they passed two laws, which, as they gave rise to nearly all the difficulties with which they were subsequently beset, it is necessary to repeat:

"1st. That no Lodge should thereafter be held without a Charter or Warrant from some accredited and legal Grand Lodge; and pronouncing all Clandestine not thus constituted.

"2d. That no Lodge confer more than the first or entered apprentice degree; reserving to the Grand Lodges alone the right to confer the second and third degrees."

Under this Constitution, as published by Brother Anderson, the two Grand Lodges went on in harmony and good feeling; but London being the place of meeting of various national bodies, as well as the great market of England, the Grand Lodge of London soon outstripped her sister in numbers, talent and influence, and her Charters were eagerly sought for, until through the instrumentality of the wide spread colonial possessions of the government, her ritual and laws had extended nearly over the globe, and gave her a position and influence which became an object of jealousy, if not rivalry, with some of her sister Grand Lodges.

The Ancient Kilwinning Masons in Scotland, so called, like the Ancient York Masons, from the town of Kilwinning, in which they professed to have practised the Scotch Ritual from remote ages, assembled and formed the Kilwinning Grand Lodge for Scotland, and claimed the sanction of antiquity for their mode of work and their laws.

The still more Ancient Carrickfeargus Masons of Ireland, so called from the town of that name, from which they hailed, assembled and formed the Carrickfeargus Grand Lodge for Ireland.

These four Grand Lodges, each within their own geographical limits, formed and exercised Masonic authority throughout the island of Great Britain, and though differing much in the Ritual of Work, yet governed by the same charges and regulations, they steadily and zealously labored for the one great end and object—the amelioration of the human family and the diffusion of the invaluable tenets of Masonry: Brotherly Love, Relief and Truth.

About this period, a few restive spirits in the city of London, feeling the stringency of the above laws, which forbid Subordinate Lodges to confer the second and third degrees, and reserving them to be conferred by the Grand Lodge as marks of distinction and rewards to those only who had rendered some essential benefit to the Craft, proceeded by bribery and persuasion to induce some misguided and inconsiderate Master Mason to assemble and secretly confer upon them these degrees, pleading as justification the well known inherent privilege of the four old Lodges, and their practice of this reserved right in their midst.

They then in turn, proceeded to impart and confer these degrees on many others, who, supposing they had received them legally, applied for admission to visit some of the legally constituted Lodges, but were detected and refused. By this means it became known to the Grand Lodge, and many and stringent resolutions were passed to arrest the abuse, but in vain.

Resolutions of pardon for past offences were passed, if accompanied with the promise of reform; but many, who had received these degrees in this illegal manner, had traveled into distant countries, been well received as visiters, and had conferred upon them higher degrees and honors; and emboldened by their success, publicly proclaimed their determination to persevere in conferring the degrees.

The Grand Lodge of England having exhausted all lenient and persuasive measures, proceeded to denounce them as Clandestine Masons; and in order to detect them more readily, made a violent and important change in their own ritual, which they ordered all chartered Lodges to adopt and practise.

The malcontents, gladly availing themselves of this capital error of the Grand Lodge, at once denounced them as innovators, and stigmatized them with the name of "Modern" Masons, while they claimed to be the pure "Ancient York" Masons, who alone had preserved the old Landmarks from desecration and removal.

The Schismatics now boldly appropriated to themselves the exclusive and honorable title of "Ancient Masons," acting under the Old York Constitutions, cemented and consecrated by immemorial observance, and taking advantage of this popular cry, proceeded in 1738 to form an independent Grand Lodge, drew up a code of laws for their government, and issued Warrants for the constitution of new Lodges "under the true ancient system of Free Masonry."

This Grand Lodge, with this imposing title, at once became popular, and men of rank, piety and talents flocked to it, its funds increased, and with them its charities multiplied, and its benevolence enlarged, until the public at large, who had all along sided with the Grand Lodge of England against the Schismatics, settled down upon the conviction that the practical object and end of all Masonry was the immediate relief of suffering humanity, and the amelioration of the passions of men. And as they daily saw men of the first rank in society and of high order of talents associating themselves masonically with each, they very naturally and justly concluded that the schism was produced and kept up by some trivial change of ritual and internal polity with which they had no concern.

The Constitutional Grand Lodge of England, conscious of the rectitude and virtue of her position, made no exertions to disseminate her teachings, and multiply her influence by the spreading of Lodges. Not so with the Schismatics, or "Ancient Grand Lodge." Knowing and feeling the inexplicable error of their position, which, while it originated in disobedience to law, had the authority of usage, and had now, in consequence of the badly considered proceedings of the Grand Lodge of England in violating a sacred principle, forced them into the attitude of preservers of the ancient Landmarks; not only did they decline all offers of amnesty for past offences and resolutions of reconciliation, but, entirely unwilling to abandon office and honors which they now possessed, they sought by every adventitious means to strengthen their position and diffuse their influence.

Let us now turn our attention for a short time to the progress of Masonry on the continent of Europe.

Masonry had been practised in France from 1700 to 1725 by such English residents as trade and speculation carried there, without Warrant or Charter for their Lodges, under the assumed primitive inherent privilege of the Old York Lodges.

The first Charter for a regular Lodge in France was granted by the Grand Lodge of England in 1725 to Lord Derwentwater, Maskeline, Higuetzy and some other English followers of the Pretender, who met at an eating-honse in the Rue des Boucheries; among whom, and at or about which time, in 1728, the notorious Chevalier Ramsay appeared and added some new degrees, or Hauts Grades, pretending to derive them from the Scotch Ritual. They, however, found little favor, until by his management Lord Harnouster was elected Grand Master of France in December, 1736, and Ramsay was installed Grand Orator.

In 1740, he went over to England and offered his Royal Arch to the Grand Lodge of England, who declined it, and gave him no countenance. The Schismatics or Grand Lodge of Ancients, however, received his overtures, and seeing that the rage for innovation was now fairly in the ascendant, they adopted it as part of their Ritual, and openly taught that Ancient Craft Masonry consisted of four degrees, including the Royal Arch, while the Moderns taught only three.

In this year Ramsay returned to France, and taught and widely disseminated his Holy Royal Arch.

This unbridled form of independent organization was not without its evils, and led to many gross and lasting departures from Masonic Law and Ritual. Among these was the most conspicuous of electing a Master for life, and when he resigned or demitted, in the lan guage of that day, to engraft him as a life-member upon all deliberative assemblages of Masons. To this evil may, we think, be traced the life-membership of Past Masters in this country; for it does not seem to have been practised anywhere else in Europe.

Feeling the disastrous consequences of this unrestrained government, in 1743 they applied to the Grand Lodge of England for a Provincial Grand Lodge, which was granted, and Count de Clermont appointed P. G. Master, under the style of "Grand Loge Anglaise de France." Clermont, however, proved very inefficient; political objections were urged against the Masonic organization; and in 1756, the "Grand Lodge of France" was formed, declaring themselves iudependent of England. This Grand Lodge to be composed of the officers elect, and of the Masters for life, of the Parisian Lodges—the Count to continue Grand Master, and to appoint his Deputies. In the exercise of this last power, he appointed a man of such rude and vulgar manners, of such low origin—by name Lacorne, that the respectable members refused to sit with him, and withdrew.

In consequence of their formal protest, he was removed, and the notorious Chaillon de Joinville appointed.

Things now reached a crisis. The officers elected under Lacorne were also displaced, and many members were expelled. These, on their part, resorted to violence to force themselves on the meeting of the Grand Lodge, until the Lieutenant of Police interfered, and ordered the Grand Lodge to close their meetings. The expelled members continued their irregular meetings. The Count died in 1771, and they invited the Duke of Chartres, (afterwards of Orleans,) to take the Grand Mastership, which he accepted.

At this time they proposed a union with the Grand Lodge, upon terms of amnesty, which being accepted, the Grand Lodge of France again resumed labors.

But during all this interval, the celebrated de Joinville, the propagandist of Prussian Consistories, had been at work diffusing his "Hauts Grades;" and these powers now claimed and exercised rights over the three symbolic degrees, and under this pretence chartered many Lodges, and assumed a position of defiance to the power of the Grand Lodge, until nothing could be seen of the pure Ritual; all was anarchy and confusion.

Again a union was proposed, and in December, 1771, the Grand

Orient of France was formed by a compromise, the Grand Lodge declared extinct, and the Duke de Luxembourg declared President. By this compromise, in its incipiency the recognition of these degrees was forced upon the Grand Lodge under the Duke of Chartres, who had been in 1770 elected Grand Master of all Councils, Chapters and Scotch Lodges in France.

A few zealous adherents to the Ancient Ritual still resisted all these encroachments, and continued to assemble as the Grand Lodge of France, until the Revolution of that unhappy time put an end to both for the time.

On the 15th of August, 1738, Frederick the Great, afterwards King of Prussia, was initiated into Masonry, at Brunswick, in a Scots Lodge, or Lodge of Ancients, being then Prince Royal. And as this monarch is to figure very largely in the future history of Masonry, more especially in the higher degrees, it is necessary to impress on the memory the circumstances connected with his initiation, and his conduct under it.

In the words of Preston, "So highly did he approve of the institution, that on his accession to the throne he commanded a Grand Lodge to be formed at Berlin, 'Les Trois Globes;' and for that purpose obtained a patent from Edinburgh. Thus was Masonry established in Prussia, and under that sanction it has continued ever since. His Majesty's attachment to the society soon induced him to establish several new Regulations for the advantage of the Fraternity; and among others he ordained—1st. That no person should be made a Mason, unless his character was unimpeachable, and his manner of living and profession respectable. 2d. That every member should pay 25 rix dollars, or £4 3s., for the first degree; 50 rix dollars, or £8 6s., for the second degree; and 100 rix dollars, or £16 12s., on his being made a Master Mason. 3d. That he should remain at least three months in each degree—And 4th. That every sum received should be divided by the Grand Treasurer into three parts: one to defray the expenses of the Lodge; another to be applied to the relief of distressed brethren; and the third to be allotted to the poor in general."

As the Masonry of Scotland is to occupy a very conspicuous position in the history of the Grand Lodge of Virginia, let us now turn our attention for a few minutes to the condition of that Grand Lodge.

The earliest authentic history we have, dates only to James I, in 1430. That monarch, renowned for his liberal patronage of the arts and sciences, assumed the title of protector of Masonry; and though not a Master Mason himself, he appointed for the Order a Grand Master, and decreed that every Mason initiated should pay him £4 annually.

The Fraternity of Free Masons in Scotland having always owned their king and sovereign as their Grand Master, when not a Mason himself, he appointed one of the brethren to preside as his deputy at all their meetings, and to regulate all matters concerning the Craft.

Accordingly, says the record, we find this eminent patron of learning countenancing the Lodges with his "presence" as the Royal Grand Master, till "he settled a yearly revenue of four pounds Scots, to be paid by every Master Mason in Scotland to a Grand Master chosen by the brethren and approved by the crown—one nobly born, or an eminent clergyman, who had his deputies in cities and counties, and every new brother at entrance paid him a fee. His office empowered him to regulate in the Fraternity what should not come under the cognizance of law courts; to him appealed both Mason and lord, or the builder and founder, when at variance, in order to prevent law pleas; and in his absence they appealed to his Deputy or Grand Wardens that resided next to the premises."

This continued the usage until 1441, the reign of James II, when William St. Clair, Earl of Orkney and Caithness, but better known to us as the Baron of Roslin, obtained a grant of this office for himself. He now countenanced the Lodges with his presence, propagated the Royal Art, and built the splendid chapel of Roslin Castle, that magnificent sample of Gothic architecture; and during the time of Grand Master Roslin, the princes and nobles built many other stately and beautiful edifices.

By another decree of this said James II, this office of Grand Master of Scotland was made hereditary to the said William St. Clair and his heirs and successors in the Barony of Roslin. Nobly, generously, and truly did this eminent family sustain the Craft under this grant, until the period we are now speaking of, 1736, when the then G. M. St. Clair indicated the advantages which would necessarily result to the Craft by having a Grand Master to preside over them of their own free choice and election, and gave notice of his intention to resign into their hands his hereditary title to the office, and requested them to look round for a suitable successor.

Accordingly he assembled the Craft at Kilwinning Grand Lodge, in the town of Edinburgh, on the 30th day of November, 1736, being St. Andrew's day, and sent in his formal transfer of the grant, and resignation of office.

In the fullness of their masonic feelings, and in gratitude for this noble and disinterested act, they proceeded to an election, when by a unanimous voice, William St. Clair of Roslin was elected, proclaimed and installed Grand Master of Masons of all Scotland.

These ancient Scotch Kilwinning Masons professed and claimed to date from the period when Mahommedanism overran all Asia, Africa and Europe, desolating and destroying the Augustan architecture, between 505 and 771, when Charlemagne and Hugh Capet succeeded in reviving the Grecian and Roman style of architecture, and became patrons of Masonry. They also at this time, 1736, professed to have saved from oblivion many higher degrees of Masonry; and from these Ramsay must have taken his Holy Royal Arch.

Let us now return to the Grand Lodge of England, in London, and survey the operation of parties there: taking the advantage of a rupture among the members of a Lodge at York, they granted a Charter to the malcontents for opening a new Lodge; which usurpation of jurisdiction was protested against by the Grand Lodge of York, but their appeal was unheeded, and the breach greatly widened by Grand Master the Earl of Crawford, who, in 1734, appointed Provincial Deputy Grand Masters for Northumberland, Lancashire and Durham, and by the constitution of new Lodges in those counties, all within the jurisdiction of said Grand Lodge.

They again, but ineffectually remonstrated. Feeling their own weakness, and being stung by the evidently assumed and overbearing conduct of the Grand Lodge of England, it is by no means to be wondered at, that seeing the respectability in numbers, rank and wealth, of the schismatics, they should have felt and indulged a secret satisfaction at the claim set up by them to the authority of the Ancient York Masons for their proceedings. They therefore quietly and silently looked on, when the malcontents in London, in 1738, openly and publicly organized their Grand Lodge, under the assumed authority and auspices of the Grand Lodge of York, claiming the captivating title of Ancient York Masons; and to make their ritual of work more captivating, if not more grand, sublime and beautiful, added a Fourth Degree, the Holy Royal Arch, which they practised in Chapters held under a Master's Warrant, and which the Grand Lodge of England stigmatized as innovation, and forbade to be practised by their Subordinates; at the same time contending that their Third Degree contained all the essentials of the Holy

Royal Arch, and in their ritual, teaching that the M. M.'s W—d was never lost.

Ramsay came over from France at this juncture, and remained a year in London, first offering his Royal Arch to the Grand Lodge of England, but meeting with no favor, he then applied to the Ancients, who, it seems from all the concurrent testimony of the time, received it. But Lawrence Dermot, a very conspicuous and influential member of the new Grand Lodge, and Grand Secretary, seeing the many glaring anachronisms which it contained, set to work and so remodeled it as to adapt it to the work and ritual of the Third Degree, as taught by the Grand Lodge of Ancients, who contended and taught that the M. M.'s W—d was lost during the erection of the first Temple, and consequently dated it from the rebuilding of the second.

About this time, 1730, a reckless, misguided man, Samuel Pritchard, published an expose of the Three Degrees as taught and practised by the Grand Lodge of England. This work, like that published in this country in 1827, produced a great excitement, and when the Schismatics established their Grand Lodge in 1738, they professed to be in possession of the Ancient York work, and consequently this expose did not affect them, even among the unitiated. This served only to increase their numbers in every direction, and consequently to add greatly to their influence and rank among Masons. The members of this Grand Lodge who travelled into foreign countries were all well received and complimented on their style and proficiency; and when they happened to be Grand or Subordinate Officers, or men of rank and distinction, returned laden with honors and marks of approbation and distinction.

The anonymous and celebrated expose of Masonry called Jachin and Boaz, was published about 1736, and as it professed to be an expose of all Masonry in the Blue Degrees, was readily seized upon by the anti-masons to lampoon and vilify the Institution; but as it worked a confirmation among the ancients of the antiquity and authenticity of their ritual among Masons, they felt rather complimented by its appearance, and gave themselves no trouble about it.

And now we have seen the condition of the unwritten or oral teachings of our blessed Institution in the several Grand Lodges of the world at this time, each claiming antiquity and immemorial usage; and it is only matter of the utmost wonder that there should have been preserved from the remotest periods of history, both traditional and recorded, so perfect an account of these degrees, and so admirable a harmony of its allegorical teachings.

Volumes have been written by its enemies to prove its modern origin. Genius, learning and talents of the highest order, in every country and in almost every language, have been put in requisition to show its origin, but all they have been able to accomplish is, to prove beyond all doubt, that though aided by the art of printing in 1420, and by the numerous manuscripts of public and private libraries before and since that period, they have utterly failed to locate a period when Masonry was not taught in both its operative and speculative character, as now demonstrated in the ritual of the Three Degrees. It remained for our own day and time to enter the lists in the settlement of this question.

Professor Stuart of Andover, in Massachusetts, set himself gravely to the task: and Col. Stone, in his notorious octavo volume of five hundred and sixty pages of letters to the Hon. John Q. Adams, upon the Morgan affair, and Masonry generally, roundly endorses Prof. Stuart's "irresistible conclusions," as he calls them.

Stuart says, the question of modern origin is proved beyond all cavil or doubt, by the Roman termination of Jubela, Jubelo, and Jubelum.

Let us for a moment examine this "proof beyond all cavil" of the Professor, and we think it will plainly appear to be "proof beyond all cavil" of what he presumes to deny. The three words of Hebrew origin, legitmate and true, in the sense and place used, pass down the stream of time, until arriving among some Ephramites in Masonry, who from some defect of voice or education, could not pronounce them aright, confirms their antiquity by an attempt to preserve them in their own vernacular tongue. A very similar, but much more barbarous, philological abuse of phonetic privilege, is found in the following authentic record:

In 1696, Sir John Locke, writing to the Earl of Pembroke, says, "I have obtained a copy from Mr. Collins, from the Bodleian Library, of a manuscript copy in the handwriting of Henry VI., or about two hundred and sixty years before that time, which contains the trial of a Free Mason before him." This manuscript we have now in print, with notes by Mr. Locke, and a wonderful curiosity it is to the antiquarian and scholar:

"To the question, How came it (Masonry) in England? the accused replies: Peter Gower journeyed into Egypt, Syria, and every land where the Venetians had planted Masonry, and winning entrance in all Lodges of Masons, became possessed of all their knowledge, and returning, established a Lodge at Groton, from whence it was taught in France, and in process of time passed into England."

Now who, my Brothers, do you suppose this Peter Gower was? Shade of our illustrious, wise and honored brother, and learned philosopher! Shall I tell the barbarous destruction of thy time-honored name? Sage of Andover, learn from this how little value can be attached to philology in proof of chronology! This Peter Gower was no less a personage than Pythagoras, the sage of Samos, in Greece, who flourished in the time of the tyrant Polycratis, about 500 years B. C. His Grecian name ending in ras, illy comported with the soft aspirates which form the termination of the refined Gaul, and therefore, to this day, they spell and write his name, "Pythagore." And here we have "proof, beyond all cavil or doubt," that the inventor or discoverer of the forty-seventh problem of Euclid was a Frenchman, according to Professor Stuart's mode of reasoning.

Col. Stone says further, by the same authority, that these words of Roman termination have no meaning in themselves, thereby proving they are not of Hebrew origin, all of which words have an intrinsic or self-demonstrating meaning.

Had this most "skilful of linguists and learned of men," as Col. Stone calls Professor Stuart, examined the whole subject with as much candor, as he has acrimony, he would have found there are three words of admitted Hebrew origin, and of good phonetic kindred, Jabal, Jebal, Jubal, which have a meaning intrinsically important to the subject under discussion, and which, by far less philological barbarity might, in passing through the various languages of the teachers of Masonry, been forced to assume the shape in which these words reached the beginning of the last century, than did the name of Pythagoras as above defined.

But enough of this by way of digression; it is only matter of astounding wonder that the Landmarks of the Ritual of Masonic work, and their speculative teachings, being orally taught under the most solemn injunctions of secrecy, should have been preserved and reached the time we are speaking of with such sameness and philological accuracy as they have. Another convincing proof of the interposition and protection of an Almighty Providence.

In the dissemination of this Ritual, the Grand Lodge of Scotland seems to have acted with the Schismatics, for though the latter granted no Charters for this continent, during the early period of their existence as a Grand Lodge, yet the Lodges who obtained

Charters from Scotland—and they were much more numerous, practised what was called the Scotch Ritual, but which was the same, or nearly so, as taught by the Grand Lodge of Ancients. Hence these two Grand Lodges, actuated by the same motive, the propagation and ultimate ascendancy of their peculiar mode of work, acted in unison. Being composed of the most influential men in both kingdoms, for their learning, piety and devotion to Masonry, their success is not a matter of surprise.

Having now given you a history of the Ritual of Ancient York Masonry, it is necessary to our task to pause and take a view of the course of legislation, dependent on and growing out of the difficulties which beset its advocates at this time.

We have seen in the former part of this narrative that immediately after the rebellion was over in 1716, the four Lodges then remaining in London met, with some old brethren, and formed and opened a Grand Lodge in 1717, and elected Brother Antony Sayer G. M.; he was succeeded in 1718, by Brother George Payne, and Brother Payne by Dr. Desagulier, in 1719. In 1720, R. W. Brother George Payne was re-elected Grand Master; and now we invite your particular attention to a portion of the record.

"It was now recommended to the brethren, the strictest observance of the communications, and that they should bring to the Grand Lodge any old writings and records concerning Masons and Masonry, to show the good usages of old. Many manuscripts were accordingly brought, for they had nothing as yet in print; but many of the most valuable concerning Lodges, regulations, charges, secrets, and usages, particularly one written by Nicholas Stone, the Warden under Grand Master Inigo Jones, were too hastily burnt by scrupulous brothers, that they might not fall into strange hands, by being printed with the contemplated Book of Constitutions."

It was at this feast, June 24, 1721, that G. M. Payne ordered Dr. Desagulier and Mr. James Anderson to collect the Constitutions and Laws into one body, to be revised and amended, and after being approved, to be printed, which was accordingly done, reported and confirmed, Dec. 27, 1721; and is the same as now called Anderson's Constitutions.

Preston, in the 11th edition of his Illustrations, (1804,) says: "In compliment to the brethren of the four old Lodges, by whom the Grand Lodge was first formed, it was resolved, 'that every privilege which they collectively enjoyed by virtue of their immemorial rights, they should still continue to enjoy; and that no law, rule or regulation to be hereafter made or passed in Grand Lodge should ever deprive them of such privilege or encroach on any Landmark which was at that time established as the standard of Masonic government.' "

This resolution being confirmed, the old Masons in the Metropolis, agreeably to the resolutions of the brethren at large, vested all their inherent privileges as individuals in the four old Lodges, in trust that they would never suffer the old charges and Ancient Landmarks to be infringed. The four old Lodges then agreed to extend their patronage to every Lodge which should hereafter be constituted by the Grand Lodge, according to the new regulations of the Society; and while such Lodges acted in conformity to the Ancient Constitutions of the Order, to admit their Masters and Wardens to share with them all the privileges of the Grand Lodge, excepting precedence of rank. Matters being thus amicably adjusted, the four old Lodges considered their attendance on the future communications of the Society as unnecessary; and, therefore, like the other Lodges, trusted implicitly to their Masters and Wardens, resting satisfied that no measure of importance would be adopted without their approbation. The officers of the old Lodges, however, soon began to discover that the new Lodges, being equally represented with them in the communications, might, in process of time, so far outnumber the old ones as to have it in their power, by a majority, to encroach on, or even subvert the privileges of the original Masons of England, which had been centred in the four old Lodges, with the concurrence of the brethren at large; therefore, they very wisely united in forming a code of laws for the future government of the Society, to which was annexed a conditional clause, which the G. Master for the time being, his successors, and the Master of every Lodge to be hereafter constituted, were bound to preserve inviolate in all time coming. To commemorate this circumstance, it has been customary since that time for the Master of the oldest Lodge to attend every Grand Installation, and taking precedence of all present, the Grand Master only excepted, to deliver the Book of the original Constitutions to the newly Installed G. Master, on his engaging to support the ancient charges and general regulations. That conditional clause above referred to, runs thus:

"Every *annual* Grand Lodge has an *inherent* power and authority to make *new* regulations, or to alter *these*, for the *real benefit* of this *ancient* Fraternity: *provided always*, that the *old Landmarks be carefully preserved:* and that such alterations and new regulations be proposed and agreed to at the third quarterly Communication preceding the Grand Feast; and that they be offered also to the perusal of *all* the brethren before dinner, in writing, *even* of the *yoüngest entered apprentice;* the approbation and consent of the *majority* of *all* the brethren present being absolutely necessary to make the same binding and obligatory."

This remarkable clause, with thirty-eight regulations preceding it, all of which are printed in the first edition of the Book of Constitutions, were approved and confirmed by one hundred and fifty brethren, at an annual Assembly and Feast at Stationer's Hall, 24th June, 1721; and in their presence subscribed by the Masters and Wardens of the four *old Lodges on the one part;* and by Philip, Duke of Wharton, their Grand Master, his Grand Wardens, and the Masters and Wardens of sixteen Lodges, which had been constituted by the Grand Lodge of England between 1717 and 1721, *on the other part.*

The four old Lodges, in consequence of the above compact, in which they considered themselves a distinct party, continued to act by their original Ancient York authority; and so far from surrendering any of their rights, had them frequently ratified and confirmed by the whole Fraternity in Grand Lodge assembled, who always acknowledged their independent and immemorial power to practise the rites of Masonry.

The necessity of ascertaining, fixing and printing the original Constitutions of Masonry, as the standard by which all future laws in the Society were to be regulated, was so clearly understood by the whole Fraternity at this time, that it was established as an unerring rule at every Installation, public and private, for many years after, to make the Grand Master, and the Masters and Wardens of every Lodge, engage to abide by, and support, the original Constitutions; and to the observance of which also, as well as the ancient charges, every Mason was bound at his initiation.

The precise period at which this invaluable usage was discontinued and substituted by the reading of the so-called charges in each degree as practised at present, we have not the means of ascertaining; but certain it is, the change was ill-advised, and has produced no good result, unless it may be in the economy of time necessary to confer the degrees: for there can be no doubt of the soundness of the old axiom, that "if anything be worth doing, it is worth doing well." These emphatic charges, so beautifully illustrative of the whole duty of a Mason to God, his neighbor and himself, are comprised in six short articles, the last containing six short sections. They should be imbedded in the memory of every wise and prudent brother as a safeguard or security against innovation and error.

Thus was the universality of Masonry, its admitted and highest glory, proclaimed to the Fraternity, and a standard of government intended to operate alike in all nations published to the world. The extreme simplicity of its provisions, and the laconic style in which those provisions are detailed, render it at once a model for all legislators, and proclaim the irresistible power of truth, reason and virtue, which form the basis of its structure. A century and a half has now passed since its promulgation in print; it has been translated into every language of civilization, and been acted on under all the incidents of local usage, policy and government; yet such are its most eccentric and peculiar features and provisions, that it has received the unqualified approbation of the good and wise in all countries. It says to king and keyser, to patrician and plebian, to the aristocracy and the plain republican, though wealth, power and the force of circumstances, may make distinctions in your ranks and conditions by the consent or rather convention of society, yet when tested by the Masonic Level of virtue, morality and patriotism, those distinctions among men are utterly untenable and useless; while the pre-eminence which attaches to a virtuous, abiding and willing application of the glorious requirements of the Masonic charges and Constitutions thus embodied, will give to its possessor a distinction and a rank, as stable as truth, and lasting as time.

The thunders of the Vatican, the terrors of the Inquisition, and the anathemas of Fanaticism, have each been tried, and signally failed, in their unholy warfare upon the humble and unpretending possessors of this distinction. Glorious and imperishable evidences of the indomitable power of Virtue and Morality! These noble achievments of inflexible fidelity to the cause of Masons and Masonry, will last through all time, and finally cause your bright names to illumine the holy records of the eternal world.

Pardon me, my Brothers, for this digression, and let us resume the narrative. Of one important fact I had neglected to inform you: The framers of this Constitution decided that all Lodges to be constituted should confer only the first or entered apprentice's degree, reserving to the Grand Lodge the right to pass and raise, and in the fullness of their gratitude to the four old Lodges, continued to them the Ancient York authority of Entering, Passing and Raising; for under that Constitution, any number of Masons, with the knowledge and consent of the sheriff of the bailiwick in which such meeting was held, had and exercised the inherent privilege of conferring any degree of which they were capable, and if at these meetings, one was a Master, Warden or Fellow Craft of the District in which such meeting was held: thus a meeting of Apprentices conferred that degree, of Fellow Crafts the second degree, and of Master Masons the third.

Thus it will be seen, there was in London at this moment, two authorities for dispensing the benefits of Masonry, alike ameneable to the same Constitutions, yet from the nature of their internal polity requiring somewhat different and modified regulations.

While this was going on in the North of England, at London, Masonry in the South was flourishing under the same Constitutions and charges as adopted by Edwin in 926, at York. They held their Annual Assemblies or Grand Lodges, elected Grand Masters, constituted Lodges, and did and performed all acts necessary for the promotion of Masonry, and maintained the title of Ancient York Masons and Grand Lodge of all England, while the Grand Lodge of London, under the title of Free and Accepted Masons, was styled the Grand Lodge of England.

The meetings of this last were held quarterly, including the Annual Communication, which was termed the Grand Feast, and at which the elections took place, and all new regulations or amendments of old ones were considered and adopted. These quarterly meetings became necessary for three reasons: 1st. To confer the honors of Passing and Raising on those recommended by the Subordinate Lodges; 2d. To exercise an immediate and continuous control over the actions of their Subordinates; and 3d. To dispense advantageously the provisions of the Grand Charity.

The honor of originating this Grand Charity Fund and Committee, is due to Francis Scott, Earl of Dalkeith, afterwards Duke of Buccleugh, during the Grand Mastership of Charles Lennox, Duke of Richmond, at the Grand Feast, in November, 1724, when it was proposed, "in order to promote the charitable disposition of Free Masons, and to render it more extensively beneficial to the Society, each Lodge may make a certain collection, according to ability, to be put into a *joint-stock*, lodged in the hands of a Treasurer, at every Quarterly Communication, for the relief of distressed brethren that shall be recommended by the contributing Lodges to the Grand Officers from time to time;" which being agreed to, was referred to a committee for the purpose of digesting certain regulations applicable thereto. This committee reported at the Grand Feast, in November, 1725, and their report was adopted; but it was not until the 24th June, 1727, that a brother could be found to act as Treasurer; at this meeting Brother Nathaniel Blakerby accepted the office, though the Grand Charity seems not to have been perfected and commenced operations until Nov'r 23d, 1729, when said Blakerby being Deputy Grand Master, aroused the Lodges to the fulfilment of the requisitions of the Grand Charity; and from this time the "Grand Committee of Charity" met regularly, and suggested certain new regulations, which were adopted by the Grand Lodge, until the Grand Mastership of Carnavan, in July, 1755, when the twenty-five articles regulating the Committee of Charity of the Free and Accepted Masons were completed, confirmed and put fully into practical operation, and have continued since.

Such, in time, became the influence and respectability of this Committee, that the Grand Lodge, on 13th December, 1733, resolved, "that what business cannot be transacted at one Lodge, may be referred to the Committee of Charity, and by them reported to the next Grand Lodge." Their number—at first eleven—was increased in 1730 to twenty-three; and five to be a quorum, provided one was a Grand Officer.

The "Grand Steward's Lodge," which came into existence on the 24th June, 1735, was effected in the following manner: In 1723, the Grand Master was requested to appoint as many Stewards as he thought necessary for the good order and government of things at the Annual Feast, and to act as to a majority of them might seem best. These Stewards were in many instances men of rank, and in all, of great respectability. In 1731, they were vested with the power of naming their successors, and in June 24, 1735, they addressed the Grand Lodge, setting forth their past services and future usefulness; whereupon it was resolved, "that they be constituted into a Master's Lodge, to be called the Grand Steward's Lodge," to be registered as such in the Grand Lodge books and printed lists, with the times and places of their meetings. Their annual number was twelve, and they were permitted to line their aprons with red, and to wear their jewels of silver, pendant to red ribbon; and subsequently were permitted to send a deputation of twelve or nine members, in addition to the Master and Wardens, to each Grand Lodge, and were required to pay half a crown each, for the twelve, to the Grand Lodge.

I have now, as briefly as I thought compatible with perspicuity, presented to you the prominent points in the History of Masonry at this eventful period. If I have been tedious, I beg you to impute it to my anxious desire to do justice to those who are soon to assume a conspicuous place in my, perhaps, too hastily written narrative.

We have already seen how the Grand Lodge of England offended the sister, nay mother Grand Lodge of all England at York, by an unjust exercise of unwarranted and assumed powers within her jurisdiction, and alienated her Masonic respect and feelings, until all correspondence ceased; we have now to witness another exercise of that arbitrary power, evidently predicated upon her inflated size, peculiar organization, and locality of existence.

It was during the Grand Mastership of Lord Petre that the corner stone of Free Mason's Hall was laid with great pomp and ceremony, 1st May, 1775; and at this meeting the office of Grand Chaplain was first instituted. This Hall was solemnly dedicated 3rd May, '76, to Masonry, Virtue, and Universal Charity and Benevolence.

Lord Petre was succeeded by the Duke of Manchester in May, 1777, and on the Festival of St. John the Evangelist, the old Lodge of Antiquity determined by a vote of the Lodge to march in procession, in the clothing and regalia of the Order, to attend Divine service at St. Dunstan's church, and back to their Lodge in the Mitre Tavern; not having obtained a Dispensation therefor, the Grand Lodge determined it to be a violation of the regulations, and passed several severe and condemnatory resolutions, which the Lodge of Antiquity resisted, pleading their immemorial Charter and privileges; and thus commenced the breach between these old Lodges and the Grand Lodge, when another circumstance occurred of still graver importance: the Lodge of Antiquity expelled three of its members for misbehavior—the Grand Lodge interfered and ordered them to be restored to membership. With this order the Lodge peremptorily refused to comply, conceiving themselves competent and sole judges in the choice of their own members, and again setting up the privileges of their immemorial Constitutions.

Matters were now carried to extremes on both sides. The Lodge of Antiquity appealed to the Grand Lodge of York, Scotland and Ireland; manifestos were published; they notified their separation, and avowed an alliance with the Grand Lodge of York, and with every Lodge and Mason who wished to act in conformity to the original Constitutions. The Grand Lodge, on the other hand, enforced its edicts, permitted the expelled members to assemble without

Warrant, as the true Lodge of Antiquity, and received their deputations into the Grand Lodge; and expelled the old Lodge, and pronounced it Clandestine, in 1779, and so continued for eleven years, or until 1790, when by the influence and exertions of Worshipful William Burch, a Past Master of the Lodge of Antiquity, a reconciliation was effected, the protests and manifestos withdrawn, and the Lodge restored to its former position in Masonry; the nominal members who had received the sanction of the society as the Lodge of Antiquity, were restored by the real Lodge, and this venerable body of Masons reinstated in all their immemorial privileges.

During all this period of turmoil and difficulty, the seceders of 1738, or Grand Lodge of Ancients, as organized in 1739, continued their Masonic operations, receiving the malcontents from each successive schism, granting Charters—domestic and foreign, and under the fascinating title of Ancient York Masons, received the approbation and patronage of men of learning, wealth and influence; and professing and practising obedience to Anderson's Constitutions, in law and usage, up to 1756, when Brother Lawrence Dermot, then Deputy Grand Master, being up to this time Grand Secretary, by order of the Grand Lodge, compiled and published the Ahiman Rezon, or "Laws of Prepared Brothers," as its Hebrew origin imports. As much has been said and written concerning this book and its author, and as it is now being very freely animadverted on by the Masonic press of this country, as well as the casuists in Masonic jurisprudence, we will here devote a few words to its history, and in these I will be as concise as possible.

Let it then be borne in memory, that the first edition of Anderson's Constitution was printed in 1721; that its style is concise, laconic, and so simple as to be a little ambigous, all which I think no one who has read it will deny; add to this the grave changes which the Grand Lodge of England made in Ritual, Usage and Law, between this time and 1738, when the second edition was printed, and it will be readily seen that some change was called for in legislation to meet those exigencies, and accordingly we find them made in the shape of new regulations, so called, under the express clause before recited as giving authority.

You will also remember, that the next year, 1739, this Grand Lodge of Ancients came into existence, destined to become a great and influential rival in the cause of Masonry; and foreseeing that event, and anxious to prevent its success, the Grand Lodge of England resorted to every legal expedient to suppress the new rival, and to give themselves eclat and celebrity at home and abroad. They multiplied their meetings, organized great and influential committees, and dignified some of them with the title of "Lodges"—as the Grand Steward's Lodge, Committee of Charity, &c. To meet these changes, certain new regulations were enacted up to 1754, when the third edition of Anderson's Constitutions was printed as carefully revised, continued and enlarged for Brother Jonathan Scott, by Rev. Brother John Entick. In this edition will be found copious extracts from the Grand Lodge records, showing the many and important changes made, and their relation to the previously existing laws; and though by no means published for that purpose, yet conclusively proving, that such changes and new regulations were necessary and incidental to the many alterations which practice and ripe experience dictated. In 1768, we find an appendix ordered to the Book of Constitutions, containing such modifications and laws as had been passed since 1754; and no other edition after the promulgation of the Ahiman Rezon (revised edition) in 1772, by R. W. Lawrence Dermot, which we have here before us, and in which, instead of first giving a literal transcript of Anderson's Constitutions, and then a copy of all amendments in the language of their enactment, he has embodied their spirit, and the most legitimate interpretation of each article; in my humble judgment, much best calculated to suppress continued cavilling as to the meaning of such laws; and under this code, this Grand Lodge, now designated in history as the Althol Grand Lodge, continued to work until the union of the two Grand Lodges in 1813, when the Duke of Sussex being Grand Master of the Grand Lodge of England, and the long desired union being brought to a grave proposition by the Earl of Moira, Deputy Grand Master, the venerable Duke of Althol resigned, and the Prince of Wales, Duke of Kent and brother of the Duke of Sussex, was chosen Grand Master, and entered at once and cordially into a negotiation with his brother for the promotion of this great and glorious object. At which time, the twenty-one articles of union were drawn up by a Lodge of reconciliation, appointed for the purpose, which twenty-one articles, as their language imports, were intended to operate as a new Constitution, as far as they went, throughout the Masonic world.

In this plan of union every position assumed by the Grand Lodge of Ancients was confirmed, expressly including the privilege and right to confer all the degrees of Masonry, and especially the Holy Royal Arch.

This important fact pleads volumes in favor of the manner in which they had conducted themselves during the seventy-five years of their insubordination to, and resistance of the assumptions of their mother G. Lodge; and the entire success which crowned their efforts to teach and perpetuate the most ancient Work and Ritual of our time-honored Institution, should require us to throw the mantle of charity over their apparent contumacy of law and order, for the time, to effect this most desirable object in the end. I repeat, apparent contumacy, because at this distance from the scene, and this remote period from the date of their disobedience, and with such an extreme paucity of authentic record of the facts and motives on which each acted, we have no authentic data on which to found a correct judgment, and as results and consequences are entirely in their favor, they demand, and should receive, our approval.

Their Ahiman Rezon, or Book of Constitutions, has been now practised under by Grand and Subordinate Lodges in both hemispheres, and nearly every language for seventy-five or eighty years, and I think we hazard nothing, when we say, it is too late to cavil at its provisions, or attempt to cast the least odium upon the compilers and writers of it. Let us rather, like good and true Masons, point out the defects, if any, which time and the experience of a century may have exposed, and by sound and clear legislation, remedy them in some shape.

But you are told Lawrence Dermot and William Preston were expelled Masons, and so they were; for no immoral or unmasonic conduct, however, but the latter, because he chose to suffer martyrdom in the cause of truth and justice, with his Lodge of Antiquity, of which he was Master during the time above alluded to, when it was condemned for rebellion to authority, assumed, but never granted, to punish for exercising privileges it had never parted with; the other, from motives of expediency, through fear of the influence of his unflinching fidelity to the cause of Masonry and of Virtue, and his untiring efforts to make that cause successful. Does not their glorious, though temporary martyrdom, in this noble work entitle them rather to our admiration and gratitude?

Again, let it be remembered that the noble pioneers in the cause of Masonry, who brought and taught it in this Western World during the last century, were many of them co-laborers and living workers in the city of London, and in some instances in the Lodges where these events were transpiring; and yet they brought with them as guides in Masonic Law and Ritual, Dermot's Ahiman Rezon, and Preston's Illustrations of Masonry. They had seen and marked well the operation of these writings in the very face and presence of the Grand Lodge of England; and does not such cotemporaneous evidence speak trumpet-tongued in their favor?

In South Carolina, in Massachusetts, in Pennsylvania, and in Virginia, the Ahiman Rezon was received, adopted and published, as *the* Book of the Law, and has continued, with some trivial modifications adapted to locality, ever since. And we have good reason for believing it was deemed sufficient for England; for we find that a committee was appointed in 1813, immediately after the union, to revise and print the Constitution and Laws, but to my knowledge they have not reported, and we are left to believe it is the law there at this time, unless, indeed, the twenty-one articles of union may have been received and adopted by them as a Constitution; since none other has been published. The great anxiety expressed on all sides for this much desired union, and the splendid pageant which accompanied its consummation; invitations being extended to sister Grand Lodges; the wealth, rank and influence of brethren enlisted on both sides; the solemnity and form used in the ratification; all prove beyond a doubt the deservedly high position which the Athol Grand Lodge had won and retained among the Fraternity by their inflexible adherence to the cause of truth, justice and Masonry.

We can now dispassionately review their acts; for their motives are only inferential, and we must admit that it required the most unbounded share of moral courage to bear the taunts and flings of insubordination to law and usage, the epithets of "Clandestine," "Cowan," and "Irregular," nay, the public announcement of expulsion which their more fortunate rivals, under the cloak of power and constitutional authority, freely lavished on them, and cotemporary journalists and writers echoed to the world.

There are writers in this country at this time, who are so thoughtless as to endorse these denunciations, and have gone so far as to stigmatize the name of Lawrence Dermott with opprobious epithets, which I do not feel justified in giving currency to, even by the bare recital of them. To show what they are pleased to term discrepancies from Anderson's Constitutions, the two have been printed and published in parallel columns. But they have not taken the trouble to investigate the impelling reasons for those modifications of phraseology. For, indeed, this will be found to be almost entirely the extent of crime, if, indeed, there is any at all. Of one remarkable fact I must inform you, which does not say much for the ingenuousness or candor of these journalists in their strictures upon the conduct and writings of Dermott and Preston; none of whom, so far as my knowledge goes, have done their memories the justice to publish the twenty-one articles of ratification drawn up and submitted by the Lodge of reconciliation, consisting of nine experienced and skilful brethren selected for the momentous occasion by each Grand Lodge, and which twenty-one articles, after being read aloud by the G. Chaplain to the assembled Lodges at Free Masons' Hall, December 27th, 1813, and receiving their unanimous sanction and approval in due Masonic form, were signed and sealed by all the Grand Officers of each body, and from that moment became the constitutional law for all England, and her Subordinate Lodges wheresoever dispersed.

To confirm and sanction the impressive solemnity of this act of Masonic Harmony and of Brotherly Love, in the double sense of those words, a representation of the ark of the covenant, which had been prepared with great care and cost for the purpose, was then brought in, and this almost holy record therein safely and solemnly deposited, for the justification of the parties to future generations.

An attentive perusal of this document will prove that the Grand Lodge of England was in effect required by the behests of truth and justice, to retract her errors, to retrace her position, and adopt the Laws and Ritual of the Athol Grand Lodge.

That it may not be supposed, and perhaps asserted, that we have given these views from a false interpretation of those articles, we present you the following authentic copy of two of them, intended, as their language expressly declares, to operate for all time throughout the world:

"Art. 2d. It is declared and pronounced, that pure Ancient Masonry consists of three degrees, and no more, viz: those of Entered Apprentice, the Fellow Craft, and the Master Mason, including the supreme order of the Holy Royal Arch. But this article is not intended to prevent any Lodge or Chapter from holding a meeting in any of the degrees of chivalry, according to the Constitutions of the said orders.

"Art. 3d. There shall be the most perfect unity of obligation, of discipline, of working the Lodges, of making, passing and raising, instructing and clothing brothers; so that but one pure unsullied system, according to the genuine Landmarks, laws, and traditions of the Craft, shall be maintained, upheld and practised throughout the Masonic world, from the day and date of the said union until time shall be no more."

The subsequent articles, as well as the record of proceedings, unequivocally prove the equality of power, right and privilege sought to be invested in, and exercised by, each of these Grand Lodges, in carrying out the stipulations of union, and will amply repay every brother by a perusal of the solemn and impressive forms and ceremonies used on that interesting occasion.

During this period of long and trying probation to which the Ritual and Constitutional Law of Masonry was subjected, another and powerful element was brought to bear upon the unhallowed efforts to popularize the various and discordant rites as they were called, of every pretender to antiquity and originality; of these there were no less than fifteen or sixteen.

As some of these Rites are still practised, and producing much confusion in the True Ancient York Ritual, I subjoin a list, somewhat in their order of antiquity:

1. York Rite.
2. Scotch Rite.
3. French or Modern.
4. Philosophic Scotch Rite.
5. Primitive Scotch Rite.
6. Ancient Reformed Rite.
7. Reformed Rite.
8. Rite of Herodom.
9. Rite of the Grand Lodge of the Three Globes.
10. Rite of Mitzraim.
11. Rite of the Temple.
12. Swedish Rite.
13. Fessler's Rite.
14. Schroeder's Rite.
15. Rite of Sweedenbourg.
16. Rite of Zinnendorf.

It would be at once curious and interesting to enquire into the points on which these variant Rites are founded, if we had time; many of which, appealing to the influence of the Christian church, sought to propitiate her favor, in propagating their favorite Ritual, by attempting to evangelize Masonry.

Never was a greater error committed, nor one, if successful, more calculated to circumscribe its usefulness, and dim the bright radiance of the most precious jewel in the crown which adorns her head and heart—we allude to the universality, oneness and indivisibility of the operation of her glorious tenets in humanizing mankind, and implanting in the breast of wayward and self-willed man those attributes of Divine perfection, so beautifully illustrated in the Masonic teachings of Faith, Hope and Charity.

The error committed, we say, was the attempt to evangelize Masonry. The means used in public was, first, the interpolation of the sacred name of Jesus in the printed and set form of prayer at initiation; and the second was the still more unphilosophical interpolation of the names of the Saints John in the printed forms of Dedication of Lodges, as Patron Saints in Masonry.

In confirmation of the modern origin of both these practices, I have already shown you, from the 11th edition of Preston on Masonry, printed in London in 1804, that neither of these names are to be found in his Illustrations of the Degrees or Ceremonies. On the Ceremony of Dedications, his language is beautiful, from the universality of its application, and its broad and comprehensive adaptation to the whole human family; by him Lodges were dedicated "in the name of the Great Jehovah, to Masonry, Virtue and Universal Benevolence;" and this, we infer, was the practice in the Lodge of Antiquity, whose usages were of immemorial origin, as he was the Worshipful Master at this time. On this subject we find the following curious and interesting tradition copied from a record preserved in some English Lodges, published in Moore's Magazine, vol. ii, p. 263, but for its authenticity he does not vouch:

"From the building of the first temple at Jerusalem, to the Babylonish captivity, Free Masons' Lodges were dedicated to King Solomon; from thence to the coming of the Messiah, they were dedicated to Zerubbabel, the builder of the second temple; and from that time to the final destruction of the temple of Titus, in the reign of Vespasian, they were dedicated to St. John the Baptist; but owing to the many massacres and disorders which attended that memorable event, Free Masonry sunk very much into decay; many Lodges were entirely broken up, and but few could meet in sufficient numbers to constitute their legality, and at a general meeting of the Craft held in the city of Benjamin, it was observed that the principal reason for the decline of Masonry, was the want of a Grand Master to patronize it: they, therefore, deputed seven of their most eminent brethren to wait upon St. John the Evangelist, who was at that time Bishop of Ephesus, requesting him to take the office of Grand Master. He returned for answer, that though well stricken in years, (being upwards of ninety), yet, having been in the early part of his life initiated into Masonry, he would take upon himself that office; he thereby completed by his learning, what the other

St. John had completed by his zeal, and thus drew what Free Masons term a parallel; ever since which, Free Masons' Lodges in all Christian countries have been dedicated both to St. John the Baptist and St. John the Evangelist."

Testimony on this important subject seems evidently to be increasing. A French writer of 1815, of great industry and application, has added the following; not having access to the work, I quote from Mackey's Lexicon, article St. John the Almoner:

"The Saint to whom Encampments of Knights Templar are dedicated. He was the son of a king of Cyprus, and was born in that island in the sixth century. He was elected Patriarch of Alexandria, and has been canonized by both the Grecian and Roman churches—his festival among the former occurring on 11th November, and among the latter on the 23d January. Bazot, who published a Manual of Free Masonry in 1811, at Paris, thinks that it is this Saint, and not St. John the Evangelist, or St. John the Baptist, who is meant as the true patron of our Order."

"He quitted his country, and the hope of a throne," says this author, "to go to Jerusalem, that he might generously aid and assist the knights and pilgrims. He founded a hospital, and organized a fraternity to attend upon the sick and wounded Christians, and to bestow pecuniary aid upon the pilgrims who visited the holy sepulchre. St. John, who was worthy to become the patron of a society, whose only object is charity, exposed his life a thousand times in the cause of virtue. Neither war, nor pestilence, nor the fury of the infidels, could deter him from the pursuits of benevolence. But death, at length, arrested him in the midst of his labors. Yet he left the example of his virtues to his brethren, who have made it their endeavor to imitate him. Rome canonized him under the name of St. John the Almoner, or St. John of Jerusalem; and the Masons, whose temples, overthrown by the barbarians, he had caused to be rebuilt, selected him with one accord as their patron."

From this it would seem we have three Sts. John, claiming to be the peculiar patron of Masonry, and each from the brilliant devotion of their lives and energies to the propagation of its holy and eternal cardinal virtues, equally entitled to the honor.

To relieve the Institution of the charge of sectarianism arising from this practise, the Grand Lodge of England, in the Union Work of 1813, ordered the Dedication of Lodges thereafter to be to "God and his service." In this country, however, we have preferred to follow the teachings of Preston and Webb, with a little change in the name, and to dedicate our Lodges in the name of the holy Sts.

John, to Masonry, Virtue and Universal Benevolence. But some of my brethren may ask, if the introduction of their names into our Ritual is a modern innovation, whence originated the custom of celebrating our annual Masonic festivals, on the natal days of these Saints, in June and December? For the same reasons they might ask, why hold Quarterly Communications in March and September?

To these questions there is, in my mind, a ready answer: Our ancient brethren were philosophers, and students of nature and her laws. Among the Druids, Magii and others, they had introduced the Heliacal worship as part of their religious rites, because they looked upon the sun in the firmament as the representative of the Eternal God in imparting light, life and productiveness to all sublunary things: the visible effect of his annual influences could not long have escaped their observation, in determining the length of days and the returns of seasons; and as the most marked of these are the summer and winter solstitial colures, as now called, at or near the 22d June and 22d December, with the equinoxes occurring at or near the 22d March and 22d September, it is quite natural, and truly in accordance with their known maxims, to say or do nothing without a satisfactory reason, that they should appoint these days as festival epochs to mark time, in the absence of gnomes, quadrants or almanacs: and so we believe they did. And when, in the last century it was sought to ingraft these natal days of our Patron Saints into the Masonic calendar, nothing was easier than by a day or two changed in these annual divisions of time, to have them fall on the 24th June and 27th December, in honor of the memories of those distinguished men, and to complete the observation of the four cardinal colures of time by quarterly meetings on or about the middle of March and September.

In Scotland, who claims the greatest antiquity for her Masonry, their Annual Festival of Free Masons is held on the 30th November, in commemoration of the natal day of St. Andrew, as the Patron Saint of the Nation. This day and Saint was selected by the Kilwinning Lodges on the occasion of the ever-memorable voluntary abdication of the Earl of St. Clair of his hereditary right to the Grand Mastership, on the 30th of November, 1736, at the Festival of St. Andrew.

From all this it seems evident that the introduction of the names of these Saints into the Masonic calendar is the work of comparatively modern Masons. Any attempt, therefore, at this day to analyze the reasons and motives which actuated these over zealous brethren to make these changes, would occupy too much of your time; let each one do this for himself, bearing in mind, that of the 960,000,000 of human beings on this globe, only 250,000,000 are Christians, in the broadest acceptation of the term, and that the high and ennobling behests of Brotherly Love, Relief and Truth, are as necessary to the temporal and eternal happiness of the 710,000,000, as it is to the Christian, that they are the blessed fruits of Faith, Hope and Charity, alike produced by, and operating on, the Chinese follower of Confucius, or the idolatrous worshipper of Mahommet, as the more humble disciples of Christ.

This is no part of my task, which is a simple and truthful narrative of the facts in Masonry which gave character to the early formation of the Grand Lodge of Virginia.

In this connection, however, it is necessary that I should introduce to your careful attention the Great and Illustrious Brother Frederick II, King of Prussia, renowned in history for his achievements, in the cabinet, in diplomacy, in civil law, and on the field of battle; this monarch had attained a fame and reputation throughout the civilized world, which far outstripped all his cotemporaries. The rapidly developed and developing influences of Masonry, at every court where it was introduced, did not long escape his notice; he established a Grand Lodge, Les Trois Globes, at Berlin, and in 1758, created the first Grand Consistory of the Hauts Grades in Masonry, as he styled them, to the number of 32 or Sovereign Princes of Jerusalem, himself possessing alone the 33d, or Sovereign Grand Inspector General. These degrees of knighthood and pseudo Masonry were many framed by him, and engrafted on the primitive degrees of Ancient York Masonry, by making them a necessary preparatory step; and desiring to propitiate the influence of the Jesuits, he sought to evangelize Masonry by the introduction and propagation of these Christian degrees, and we might almost add a profanation of the name of Jesus and the holy Saints John. Finding the task a difficult one, by his own unaided exertions in Prussia, he called a Grand Consistory of the Royal Secret at Paris, in 1761, and appointed Chaillon de Joinville his representative and deputy. This Consistory, then, by his authority, created a Consistory for the northern, and one for the southern divisions of the United States, each to consist of nine created Sovereign Grand Inspectors General: and commissioned Stephen Morin as his Deputy, to carry out these provisions, which he did by appointing Isaac Da Costa, Sovereign Grand Inspector General for the southern, and Moses M. Hayes, Sovereign Grand Inspector General for the northern sections. Arriving in this country on their mission of Masonic propagandism, Da Costa soon died, and was succeeded by the appointment of Joseph Myers to that office. Fortunately for Masonry, but unfortunately for the views of Frederick II, both these Inspectors General were Israelites, and were educated gentlemen. The humble speaker, who now addresses you, received these Degrees from the last named in this city, and so beautiful and illustrative were his lectures, that he found no difficulty in recognizing them as the pure and genuine Ancient York Ritual of Masonry in the four or five first Degrees; the other 27 or 8 being ornamental or side degrees, as Brother Myers always characterized them; and a full and entire copy of which he used as written out, not deeming them Masonry in any sense. Indeed, it is now an established fact, that many of these degrees underwent great changes at that meeting in Paris; this we may fairly infer to have been brought about by the influence of the Chevalier Ramsay, to whom I formerly alluded as the inventor of a Royal Arch Degree, which had been repudiated by the Grand Lodge of England; and the still greater influence of Lawrence Dermott, who had introduced it into the Ritual of the Athol Grand Lodge, and immensely increased its weight and respectability in numbers and talents thereby. A very cursory view of the facts and circumstances now transpiring, will serve to convince us that Dermott, who hailed from and received the support of the Grand Lodge of Ireland, would not fail to avail himself of the proffered influence on this occasion of the Grand Lodge of France, through Ramsay, who was then Deputy Grand Master; of Prussia, through De Joinville, the Vice Grand Master; and of the Grand Lodge of Scotland, through the Duke of Athol, then its Grand Master; in building up into stately and comely form this sublime Degree, which gave him such ascendancy over his rival, the Grand Lodge of England.

Such was the state of Masonry, my Brothers, in the Old World, when our narrative commences the history of the origin of the Most Worshipful Grand Lodge of Virginia, which is, as we shall presently see, almost necessarily a history of the introduction of Masonry into the United States in a chartered or constituted form.

We have before us a copy of Wor. Brother Jonathan Scott's Manual and History of Masonry, printed at London in 1759, in which is given, what is unquestionably authentic upon that subject, a list of all the regular Lodges on the registry of the Grand Lodge of England, and among them we find the Royal Exchange Lodge, No. 172, chartered in the town of Norfolk, in the state of Virginia, December 22d, 1733—meetings held first Thursday in every month, so that it must have gone into operation and reported its code of by-laws.

From facts which have reached us through persons, there can be very little doubt that occasional Lodges were held and degrees conferred without Warrant, before and subsequent to this date, at many places in Virginia, under the immemorial usage of the Ancient Grand Lodge at York.

We have also evidence from the records of Falmouth Lodge, in Stafford county, that in the absence of a Warrant from any Grand Lodge, the competent number of Master Masons being met and agreed, acted under this immemorial usage, only asking the sanction of the nearest Lodge in writing; and which document operated as their Warrant, as will be seen by the records of Fredericksburg Lodge, No. 4, in granting this privilege to the Masons of Falmouth. We are also justified in inferring that the Military Traveling Lodges may have in many instances imparted the Degrees of Masonry to persons of respectability residing at or near their place of encampment, and on leaving gave them a Warrant to confer these Degrees on others, in lieu of a certificate of enrolment.

The records and Warrants of these "particular Lodges" were lost or destroyed during the American revolution, and when, during the present century, these Lodges have sought for the evidences of their organization among the archives of Grand Lodges in this and other countries, they have failed to find them, because no return of the acts of many of these Military Lodges has ever been made.

From an equally authentic source, the Free Mason's Pocket Companion, printed in Edinburgh in 1765, which we have also before us, we find in a list of regular Lodges under the Grand Lodge of Scotland, St. John's Lodge, No. 117, chartered for Norfolk in Virginia, June 1, 1741, and one for Blanford in Virginia, about the same date, under the same authority, No. 83; and York Lodge, at Yorktown, under the Grand Lodge of England. At this time, and a little subsequent, we know from our own records there were Lodges at Fredericksburg, Hampton, Gloucester, Cabin Point and Port Royal; there were also many Traveling Military Lodges up to and during the war of our revolution. From which of the many Grand Lodges then existing in Europe, these Lodges derived their Charters, unfortunately we have now no reliable information, and we are left to infer their origin from their mode of Work and Ritual; this we shall find to have been a modification of the Scotch and Athol teachings more especially, and almost conclusively from the introduction and exercise of the Holy Royal Arch, as well as their adoption of the Ahiman Rezon of Dermot, as their Book of Constitutions.

The great paucity of Masonic records, the chariness of writing too much which characterized all our older brethren, added to the vandal character of the British in firing all our towns and public buildings during the war, has deprived posterity of many valuable documents which could enlighten us on this most interesting period of our early Masonic history. The first page of our record says, "We find that the Lodges in this State hold their Charters from five distinct and separate authorities, viz: the Grand Masters of England, Scotland, Ireland, Pennsylvania and America (the last at second hand)." But which of the Lodges, or how many, were attached to each jurisdiction they do not say; nor have we any means of stating their origin with more precision than we have already done.

Suffice it to know that the Masonry of Virginia was at that time in the hands of as talented, as pious, and as firm a set of men as the world has ever seen. These were her ministers, who were generally highly educated Scotchmen; her merchants and mechanics, who were as generally prudent, enlightened and methodic Scotchmen; her school teachers, who were her Scotch divines, and who made this occupation tributary to the meagre support which the sparsely settled colony gave them for preaching; and when we add to this fact the well known devotion of all Scotia's sons to her usages and laws, it is matter of little wonder that they should endeavor to teach and diffuse Scotch Masonry; and so in the sequel we shall find they did.

The glorious war of the revolution was proclaimed to the world on the 4th July, 1776, at Philadelphia, and the gauntlet of independence thrown to the mother country by this infant nation, as an earnest of eternal separation from her politics, laws, and form of government. In May, on the 6th day, 1777, a portion of these same devoted patriots and enlightened Masons, met at Williamsburg, by the representatives of five of the eight constituted Lodges then in Virginia, after legal Masonic notice to all. We say eight, because, though it is known there were or had been several others working under authority, yet from the many difficulties arising from the French and Indian wars, which indeed were not terminated at this time, their records, charters, &c., had been lost or destroyed, these eight were all that presented legal evidence of constituted existence; and at the Grand Lodge in 1786, the committee appointed to settle and regulate their rank, reported—

No. 1. Norfolk Lodge, constituted June 1, 1741.
" 2. Port Royal Kilwinning Cross, Dec. 1, 1755.
" 3. Blandford (Petersburg), Sept. 9, 1757.
" 4. Fredericksburg, July 21, 1758.
" 5. Hampton, St. Tamany, Feb'y 26, 1754.
" 6. Williamsburg, Nov'r 6, 1773.
" 7. Botetourt (Gloucester), Nov'r 6, 1773.
" 8. Cabin Point Royal Arch, April 13, 1775.

That there were others, equally, nay perhaps more, efficient in diffusing the truth and light of Masonry, is proven by a letter written in 1843, by R. W. Jno. Barny, the Grand Lecturer of Ohio, to Brother C. W. Moore, of Boston, in which he says, "Capt. Hugh Maloy, aged 93, is now living in or near Bethel, Clermont co., who was initiated in 1782, in General Washington's Marquee; General Washington presided in person, and performed the initiatory ceremonies!"

In a plain, but forcibly couched preamble, addressed to their brethren throughout the world, they declared the reasons which actuated them as patriot Masons, to sever their allegiance from all foreign Masonic governments, and to constitute a Grand Lodge, with officers, laws and ritual of their own selection. They accordingly drew up a code of laws and regulations for their own government, and submitted a verbal ritual, which received the sanction of an adjourned meeting of the Convention on the 13th day of October, 1778, composed of deputies from the Lodges at Norfolk, Port Royal, Blandford, Williamsburg, Gloucester and Cabin Point. The records of the first meeting of this Convention show, they presented the name of Brother George Washington, as a Mason fit and proper to be the first Grand Master of Masons for Virginia, which honor, when informed of, he declined for two reasons, alike characteristic of the Mason and the man: first, never having been Master or Warden of a chartered Lodge, he did not think it legally proper to accept; and second, his country having claimed his services in the tented field, his time would be wholly occupied in those arduous duties. How deeply characteristic of the Mason and the man, whose symmetrical and colossal proportions in every attribute which constitute true greatness, had already placed him high and conspicuous among his cotemporaries, an exemplar of virtue, patriotism, and inflexible fidelity to law and order! And here we may point you to a most remarkable evidence of what we have frequently lamented—a too laconic method in keeping records among the older Lodges.

In Fredericksburg Lodge, No. 4, will be seen, as the records of the transactions of a meeting, "George Washington made Apprentice November 4, 1752;" and again, "George Washington passed Fellow Craft March 3d, 1753;" and finally, "George Washington raised Master Mason, August 4, 1753."

Little, indeed, could Fredericksburg Lodge, No. 4, have realized the momentous act she was then engaged in, both to herself and mankind, in all future time, or we may be assured the record of it would have been made with far more fullness of detail, if not clothed with all the pomp and circumstance of some mighty event which was to carry her envied name, with that of her adopted Brother, to every confine of civilization. How sacredly he carried out the teachings of her holy, moral and Masonic Ritual in after life, this simple fact, above alluded to, abundantly proves.

His decision being made known, the Grand Lodge was organized at the second meeting, by the unanimous election of Wor. Brother John Blair, P. M. of Williamsburg Lodge, No. 6, as M. Worshipful Grand Master, who was pleased to appoint the Rev. Brother Robert Andrews D. G. M. These officers were succeeded by James Mercer and Edmund Randolph, in 1784; by Edmund Randolph and John Marshall, in 1786; by Alexander Montgomerie and Thomas Matthews, in 1789; and by Thomas Matthews, in 1791, who declining the right and honor of appointing his Deputy, the Grand Lodge unanimously elected Dr. John K. Read as Deputy, and requested him to draw up and report the Constitution as adopted, and the charges and Ritual as far as the latter could be written; this it seems he did by a reprint of Dermott's Ahiman Rezon, as the Constitution, and of Preston's Illustrations, as the Ritual, in 1791; which has continued the laws, with some modifications, to this day; though the Ritual, as taught professedly from Preston, has undergone great changes, and more nearly assimilated to the Ancient York.

Under the auspices and patronage of these exemplary and highly distinguished statesmen, jurists, divines, patriots and scholars, Masonry took her proud stand on the continent of America as an organized Institution, and co-laborer with the religion of the country, in disseminating the inappreciable tenets of Brotherly Love, Relief and Truth, and of firmly uniting men of every country, sect and opinion, into one common family of devoted patriots and brothers.

Our gallant sister in the memorable struggle for equality of rights and privileges, and freedom from oppression and imposition, the then far distant state of Massachusetts, seems also to have been impressed with the early importance of some form of Masonic organization; she, however, pursued an entirely different course to effect it. Her primitive Masons being, though like ours, the initiates of most, if not all, the conflicting jurisdictions of England and Scotland, and each prejudiced in favor of the Ritual of his adoption. They commenced their organization by the interposition of Provincial Deputy Grand Masters, and at once and immediately by patent from the Grand Lodge of England, granted to R. W. Henry Price, in 1733, opened a Lodge at Boston, called the "St. Johns' Grand Lodge," on the 30th day of July; though their first regularly installed and invested Grand Master, was R. W. Robert Tomlinson, in April, 1737.

It seems the wave of schism reached our shores at this time, for the Ancients about this time applied to Lord Aberdeen, and received a grant to open St. Andrew's Lodge, No. 83, and in 1769, the Earl of Dalhousie constituted it a Grand Lodge, by the appointment of the Illustrious Brother Joseph Warren, as Provincial Grand Master under the Scotch Ritual. This, then, became "the Massachusetts Grand Lodge;" their authority, as might be anticipated, was violently opposed by the St. Johns' Grand Lodge.

A third and still more powerful element of discord was now brought upon the stage, for the Duke of Athol constituted Ancient York Lodge, No. 169, at the house of Mr. Alexander, Battery-Marsh, in Boston, to meet first and third Tuesday in each month. This movement was at the instance and request of the *real* Ancients then in Boston.

Such conflicting exercise of unsettled usage might be expected to give rise to jealousies, bickerings and heartburns, and so it did: the St. Johns' Grand Lodge remonstrated against the encroachments of its rival, the "Massachusetts Grand Lodge;" and both these against the Ancient York Lodge. It was not until 5th March, 1792, these difficulties were settled, when the two G. Lodges met for the last time, and formed a union, by the appointment of seven electors, to choose a Grand Master, when Brother John Cutler was elected. The Book of Constitutions, a reprint of Dermot's Ahiman Rezon, was at this time ordered, and Masonry from this date commenced a prosperous and successful organization under, and as the "Grand Lodge of Massachusetts."

From this it is apparent the planting and propagation of Masonry in the two colonies was steadily, almost *pari passu*, put under two essentially different modes of organization. Our sister commenced with the Provincial Grand Lodge system, and though this gave them the advantage of early and authentic record, yet this is more than compensated for by the notices of schisms and quarrels which such records present.

Virginia, it seems, never sought or tolerated the Provincial Grand Master system in Masonry, preferring the quieter, more efficient, but less ostentatious method of permitting any number of Masons good and true, to assemble under Warrant or Charter, and dispense the light and blessings of Masonry as to them seemed best, either in Military Traveling, or in Local Lodges, provided they adhered to the ancient Landmarks. For these reasons, it is, that her early records are so very rare and scarce, yet those which have reached us from these subordinates, present nothing but Harmony and Brotherly Love among the patrons and advocates of Masonry, in whose hands its holy teachings were practised, and exercised, as well in the daily pursuits of private or public life, as in their humble and unpretending Lodges.

New Lodges were chartered in this and sister states—new Grand Lodges were formed for each State jurisdiction; and the patriots and statesmen of each, as they became enlightened by the moral teachings of the Lodge, drew largely upon the wise polity of its internal form of government for those blessed features so admirably adapted to the wants of man, when struggling for the supremacy of equal rights, and the suppression of all privileges, hereditary and acquired, except those predicated on virtue and merit.

It is not at all matter of surprise that men, devoted heart and soul to the propagation of these glorious principles and truths, the confirmation of which they knew would perpetuate their names in a blaze of glory, to all future time, should have found little leisure to study or practise the little details of the Work and Ritual; and such we shall find was the fact until the Grand Lodge found it necessary to appoint visiters or lecturers to visit the several Lodges and heal the discrepancies, in 1797; these officers were then called Inspectors, and in one form or other have been in vogue to the present time. These discrepancies were necessarily greatly multiplied by the fact that the Grand Lodge of Virginia had adopted the Ritual of the Athol Grand Lodge, so far as to assert by law that they had the undoubted right to confer all the Degrees in Masonry, and consequently the Royal Arch. Acting under this authority the Lodges, by virtue of their Master's Warrant, held what they termed Royal Arch Lodges or Chapters, and conferred the Royal Arch and all the preparatory Degrees as Past, Mark, and Most Excellent Masters; the mode of work varying somewhat in each of these Degrees, according to the Ritual from which they were taught.

In some instances the Grand Lodge granted Charters for Mark Lodges, as an independent Degree, one of which was held in this city for many years, and even continued its operations some years after the organization of the Grand Chapter; indeed, we received the Mark Degree in that Lodge in 1816, ourselves. This practice led necessarily to some of the apparent discrepancies which appear in the Ahiman Rezon from Anderson's Constitutions. It also led to a difference in the clothing of some Lodges; for while by the laws of the Grand Lodge of England, the livery of her subordinates was confined to white lined with blue, the Scotch Ritual, practising the Royal Arch, permitted her subordinates to wear red, purple, blue or white, and it is only within a few years that Fredericksburg Lodge, No. 4, and Alexandria Washington Lodge, No. 22, have dropped the scarlet livery and adopted the blue; and St. Johns Lodge of Norfolk, for many years, wore purple; while a large number wore white, so ornamented with blue as to characterize its livery blue, until the designation of Blue Lodges has become proverbial as applicable to all Master's Lodges of the three first Degrees.

At what time Chapter No. 1, at Norfolk, or No. 2, at Staunton, commenced their operations as a distinct organization under their Master's Charter, I have not been able to learn; but Richmond Chapter, No. 3, commenced its separate existence under the Charters of Richmond Lodge, No. 10, and Richmond Randolph Lodge, No. 19, in 1792, and has kept up a continuous record of work to this time.

These three Chapters, being all in the state, assembled after due notice, in the borough of Norfolk, on the 5th May, 1808, and organized a Grand Chapter, passed a code of by-laws, elected officers, and assumed a separate and independent existence, and adopted as their Ritual the Holy Royal Arch of the Scotch Rite. Their title now became the "Most Excellent Supreme Grand Royal Arch Chapter of Virginia," and at this meeting, says the record, "the Most Rev. Robert Brough (of chap. No. 1,) was installed Most Rev. Supreme Grand High Priest of the Most Excellent Supreme Grand Chapter of Royal Arch Excellent and Super-Excellent Masons of Virginia," with all the honors. This organization was effected without notice to, or consent of the Grand Lodge, nor has it ever been officially recognized to this day. The various Mark Lodges have silently passed out of existence, and that Degree, by the same tacit consent, has passed under the jurisdiction, and been merged in the

Ritual of the Grand Chapter, which now numbers some forty or more subordinates.

Under the Work and Ritual of Scotland, or, as it is sometimes called, the "Rite Ecossaise," these two Grand Bodies continued to work in 1814, when your humble speaker first saw light in Masonry, in that most respectable Lodge, called St. Johns, No. 36, of this city. In this Lodge I was passed and raised in the course of the year, and took the Mark Degree in the Richmond Mark Lodge; in the winter I appeared in the Grand Lodge as a visiter, and was remarkably impressed with the mode of work. During the ensuing year I received the Past, Most Excellent and Royal Arch Degrees, in Richmond Chapter, No. 3, and became a member of both bodies. During the winter of 1815, I attended the Convocation of the Grand Chapter, where I met many of the oldest and best informed Masons in Virginia, and communicated freely to them my, perhaps unfounded, misgivings of the antiquity or authenticity of the Ritual they had adopted, and anxiously inquired if there were any books or records to be obtained which would shed any truthful light upon the subject. Among the Masons whose counsel I sought, was the M. W. Solomon Jacobs, a P. M. of Richmond Randolph Lodge, No. 19, and who had presided over the Grand Lodge of Virginia from 1810 to 1813, and whose address in resigning the chair I had just read with great pride and pleasure. He was also a well educated Israelite, and man of high standing in the community, as well as with the Fraternity. Having adverted in his address, in strong and emphatic language, to the dangers of sectarianism to the universality of Masonry, I approached him with more confidence, and being as a citizen somewhat on terms of intimacy with him, had frequent and free discussions of my views. The result was, his liberal mind rose at once above the petty fears of innovation; he admitted the apparent inconsistencies of his mode of work with his so-called lecture in the Lodge, and he became an advocate for the revival of the Ancient York Ritual in its purity, if possibly to be obtained.

At this part of my narrative, my Brothers, justice to the subject renders it necessary I should speak of myself more conspicuously than is at all compatible with propriety or self-respect. All my colaborers in this interesting work, with one exception, M. E. James Penn, and he in a distant State, have passed from this earthly tabernacle to that "house not built by hands, eternal in the heavens," where we hope and trust they are reaping the rewards of a well-spent life. To those mansions of the departed spirits of my zealous brothers, these grey hairs, and these aids of declining vision, too plainly admonish me I was hastening, when I received your polite request to give you the information which, upon reflection I was soon convinced, you must receive from me or loose forever. Under this impression I could not hesitate, though at the unenviable cost of seeming to speak too much of myself. You will therefore, and for these reasons, pardon my style, while I proceed with my narrative of the Grand Lodge of Virginia.

I perused attentively all works and records within my reach, and soon convinced myself that the want of memory in some Masters, of education in others, and application in most, had in a very great degree confounded the true and false teachings in the details of Work. I became also deeply alarmed at the peril of the glorious universality of action of the tenets of Masonry, by the success of the efforts of the propagandists of Prussian Consistories to engraft upon its beautiful code of moral discipline their sectarian doctrines. These convictions and alarms were freely and frankly communicated to my young brethren, many of whom became at once converts and ready supporters.

I then sought to propitiate the influence of old and experienced Masons in the cause of reform, and held many and lengthened interviews and conferences with them; but the powerful influence of long established practise and habit made them very unwilling listeners to what they at once characterized as innovation, and not reform. Among the books placed in my hands by one of the most experienced of them, the late Past Grand Secretary, Wm. H. Fitzwhylsonn, was Thomas Smith Webb's Monitor, early edition; upon a careful perusal of it, I thought I saw the true Ancient York Work, and I immediately instituted a correspondence with the most skilful and experienced Masons of Connecticut, Rhode Island, (his native State,) and Massachusetts, all of whom united in extolling his Monitor, and recommending his work and lectures.

With these aids, I entered the Grand Lodge in 1816, as the representative of Lodge, No. 36, and commenced the work of reform in earnest. At the suggestion of the above skilful Masons, I wrote to Brother Jeremy L. Cross, who they assured me was well versed in the Work and Lectures of M. W. Thomas S. Webb. He came out in 1817, endorsed by a letter of recommendation from the M. Wor. Thomas S. Webb, and from him I and several others learned the Work and Ritual critically correct, as taught by the distinguished Webb.

This Ritual supplied many anachronisms in date in the Scotch work, and rendered the chronological arrangement more truthful; it also, in a word, liberalized the Institution, and made its glorious universality more applicable to the moral wants of mankind.

The esoteric teachings of the Lodge had, up to this time, been accomplished by means of painted floor cloths, containing a confused arrangement, if I may be allowed the expression, of the Masonic emblems in all the Degrees. In some Lodges they had succeeded so far in method as to have one floor cloth, with its appropriate emblems, for each Degree. These floor cloths, however, for all practical uses, were confined within the walls of the Lodge. To remedy this serious obstacle to the successful propagation of the work, it was suggested that a pocket floor cloth, in book form, containing the dissected emblems, was indispensably required, and which should contain the Constitution, charges and ancient forms of public and private ceremonies, &c.

Having agreed upon the outline, and most of the detail, Cross returned to New Haven to publish the work, with a promise as soon as it was completed to send it for circulation, and to come himself, or send a well qualified reader of the hieroglyphics. In the meantime we were busily employed in teaching, all who applied, the mode of work, and thus kept ourselves also very bright, masonically speaking, in the oral teaching.

During the Communications of the Grand Lodge for 1817 and '18, we frankly and freely exposed our views and intentions to all the members, individually and collectively, and knowing that the great struggle was to be made before the Grand Committee on Work, annually appointed, we sought by every possible legitimate means to indoctrinate them, and secure their influence. This we found an extremely arduous task, for the old and experienced Masons, who very legitimately had the ear of the Grand Master, and who now spoke of us as innovators, and treated our teachings as such, took good care to put upon that committee the oldest and most skilful Masons, and such, if their memories justify the epithet, as were most deeply bigoted in their old routine.

In the fall of 1819 the work was printed, and Cross sent me 2,000 copies; these I distributed freely; though to my great surprise and mortification, if not, as I feared, to our entire discomfiture and defeat, instead of sending a book of plates, with a reader to circulate and teach it, he sent the book with a reading, and a vast deal too much of it. The old Masons expressed themselves horror struck at the threatened exposure, and used their suspicions formidably against us. Of this state of things I again apprised Brother Cross, and on the 26th November, 1819, he procured the services, and sent to me with a letter, a reader, in the person of Wor. James Cushman, a well skilled and highly respectable Mason.

The session of 1819, December 13, now came on, at which we all knew the great and final struggle was to be made. The great interest felt, induced the oldest and most influential of the Fraternity to assemble from all parts of the State, and by concert, to prepare themselves for the contest. The Grand Working Committee was carefully organized, and every legitimate means resorted to, to fortify their position—47 Lodges, out of 78 working, were represented. I appeared as one of three representatives from Richmond Randolph Lodge, No. 19, and a few of our colaborers represented other Lodges. We presented the work through Wor. James Cushman, and pressed an exemplification before the Working Committee by catechetical examination between him and myself. We succeeded before the Committee, and they reported through us to the Grand Lodge, the work entire. Here we exemplified again, and after elaborate discussion and dissection of every part, it was adopted by the Grand Lodge on Friday morning, December 17, 1819, and ordered to be taught in all the Lodges by a Grand Lecturer—Brother Cushman receiving the distinguished honor of that office, by election.

I cannot pass over an interesting anecdote which occurred at this meeting, particularly as it enured most happily to our success, and seems to prove the continued interposition of an ever-watchful Providence in protecting and preserving our time-honored Ritual.

You will recollect we were styled innovators, moderns, interpolators, &c.; we were tauntingly charged with going north for light, and were repeatedly assured that this was not the work or teachings of our illustrious Brother Wm. Preston, P. M. of the Lodge of Antiquity. In the midst of these asseverations, Brother George Richards, a representative of the youngest Lodge in the Communication, Olive Branch, No. 114, (prophetic name!) arose, expressing great earnestness in his manner, and as great surprise at the opposition, expressed, and said, "I am the son of the Rev. Dr. Richards, who published the first edition of Preston's Illustrations of Masonry in this country, and who was made a Mason in the Lodge of Antiquity, in London; from him I received my degrees, and this is the work as he taught it from that book; and though I have never seen either of the brethren now exemplifying, until this time, I think I can take either of them and go through the work as given by them." Never was aid so efficient and so opportune! We carried our cause triumphantly by its truthfulness; and may it continue while sustained by that imperishable pillar, until time shall be no more!

It happened also, at this Communication, that our late talented and skilful Brother Dr. James Henderson, who had been engaged upon the work for two or three years, had now reported a copy of the Ahiman Rezon, with a well arranged digest of it, and the laws of the Grand Lodge then in force, as a proper code for the government of the Craft, which they did me the honor to refer to a committee of which I was made a member. We reported in favor of it at the ensuing Grand Lodge (1820), and thus was established the Law and Ritual under which we are now working.

Our labors in the cause of reform had not yet ended, the work in the Royal Arch and appendant degrees of Past, Mark, and Most Excellent Master, had deviated still more palpably from this Ritual, and the changes necessary to be made to conform them to it, were so great as almost to appear radical. The abiding and deep interest which the members of the Grand Lodge felt in those degrees, from the fact that they had been exercised and taught, by and under its authority, until tacitly surrendered to the Grand Chapter, at its organization in 1808, at once afforded us much aid in the proposed reform. Many who warmly opposed the recent change in the Lodge work, attended the lectures of Brother Cushman, became highly gratified, and by being adepts in that, were already prepared for the expected improvement in working the higher degrees.

I had entered the Grand Chapter in 1818, as a representative of Richmond Chapter, No. 3, and was at once complimented with the office of Grand Secretary, or Scribe, as then called. I found all its members, for they were few and old Masons, members of the Grand Lodge, and at once, with all the freedom and frankness which had been used before, exposed to them our views, and the extent of reform needed to meet those views.

At the Convention in 1820, for there was none held in 1819, we presented the work as laid down in the before mentioned Pocket Floor Cloth, and by request exemplified it in open Grand Chapter, through Comp. James Cushman. Its truthfulness at once carried conviction everywhere, and upon a vote, it was unanimously adopted as the Ritual of the Grand Chapter of Virginia, on the 18th day of January, 1820, and M. E. Samuel Jones, P. H. P. of Richmond Chapter, No. 3, was elected and installed Grand High Priest. At this meeting, also, the Constitution and Laws of the Grand Chapter were referred to a committee, of which I had again the honor of being a member, for revision and adaptation to the changes made.

We reported to a special Convocation held in Norfolk the 1st day of May, 1820, when it was approved and ratified unanimously, and M. E. Mordecai Cooke, of Portsmouth Chapter, No. 11, was duly elected and installed first High Priest under it.

From this time Royal Arch Masonry began to be studied and appreciated for the sublime beauty of its Ritual and its holy reverence for that most precious relic the book of the law and the testimony, whose record contains the divine and eternal truths and principles on which our beloved and time-honored Institution is founded, and is the same which, during the reign of that good king Josiah, and when Hildiah was high priest, and Shaphan scribe, was found while repairing the temple, 370 years after the dedication thereof; and which, when read by Shaphan, the scribe, and interpreted by Huldah, the prophetess, caused the knees of the whole court to smite with terror, at the near approach of the government of God, on their idolatrous desecration of his holy temple, altar and name.

I cannot conclude this incidental, though necessary, sketch of the Grand Chapter of Virginia, without relating a characteristic and interesting anecdote of the M. E. Samuel Jones, the above named first Grand High Priest, and the architect of Mayo's bridge, in 1793. I had it from his own lips, and he took much pride in recounting it to me, and many others; it was further corroborated by the preservation and production of the record, in his own handwriting.

It is well known to many now living, that at the above date Richmond was, though an incorporated town, a very small one, and the access to it very difficult, by reason of the newness of roads and great want of the facilities of travel and transportation of men and property. An enterprising and wealthy citizen, Col. John Mayo, undertook the construction of a bridge across the James river, at the foot of the falls, and near its present location. For this purpose he contracted with Mr. Samuel Jones as architect and superintendent, who was then a Master workman in the three first degrees of Masonry only.

"In so large an undertaking, (said Brother Jones,) I found myself surrounded with many and perplexing difficulties, involving my character for competency and honesty. The timbers were felled and prepared in the forests of Chesterfield, some miles off; the stones fitted and squared at the quarries of James river, some distance from the bridge, from thence they were brought on wagons to the shore, and thence on floats to the pens for the columns of the bridge. I had a large body of men, white and black, in my employ, with whom I was unacquainted, and who, as might be expected, were desirous to make the most by their work. I had bearers of burden, and hewers of wood, squarers of wood and stone, and workers in metal; these I classed according to capacity, and paid them in proportion; but I was continually liable to imposition from unskilful workmen sending up work unfit for use, and from unworthy workmen claiming wages for work not performed. To obviate these difficulties, I required each man to select a mark of some kind to be placed upon his work, and to send a copy of it to be recorded by my chief clerk. The general price or wages of competent workmen per task or day's work was known or fixed, but there were many not skilful workmen, with whom I had agreed on a stipulated price. I could not offend the self-pride of those by exposing the amount of their wages. I, therefore, to overcome all these difficulties, required them to appear on the sixth day of the week (Saturday) at my clerk's office, where I had a private wicket door made, into which one was admitted at a time, and required to present his mark. On the clerk's book was a column for inspected and rejected work, where this mark appeared, and opposite a column of amount due; this enabled me to settle squarely with each, silently and in good feeling, and at the same time do justice to my patron and principal, and to keep in my possession proof of both transactions. And when the bridge was completed, we celebrated it with a fest, and this record was exhibited."

When I entered the Mark Lodge, then working under a Charter from the Grand Lodge, in 1816, I found R. W. Samuel Jones, Master; and taking peculiar pleasure in working out the Degree of a Mark Master.

I think you will unite with me in saying, that had these incidents occurred a few hundred years ago, they would have entitled their author to, and obtained for him, the cognomen of Grand Master of all Mark Masons for Virginia, while erecting this bridge over the noble Powhatan.

I have thus endeavored, to the best of my feeble abilities, to give you a correct narrative of the origin, rise and progress of our much venerated mother, and in connection, as a necessary incident, the origin and condition of the materials of which her frame work was composed. The wisdom, sagacity, and virtue of her founders, needs no higher eulogium than a bare recital of the actual fact, that, though now in operation for three-quarters of a century, nothing but harmony and brotherly love pervades her jurisdiction. That in time she has been the blessed source from whence sprang into high, honorable and successful existence, in the then almost wilderness of the West, our sister Grand Lodge of Kentucky, within whose temple has often sounded the silvery voice of that gifted Virginian, as Grand Orator, and over whose wise aud harmonious deliberations he early presided as G. Master—a magnificent solution and bold exemplification of Masonic wisdom in conferring reward according to the broad level of merit. Our Brother Henry Clay, the native Demosthenes, unassisted by any adventitious aid, ascends the ladder of fame, until, having grasped its topmost round, he plants himself on the broad level of equality, in the very presence of the kings, princes and potentates of the old world; and the wisest and best of senators and statesmen in the new; the admired cynosure of all observers. The Mason who "would rather be right, than be President of the United States"!!! That she has issued Charters for the District of Columbia, and for North Carolina, before the date of their respective G. Lodges. That even the province of Caracas has sought and obtained her Warrant for a Lodge; and above all, that she has continued in friendly and brotherly correspondence with every sister Grand Lodge on this continent, and with most others over the globe; yet such has been her virtuous bearing towards equals and subordinates, that the calm sunshine which has irradiated her brilliant march, has never for one moment been bedimmed by the smallest cloud of discontent, jealousy or strife. The laws which have governed her policy, foreign and domestic, have been, in fact and in truth, the "Ahiman Rezon," or laws of "Prepared Brothers," as those words import. They are the same, with few or trivial amendments, at this day, as those bearing the same name under which her organization commenced. Her pure and beautifully illustrative Ritual is now the admiration of all to whom it is disclosed, and her proficients are sought in all our sister jurisdictions, as workmen of rare and exquisite skill, in preparing, fitting and adjusting the materials for that holy temple, that house not built with hands, eternal in the heavens.

Her Grand Officers, who officiated at her holy altar and within the portals of her sacred temple, have been men of great purity of purpose, of practical virtue, and exemplary morality, winning and receiving respect, esteem and veneration, from equals and subordinates.

From her first Grand Master, that devoted patriot, the M. W. John Blair, who, though the son of a former government under colonial government, became so deeply imbued with the great principles of civil liberty, and so ardent and influential an advocate for the equal rights of man, that he was appointed one of the councillors of state under the state government, in 1777—an office at that time of the gravest importance; the acceptance of which involved his life, and forfeited it to offended sovereignty, and the proper administration of which involved his character for competency and fidelity in the discharge of the high and responsible duties it imposed. Yet, amid all these embarassing engagements, such was his high appreciation of the utility of the teachings of Masonry in morality, virtue, discipline and good government, to the condition and wants of civil society, at that eventful epoch, that he did not hesitate to leave the councils of state for a time, in 1778, to meet and unite with his brethren of the Mystic Tie; to minister at her sacred altars, and use his greatest efforts to propagate her invaluable tenets of Brotherly Love, Relief and Truth; and her utter repudiation of all distinctions and privileges, except those which are conferred by merit alone; and her lasting attachment to and veneration for her officers, the possessors of those distinctions and privileges, so highly exalted by being won and received as the reward of a self-imposed exercise of her cardinal virtues.

Of Edmund Randolph, whose honored name gave title to one of the Lodges I have now the honor to address, and at whose particular instance this narrative is written, and well has she sustained the proud honor of that title from the day she received it, October 19, 1787, to the present time, by her inflexible observance of, and obedience to law and order, by her skilful and strict exemplification of Work and Ritual, and by her harmony and exemption from schism. It is due to truth to state, however, that not to have maintained this distinction among her equals, would have been to subject her fair name to the merited opprobrium of not improving the adventitious advantages with which she has been signally favored: 1st, in her locality at the emporium of Masonry in Virginia; 2d, in having several of our M. W. G. Masters to preside over her deliberations, and direct her Work and Ritual; and 3d, in having every G. Secretary an acting member, and often an officer, to keep her advised on all subjects of law and usage. He, too, eminently conspicuous among his cotemporaries, was a member of the congress of the United States from 1799 to 1782; of the Federal Convention of 1787; was Governor of Virginia in 1789, and Secretary of State of the United States in 1793, under our illustrious Brother George Washington; and yet found time and inclination, as M. W. G. Master, to preside over the deliberations and workings of this Grand Lodge, in 1786, and to superintend and give direction to the weighty influences of the teachings of the Craft.

Of the venerated and almost idolized, the pure and virtuous John Marshall, M. W. G. M. in 1793, whose sainted name has also given title to one of your sister subordinates, Marshall Lodge, No. 39, of Lynchburg, and the banner Lodge of this jurisdiction in numbers, if not in skill and Masonic observance of law and order. He it was whom the Hon. John Adams selected, and the Senate confirmed, as one of a commission of three to form a mission to France in 1797, in the words of the message, "to dissipate umbrages, remove prejudices, rectify errors, and adjust all differences;" a holy mission indeed! and well was he fitted for it by the even tenor of his amiable, distinguished and exemplary life. Never shall I forget the manly, Masonic and dignified bearing, with which, twenty-seven years after, he met and received in this city, in this Lodge, as the temporary presiding officer, the gallant and noble Frenchman and Brother Mason, General Lafayette, the man who acted so conspicuous a part in the exciting incidents which formed the basis of the above mission. Nor can I forget the moral lesson deeply engraved on my then youthful mind, when, instead of the adulatory and almost fulsome language he had everywhere been wont to be received with, in public, the orator of the day, that firm, republican Mason, Wor. James Henderson, Master of Manchester Lodge, No. 14, arose, advanced and, taking the General by the hand, said, as he entered the Lodge room, "Brother L. I am glad to see you, and in the name of the Fraternity here assembled, do offer you a cordial welcome to our hospitalities and the Masonic festivities in honor of your presence."

Here, said I, is a splendid illustration of the Masonic teachings and confidence inspired by the level of merit in well regulated minds; the unpretending practitioner of medicine in the village of Manchester, thus meets and addresses the noble Marquis De La Fayette, of France, whose nod had directed armies, and whose presence had been craved to protect a king and queen from an infuriated mob in their own mansion. Proudly bowing to the prestige of hereditary title, wealth, rank and influence, he plants himself on the broad level of Masonic equality, receives him as a Brother Mason, good and true, and in that exalted character, introduces him to the Fraternity of Richmond.

But let me not waste your precious time, and weary your already too highly taxed patience, by attempting to recount the virtue and inflexible fidelity of each of the long list of Grand Masters who have presided over your work as Masons, "who needeth not to be ashamed," for the last seventy-five years; suffice it to say, "by their works ye shall know them."

Of this long list of virtuous and enlightened Masons a very large proportion have passed away from the busy scenes of life, a few only remain co-workers with you of this day in the high and holy cause of disseminating the glorious principles of our hallowed and hoary mother; look well to the bright escutcheon of her fame, and see that its pure and spotless surface be never dimmed or defaced, by any blot or stain of your creating, or permitting to be created. Under the invincible banner of Brotherly Love and Affection, rally as her children around the precious and priceless jewels which adorn her hoary crown, those great Cardinal Principles of Masonry, which, through a succession of ages, have reached us unchanged by time and uncontrolled by prejudice; imperishable evidences of the continued protection of an overruling and eternal Providence, who, when he commissioned the Genius of Masonry, and sent her forth, on his holy errand of love and affection for the whole human race, as one common family of friends and brothers, armed her with the invincible panoply of truth and justice, as a safeguard and defence against the fiendish machinations of the dread demon of discord and anti-masonry in all ages. The wretched and disgusting implements of warfare used in this unhallowed crusade in the old world—the thunders of the vatican, the terrors of the dungeon and of the relentless inquisition, the galling chains of petty tyrants, and the demoniac falsehoods of infidelity and anti-religion, hurled by bigots and fanatics—withered and fell harmless under the impenetrable ægis of Almighty Truth. In a few revolving years all was peace and quiet in her honored temples, and the High Priests of Brotherly Love and Harmony resumed their precious exercises around her holy altars.

A few short years passed away, and with them those halcyon days of Harmony and Brotherly Love, by the appearance of the fell demon of anti-masonry in the new world, and in our midst. This hydra again erects his accursed crest, having exhausted his artillery of the old world; the dread of anathema, to intimidate the mind, and the tortures of the dungeon, to convert the nerve strings of human sensibility into physical suffering. He assumes, and wears that inestimable, but oh! how often profaned badge, of an American citizen, freedom of speech, and toleration of opinion; and in sacrilegious desecration of the names and memories of the sainted Masonic patriots of our revolution, before alluded to, who dying bequeathed it to us for far nobler and more useful purposes. Under protection of this honored badge, he stalked forth in open day, and by the assiduous propagation of unfounded charges, and malignant falsehoods, poisons the pure fountains of Fraternal Love and Harmony.

Fortunately, perhaps, for Masonry in this commonwealth, he selected, as a more fitting theatre for his abominations of law and order, the crowded cities, towns and villages of our northern and eastern neighbors. He enters the domestic circle, and at the once peaceful fireside, severs the ties of consanguinity, arraying father against son, and the still more enduring ones of husband and wife; he enters the halls of justice, and infuses distrust on judge, and witness, and jury; he appears in the hall of legislation, federal and state, and there, appealing to the most groveling and detestable of all passions and prejudices, the dreaded influence of the envied power of truth and virtue in associated form, he seduces statesmen and senators, wise, upright and reliable on most other subjects, by this detestable mode of reasoning, until they become fools, knaves, and panders to this unholy minister of discord; and this too, in many instances, over their own signatures. He invades the holy church of God, and there, by the oft-repeated, and as often refuted, hell-born charge of infidelity, he converts the sacred communion into an arena of the bitterest animosities and vituperations, until the holy man who officiates at this most hallowed and sacred rite, bending under the weight of years and poverty, and in view of the momentous responsibility of his calling, is required to resign his post, or abjure his Masonry. If angels are permitted to weep, it is at such a sight! Emboldened by success, he finally dared to invade the sanctuary of the Lodge, and in the presence of the Eternal and Great I AM, around his holy altar, on which lay open his divine will, as recorded in the book of the law and the testimony, to preach distrust in her holy Ritual as taken from that sacred volume.

Here the great battle was fought, here the death struggle for victory was to be made; here and there a few timid and unskilful brothers—timid because unskilful, yielded to the syren song of expediency, and either withdrew their attendance, or advised, or favored a suspension of work. In a few Lodges their lights were extinguished, and the sound of the gavel ceased; but this was in states where they had been so unguarded as to ask and receive Charters, or acts of incorporation, of certain vested rights; here, executive power was brought to bear upon them, and to avoid force, they submitted, resigned their Charters, and ceased work.

In charity, let us now pity and forgive the timidity and caut io of these exceptions to the mass, who gained the glorious victory over such a fearful array of formidable obstacles. Thanks, devoutly thanks to God! for the victory; hosannas to the invincible ægis with which he armed the Genius of Masonry on his holy errand, on whose glittering surface shines forth, in indelible characters, "Truth and Justice!" her victory is complete; and her altar fires are now relumed, and burning with a brighter, purer, and more fervent brilliancy in the cause of Brotherly Love, than they have ever done; and are daily increasing in numbers, not only in every section of this happy country especially, but in every part of the civilized world. While the discomfited demon, amid the lurid glare of calumny and detraction, gropes his way back to the dark dungeons of falsehood and error, there may he gnaw his chains in helpless anguish, among the loathsome volumes of Plott, of Pritchard, Barruel, Robinson, Stone and Adams; and may no mortal man have mercy on him or his ignominious cause! Of his unearthly retinue, one fiend still lingers in our midst—the serpent of discord is at work in a sister jurisdiction; and from the formidable array of shapes he has assumed, will require as much at their hands as the club of a Hercules ever accomplished. Already the wail and lamentation of our sisters are heard in all their jurisdictions, over the condition of that part of our Masonic temple. Sympathies, loud and deep, are expressed for the distracted and degraded state of her household. Our young sister of Missouri speaks out in the agonized fullness of her heart, and says to New York, yield your implements of Masonic work into the experience and skilful hands of our old and tried sisters, the first-born of our common mother, Massachusetts and Virginia; let them examine your materials, and by the decisions of their judgment abide. Such as will not stand the test of the overseer's square, let be rejected as unfit for use. And though your edifice may be materially reduced in size, its several parts will then present that uniformity of finish which can alone give stability and firmness. Let them then place the trowel in the hands of some well-selected and skilful Master, to spread the cement of Brotherly Love on all its joints and bonds of union; and by future, firm, though well-regulated use of the mallet of discipline, perpetuate that comely Order of Harmony and Peace—

> "Which nothing earthly gives, or can destroy,
> The soul's calm sunshine, and the heart-felt joy."

FORM OF RETURN.

Return of ——— Lodge, No. —, to the Grand Annual Communication of the M. W. Grand Lodge of Virginia, to be holden in the City of Richmond, on the second Monday in December, A. L. 58— *A. D.* 18—.

Officers.

Worshipful A. B., Master.
C. D., S. Warden.
E. F., J. Warden.
G. H., Secretary.
I. K., Treasurer.
L. M., S. Deacon.
N. O., J. Deacon.
P. Q., Steward.
R. S., Tiler.

Past Masters.

T. U.
V. W.

Note.—No one can rank as a Past Master, unless he has been duly elected and installed Master of a Lodge.

Master Masons.

A. A.
B. B.
C. C.

Fellow Crafts.

D. D.
E. E.
F. F.
G. G.
H. H.

Apprentices.

A. B.
C. D.

*Removals or Withdrawals.**

D. E.
F. G.

*Suspensions.**

R. S.
S. T.

Note.—Opposite each name is to be put the time when the suspension took place, and the term of its duration.

*Expulsions.**

R. G.
R. F.

*Deaths.**

M. L.
L. M.

Names of Master Masons, not Members of Lodges, residing in vicinity.

A. B.
C. D.

N. B.—It is necessary that every Lodge should forward by their Representatives the annual contribution, which is *Fifty Cents* per Member, (and none are members but Master Masons;) but no Lodge can pay less than *Ten Dollars.*

* In the List of Suspensions, Expulsions, Withdrawals, &c., no names should be mentioned which have been mentioned in any former Return, lest an unnecessary repetition of them be found in the list which accompanies the Proceedings.

There are —— members belonging to —— Lodge, No. ——.

The Fee for Initiation in Lodge No. —— is ——, for Passing, ——, and for Raising, ——.

The Lodge No. —— meets at ——, on the —— day of every month.

Brother —— is recommended by this Lodge, as the District Deputy Grand Master, for District No. ——.

Our Post Office is ——.

A—— B——, *Master*.

[SEAL.] *Teste*,

G—— H——, *Secretary*.

FORM OF CERTIFICATE OF CREDENCE.*

To all whom it may concern, greeting:

KNOW YE, That the bearer hereof, our trusty and well beloved Brother A—— B——, (*here, if he be master or warden, mention it*,) is duly authorized to represent Lodge No. ——, in the Grand Lodge of Virginia, at the Grand Annual Communication to be holden in the City of Richmond, on the second Monday in December, Anno Lucis 5866: then and there, in behalf of the said Lodge No. ——, to deliberate and act as may, in his judgment, best comport with the interests of the Craft in general, at all times governing himself by the customs and regulations of the said Most Worshipful Grand Lodge. And that he may be duly received and accredited, we have furnished him with this Certificate, this —— day of ——, Anno Lucis ——.

A—— B——, *Master*.

[SEAL.] *Teste*,

G—— H——, *Secretary*.

* Each of the Representatives must be furnished with a Certificate under Seal of his Lodge; they should also have with them the Jewels and Clothing of their Lodge, and must reside in the Masonic District.

MASONIC SONGS.

ENTERED APPRENTICE'S SONG.

Come, let us prepare,
We brothers that are
Assembled on merry occasion:
Let's be happy and sing,
For life is a spring
To a Free and an Accepted Mason.

The world is in pain
Our secrets to gain,
And still let them wonder and gaze on:
They ne'r can divine
The word or the sign
Of a Free and an Accepted Mason.

'Tis this and 'tis that,
They cannot tell what,
Nor why the great men of the nation,
Should aprons put *on*,
And make themselves one
With a Free and an Accepted Mason.

Great Kings, Dukes and Lords,
Have laid by their swords,
Our myst'ry to put a good grace on,
And ne'er been asham'd
To hear themselves nam'd
With a Free and an Accepted Mason.

Antiquity's pride
We have on our side,
To keep up our old reputation:
There's nought but what's good
To be understood
By a Free and an Accepted Mason.

We're true and sincere,
And just to the Fair;
They'll trust us on any occasion:
No mortal can more,
The Ladies adore,
Than a Free and an Accepted Mason.

Then join hand in hand,
By each brother firm stand,
Let's be merry and put a bright face on:
What mortal can boast
So noble a toast
As a Free and an Accepted Mason.

Chorus.—No mortal can boast
So noble a toast
As a Free and an Accepted Mason.

THE MASON'S ADIEU.

Adieu, a heart's fond, warm, adieu,
Ye brothers of our mystic tie;
Ye favor'd and enlightened few,
Companions of my social joy;
Tho' I to foreign lands must hie,
Pursuing fortune's slippery ba';
With melting heart and brimful eye,
I'll mind you still when far awa'.

Oft have I met your social band,
To spend a cheerful, festive night:
Oft honored with supreme command,
Presiding o'er the sons of light:
And by that hyeroglyphic bright,
Which none but Craftsmen ever saw,
Strong mem'ry on my heart shall write,
Those happy scenes when far awa'.

May freedom, harmony and love,
Cement you in the grand design,
Beneath th' Omniscient eye above,
The glorious Architect Divine;
That you may keep th' unerring line,
Still guided by the Plummet's law,
Till order bright completely shine,
Shall be my prayer when far awa'.

And you, farewell, whose merits claim,
Justly that highest badge to wear,
May heaven bless your noble name,
To Masonry and Friendship dear:
My last request permit me then,
When yearly you're assembled a',
One round, I ask it with a tear,
To him, your friend, that's far awa'.

And you, kind-hearted sisters fair,
I sing farewell to all your charms,
Th' impression of your pleasing air
With rapture oft my bosom warms.
Alas! the social winter's night
No more returns while breath I draw,
Till sisters, brothers, all unite,
In that Grand Lodge that's far awa'.

FOR FESTIVALS.

Come strike the *tune* that e'er imparts
Such thrilling charms divine!
That warms with love Free Masons' hearts,
For Auld Lang Syne,

For Auld Lang Syne, my dear,
For Auld Lang Syne,
That warms with love Free Masons' hearts,
For Auld Lang Syne.

The *Fair* first claim the Masons' care,
(We bow at beauty's shrine,)
To Masons a' they e'er were dear,
In Auld Lang Syne,

In Auld Lang Syne, my dear, &c.

Then Masons *charge* your glasses high,
With this bright sparkling wine;
And toasting drink "*to woman's sigh*,"
For Auld Lang Syne,

For Auld Lang Syne, my dear, &c.

Our Master next we proudly cheer,
And *mark* his jewels shine!
Oh! may we often meet him here,
For Auld Lang Syne,

For Auld Lang Syne, my dear, &c.

Within due *bounds* he makes us steer,
By the GREAT LIGHT divine!
And teaches us our acts to square,
By Auld Lang Syne,

By Auld Lang Syne, my dear, &c.

Our Wardens next we cheerful greet,
  May *peace* their brows entwine;
On *Friendship's Level* e'er we meet,
          For Auld Lang Syne,

  For Auld Lang Syne, my dear, &c.

Such noble feelings warm each heart,
  Such sentiments divine;
That on the *Square* we ever part,
          For Auld Lang Syne,

  For Auld Lang Syne, my dear, &c.

Now to the Craft where'er they be,
  Working by *rule* and *line;*
Long may they live both blest and free,
          For Auld Lang Syne,

  For Auld Lang Syne, my dear, &c.

And when we quit our Brethren here,
  The Craft above to join,
May ev'ry act prove *just* and *square,*
          For Auld Lang Syne,

  For Auld Lang Syne, my dear, &c.

ERRATUM.

Page 253, paragraph 6, after the word "advanced," in the 4th line, insert "and prove himself proficient, on the first section at least, of the degree from which he prays to be advanced."

NOTE.

Sec. 6, of Article V, of the Code of By-Laws, until altered to accord with a resolution of the Grand Lodge, read as follows:

"Should any member absent himself from the Lodge for twelve months successively, or be in arrears to the Lodge to the amount of —— dollars, he shall thereby absolutely forfeit his seat as a member; but should he come forward either personally or by proxy, discharge his dues, and offer a reasonable excuse for his delinquency, he may be reinstated, provided on a ballot a majority of the members present agree thereto."

INDEX TO METHODICAL DIGEST.

A

B

C

D

E

F

G

N

O

P

Q

R

S

T

U

V

W

www.ingramcontent.com/pod-product-compliance
Lightning Source LLC
LaVergne TN
LVHW020125110826
845151LV00001B/281